MASTER OF THE

Girl Pat

MASTER OF THE
Girl Pat

DOD ORSBORNE

EDITED BY JOE McCARTHY

DOUBLEDAY & COMPANY, INC., GARDEN CITY, NEW YORK, 1949

$\mathcal{S}$OLID AND SENSIBLE PEOPLE, WHO WANT THEIR SON to take that nice steady desk job in the utilities company with two weeks' vacation every summer and a retirement pension at sixty-five, may find Dod Orsborne and this book rather incredible, if not downright unbelievable. Orsborne is a Scotchman and a subject of the King. Yet his life story sounds like the adventures of a hero in a Milton Caniff comic strip. That seems to be a contradiction. We have been brought up to think of the inhabitants of the British Empire as rather cautious and conservative people, much less adventurous than the Americans. And even the most adventurous Americans, the pioneers of the old West, did not strike out into the plains merely for the thrill of facing the Indians. They were seeking a piece of land where they could settle down. It may be difficult for many of us to swallow the concept of Orsborne as a twentieth-century British subject who is always willing to drop anything to get into something more dangerous in a more remote part of the world. After all, the Britain of Churchill and Attlee is not the Britain of Sir Francis Drake.

But those of us who shared the discomforts and the occasional pleasures of the past war with members of the Empire forces know differently. The soldiers and sailors of the United Kingdom and Canada and Australia and South Africa and New Zealand believed firmly in tea and thick woolen socks. Unlike our General Mark Clark, who once quartered his staff in trailers in a park beside the available hotels of Florence so that his Fifth Army could maintain its record for living roughly "in the field," the Empire lads saw no point in sleeping on the ground if there was room in the back of a truck for a comfortable cot bed. Still, they were always ready to do the damnedest things. James A. Michener in his *Tales of the South Pacific* describes two New Zealanders fighting bitterly for the right to fly a dangerous patrol during the Battle of the Coral Sea. He also describes the mild-mannered remittance man from the little town near London who sneaked into Bougainville behind the Jap lines to broadcast daily intelligence reports to the Americans at Guadalcanal. There were university graduates in the Commandos who piloted one-man submarines alone through hundreds of miles of water. Their mission was to fasten the submarine, itself a time bomb, to the underbelly of a German battleship and then to leave it and to board the battleship and inform the commander that his ship was doomed. In New Guinea there was always an Aussie who could be counted upon to walk straight into a troublesome enemy machine-gun position, saying to his mates, "Are we going to let this bugger hold up the whole bloody war? Say good-by to Sheila for me."

Orsborne would have passed unnoticed in the collection of Britishers that I ran into one bright and sunny October morning in 1944 at Megara, twenty-odd miles from German-occupied Athens. The first one of them that I saw was a major who stood beside a reconnaissance car in the village square, speaking calmly into a walkie-talkie radio while the natives gaped at him. He wore one of those Scotch caps with two ribbons hanging down from the back of it and a battle jacket and brilliant green-and-black plaid regimental dress trousers, tapering narrowly at the cuffs, the first pair I had seen outside of the high-toned Scotch whisky advertisements. He was not more than eighteen years old. The others were an odd mixture of Navy, Army, and Marine officers and men, all of them young and most of them with the kind of looks that an American co-ed would pronounce pretty darned smooth. The outfit was called the Special Boat Service and its commanding officer was the Earl of Jellicoe, aged twenty-eight, son of the naval hero of World War I. They had been hand-picked for dangerous work and the earl had obviously chosen his own friends from the right clubs and the right sets at Oxford and Cambridge. ("Do you really think Reggie won't be a bore on this sort of a show?")

When they wanted to find out whether a road was mined, they drove a jeep over it.

They were in Megara on an interesting but harebrained mission of their own making. They had been in on the invasion of the Peloponnesos two weeks before and they had been ordered to occupy Corinth and to stay there. But Corinth was a bit dull for them. A large British invasion force was scheduled to take Athens from the sea the following week. The Special Boat Service decided that it would be rather a good joke to dash across Greece and capture Athens before the invasion force arrived. The earl had only about one hundred men and there were a great number of Germans between Corinth and Athens. But he started for Athens and the Germans fled before him, assuming that his little party was advance reconnaissance for a large force. At Megara he joined forces with some British paratroopers who had dropped there and the Special Boat Service was comfortably settled at the bar of the Grand Bretagne Hotel in Athens three whole days before the invasion force marched into the city. I talked about them with the Tommy who drove one of their vehicles. He said, "They never did anything in civilian life except hunt foxes and look for thrills. They're merely doing the same thing now."

Dod Orsborne is not, of course, a fox-hunting man but the point I am laboring to make is that his reckless outlook on life is not an uncommon one in the British Empire and, when you consider that outlook, this book is not improbable. When he wrote the manuscript, Orsborne sometimes had difficulty getting the exact details of certain incidents straight in his mind. Once he described something to me as happening at Dakar and wrote it as happening at Djibouti. But there is no doubt that it actually *did* happen. He was not making it up. A man like Orsborne, who feels sincerely that life is not much good unless it is constantly risked, would not have to make up this sort of a book.

If you think *this* stuff is incredible, you ought to see some of the things that we had to leave out.

And if you think it is incredible, a half hour in the presence of the skipper of the *Girl Pat* might change your mind. At the age of forty-five Orsborne is a restless and energetic man who seems as though he is eager for you to suggest an expedition. Any kind of an expedition. He wears a short, pointed reddish beard that combines with his pointed face and slightly slanted eyes to give him the appearance of a faun, or, to be blunt about it, of a Satan. You expect him to have hoofs instead of feet. He speaks with a Scottish brogue and instead of laughing normally he arches his eyebrows and pops out his eyeballs and throws back his head and emits one reverberating "Hah!" which causes the neighbor on the porch next door to look up startled from the pages of the newest historical novel. His eyes have the glint of a born hell-raiser.

That's what he is. As he tries to point out in his story, Orsborne is simply a man with an extraordinary capacity for getting into trouble. A Peck's Bad Boy who never reformed at adolescence. He mentions in the book many close escapes from death but he does not include among them the attack of pneumonia he suffered as a child. The doctor gave him up and told his mother not to bother doing anything more for him. The case was hopeless. But his mother ignored the doctor and sat up all night administering hot poultices and whisky and in the morning Dod began to recover.

"And time and time again after that," his sister says, "Mother would shake her head and say, 'Now look what Doddie's gone and done. Why didn't I follow the doctor's advice?' He was the kind of a boy who would tear a piece of crust off the bread while he was carrying it from the baker's and reach inside and eat out all the dough. Then he would replace the piece of crust. My mother would slice the loaf and find that it was hollow."

My wife once made a comment about Dod Orsborne which sums him up as well as he can be summed up.

We were sitting with him one night after dinner and he was talking about the things that only he can talk about: His annual visits to a lonely lighthouse keeper in the Flannan Islands. The method of opening a safe, taught to him by a convict at Devil's Island, by balancing on top of the safe a blob of mercury on a cigarette paper on a cocktail glass. The time he straightened out the Archbishop of Canterbury on a few interpretations of the Bible. The old man in Ireland who gave him a drink from a bottle that was being saved in a coffin under the old man's bed for the old man's wake. His seagoing friend from Grimsby, a character known simply as The Horse, who vowed in 1939 that he would never go to war and then turned up on the beach at Normandy on D-Day, playing the bagpipes. The ring, given to him by a Chinese shipowner in Australia, which gets him extra special service in Chinese restaurants. The captain of his whaling vessel who was called Screaming Jimmy and who always wore at sea a derby hat. And then, as always, a few stories about his favorite country, India, and the people and the animals he has known there. At this point my wife managed to get a word in and asked if he had ever read *Passage to India.*

"No, I haven't," Dod said. "I haven't read a book in—let's see. I haven't read a book in fifteen years."

"You don't need to," my wife said.

JOE MCCARTHY

For Mercia and Bert

CHAPTER 1

I T WAS ONE OF THOSE TIMES WHEN THE ROYAL NAVY and I were not speaking. As usual, I had rubbed some of the old school tie people in the Admiralty the wrong way. This was September 1940, when the Battle of Britain was at its height and the threat of a German invasion of England was imminent. The Admiralty said it needed every available man. I had not gone to Oxford or Cambridge but I had been at sea since I was fourteen and I had held a captain's ticket in the merchant fleet since I was twenty-one. I had seen naval combat as a youngster in World War I and, disguised as a fishing-boat skipper, I had served as a Naval Intelligence agent in the Mediterranean during the Abyssinian and Spanish wars. So I felt I was entitled to a captain's commission. The old school tie people in the Admiralty felt differently. I watched them hand Royal Navy Volunteer Reserve commissions to a bartender I knew from a waterfront pub in Southampton and to a clerk from a timber merchant's office whom I had actually taught to row a boat the year before. But they handed me nothing.

While I was deciding what to do next I stayed in London, seeing a lot of Lucille and killing the rest of the time working as a courier for my friend Donald Gillies. Donald's advertising firm was doing a great deal of highly secret work for the Admiralty and for the War Office. His downtown office at Shell Mex House on the Strand had been bombed and he had to move to a place outside the city. He needed somebody to carry confidential documents and messages out there from the government offices, a task that was not easy during the German air raids, which were then very bad. I took it over.

One day I was with Donald at Whitehall and we started to make our way across London to his apartment in Chelsea. I suggested stopping at a certain pub I knew for one drink.

"I don't really feel like a drink," Donald said.

"Oh, come along," I said. "Just one."

We had the drink and then we hailed a cab and continued toward Chelsea. The air raid alarm sounded and the bombs began to fall. As we neared the apartment building where Donald lived we saw a land mine descending by parachute and landing on its roof. The whole side of the building crumbled and the rest of the structure broke into flames. The cab stopped with a jolt.

Donald turned to me. "Not much use our going there now, Dod," he said.

The cabby glanced at us. "Better come with me instead, gents," he said. "I know where I'm going. Down that bleeding shelter over there."

We followed him. Bombs were whistling and exploding all around us. It was early in the evening and the shelter was packed with people who had been on their way home from work. As we joined them there was a tremendous blast outside. The cabby was nervous about his taxi and ran upstairs to have a look at it. "She's safe and sound," he reported. "Just a little dusty."

I noticed in the shelter two women in their thirties, apparently sisters. One of them was holding her hand over her mouth. "Oh, please let me go back and get them," she was saying to the other woman. "I must look perfectly frightful." The other woman laughed and reached into her own mouth and removed her lower teeth. "Here," she said. "Have half of mine."

Donald and I recognized an older woman in a mink coat who was sitting near the door of the shelter. She had occupied the apartment above Donald's and she was known as the neighborhood snob. The local tradespeople were forever complaining about her overbearing and condescending manners. Sitting next to her was a ragged little woman who held in her lap a basket of white heather that she had been peddling in the streets. A night watchman approached them with a billy can of tea that he had brewed over a spirit lamp.

"There ye are, lady," he said to the woman in the mink coat. "Have a mouthful of char. There's no milk nor sugar but it'll wet yer whistle."

Donald and I were astonished to see her thank him politely and take a swallow from the can. She passed it to the heather woman. "It's quite nice, my dear," she said. "Have you far to go when the all clear sounds?"

The heather woman explained that she had to go all the way to the other side of London.

"You poor thing," the woman in the mink coat said. "Why don't you come home with me? I live only in the next block. You can return to your place in the morning."

I thought Donald's eyes would drop out from amazement. The heather woman declined the invitation. The lady in the mink coat had no idea, of course, that her apartment in the next block no longer existed. A few minutes later, after we watched a fight between two dogs that caused more panic in the shelter than the German bombs outside, I nudged Donald and told him I wanted to go to Lucille.

"Why not wait a bit?" he asked. "Perhaps it will be safer in a half hour or so."

I said I was worried about Lucille and wanted to go now.

Donald said he'd go along with me. The cab driver, who was listening, said he'd drive us. "Might as well die in the fresh air as suffocate to death in here," he said.

The all clear sounded shortly after we reached Lucille's house. Donald and I had tea with her and then we stretched out on the floor and tried to get a few hours' sleep, knowing that we would not have much peace before the next raid. We were right. The next raid came at midnight. We went outside to look at it. The sky was lit with the glare of burning buildings. A plane burst into flames directly over our heads. We ran into the house to get away from it and there was a terrific explosion. The house rocked. Furniture was thrown against us and the windows were blown out by the concussion. We found big jagged splinters of glass sticking into the walls and the floor but none of us was hurt. In all the years I had known her, that was the only time I ever heard Lucille use improper language. She looked at the sky and shook her fist.

"You bastards," she said. "You didn't get us that time."

In the morning we found that the plane, with its cargo of bombs, had crashed into a garage down the road. The garage and six adjoining houses had completely disappeared. Half of an automobile was lying in the garden outside Lucille's back door. Her own car in

3

front of the house was undamaged and she insisted upon driving us to Chelsea to see if anything could be salvaged from Donald's apartment. As we were getting into the car an old lady put her head out of the shelter across the street and called to us.

"Excuse me, gentlemen. Has the all clear sounded yet?"

We told her it had sounded several hours ago.

"Mercy," she said. "I've been here since six o'clock."

The old lady had not heard the air raid alarm at midnight and she had slept through the entire bombing. When the all clear sounded at six in the morning she awoke and dashed to the shelter, thinking it was the beginning of a raid. She had been sitting alone in the shelter ever since.

We drove down Brixton Road. Firemen and emergency workers were digging for bodies in the ruined buildings. As we reached Donald's street in Chelsea a policeman stopped us and told us we would have to detour.

"You can't pass here," he told us. "There was a direct hit on that air raid shelter. They've already removed ninety-eight bodies and they're still digging."

It was the same shelter Donald and I had been in the previous evening. We asked what time it had been hit. "Around eight-thirty," the policeman said. That was approximately ten minutes after we left it to go to Lucille's house.

"Well, Dod," Donald said, "the two old ladies went home together after all."

That evening Donald and I went to his temporary office in the country, thirty miles from London. We sat down after dinner in his makeshift living quarters upstairs and listened to the sound of another raid on the city. I picked up an old magazine and began to read it and while I turned the pages I noticed Donald staring at me rather curiously. I winked at him and went back to the magazine but I could feel his eyes still on me. After a moment I looked up again.

"What's eating you?" I asked.

He kept on watching me steadily, rubbing the stem of his pipe against the corner of his mouth.

"Dod," he said, "I want to ask you something."

I put down the magazine.

4

"Do you ever hear some person or some voice that tells you to do certain things?"

"Well," I said, "I have dreams like everyone else, if that's what you mean."

"No, that's not what I mean," Donald said. "Let's take, for instance, yesterday evening when we left Whitehall and you talked me into stopping for that drink. Did you really feel as though you wanted a drink?"

"I didn't need a drink, I suppose. It just seemed a good idea."

"Why did it seem a good idea? And when we were in the shelter, why did you suddenly make up your mind to visit Lucille?"

"Oh, I wanted to see if she was safe. When you care for a girl, you worry about her during an air raid."

"It's not as simple as that," Donald said. "Good Lord, man, don't you realize that if you hadn't suggested that drink—that drink neither of us particularly wanted—we would have reached my apartment fifteen minutes earlier and we would have been there when it was destroyed. And if you hadn't suggested going to see Lucille we would have been in the shelter when the bomb hit it. All the people who were in that shelter are now dead, except you and me and the cab driver. Dod, why is it that nothing ever happens to you?"

"What do you mean?" I said. "Things are always happening to me."

"You know what I mean. That time in Spain when they put you before a firing squad and then let you off."

"They were only trying to frighten me," I said.

"Perhaps. But there was that business with the *Girl Pat*. You sailed that small boat across the Atlantic from Africa to South America with no fuel, no food, no compass, and no navigation charts. Nothing but the stars and a school child's atlas. And you landed it safely. Anyone else would have perished. And this last thing a few months ago, the parachute jump in Holland. You actually tried to give yourself up to the Germans and they refused to touch you."

"It must be something more than luck," Donald said. "It seems supernatural, downright uncanny. Nothing happens to you and it's no fault of yours that it doesn't. God knows, you take enough risks. You must have a guardian angel."

I laughed at him and we had a drink and went to bed. But before I went to sleep that night I thought a long time about what Donald

5

had said. I had never thought about it before but it was indeed true that all through my life I had been escaping death by narrow margins. I thought of some of those escapes.

There was that tiger in India. I had stood face to face with him for at least two minutes. He was only fifteen feet from me and, while he stared at me, he feinted at me a few times with his paw and snapped at me with bared teeth. He was trying to make me move. I was so completely paralyzed by fear that it was impossible for me to make any kind of movement. Every muscle in my body was frozen stiff. I could not even reach for my rifle, which was hanging on its sling behind my shoulder.

Finally, after what seemed like three months, the tiger relaxed and turned his head away from me, as though he was disgusted. I managed to twist my shoulder and slide the rifle down my arm and into my hands and I fired at the tiger and killed him. I realized afterward that the paralyzing fear had saved my life. If I had been able to reach for the rifle before the tiger turned his head he would have leaped on me.

And there was the time I was stabbed by the girl in Norway.

When I was the skipper of a trawler in the twenties, I stopped regularly at a small port in the fiords of Norway. There was only one good inn in the town and I became friendly with the innkeeper's daughter. She worked as a waitress in her father's place. In the afternoon, when she was not serving meals, she visited me in my cabin on the ship. I was wearing a ring, a cheap thing that had not cost two pounds, and she took a fancy to it. She was always trying it on and admiring it but for some reason I never gave it to her.

One time when I was in that town I met an old acquaintance, a Belgian captain, who asked me to spend an evening with him and two Norwegian sisters he had met on a previous voyage. We took the girls to dinner at the inn. The sister I drew turned out to be an exceptionally attractive girl. She, too, admired my ring. I did a very stupid thing. I took it off and presented it to her, just at the moment that the innkeeper's daughter was serving the soup at our table. The innkeeper's daughter dropped the soup and screamed and began to pull hair from the heads of both sisters.

The next thing I knew, the Belgian and I and another seaman were fighting four Norwegians. The innkeeper's daughter picked up a knife and stabbed me twice, once in the abdomen and once in the back of my neck. I staggered away from her with the knife sticking out of the back of my neck. The Belgian stopped fighting long enough to pull it out.

I stumbled out the door and walked away from the inn and sat down in the snow. I sat there a long time, trying to pull myself together, because in addition to everything else I happened to be quite drunk. I could feel the blood from my neck running down my back, and my pants were full of blood from my abdomen.

Finally I stood up and walked to the dock and went aboard my ship. I called the mate and told him to round up the men because we were sailing for England.

"When?" he asked.

"Now," I said.

I went to my cabin and took a bottle of iodine from the medicine chest and poured it on my wounds. I also located a bottle of rum and took two long drinks from it. Piloting a ship through the Norwegian fiords is a tricky job. The mate did not have enough experience to handle it. When the crew was aboard I took a third drink of rum and went up and took the wheel. I stood at the wheel for the next eight hours until we were safely in the open sea. Then the mate took over and I went to my cabin and fell asleep.

When we docked in England I went to a doctor and showed him the knife wounds. "There's nothing for me to do," he said. "They have both healed perfectly."

I thought, too, that night about my mother's description of how I was carried home to her unconscious when I was three years old. My sister and I had wandered away from our house in Scotland and gone to play on the bank of a nearby river. I slipped and fell into the water. The current was swift and strong and I was carried away by it. A fisherman, who happened to be walking by, saw my sister crying on the riverbank and then noticed my blond curls rushing downstream. He dived in and saved me. I remembered also the *Dandani*. I had shipped on her as an able-bodied seaman at the age of sixteen after I was discharged from the Royal Navy for lying about my age. (Even in World War I, I had my troubles with the Admiralty. They took a dim view of my signing up as a seaman when I was only fourteen.) The *Dandani* nearly foundered in a terrible storm between the Orkney and Shetland islands and drifted rudderless and waterlogged for nine days before she

7

was picked up and towed to Aberdeen by a steam trawler. When we landed I found my family mourning me as dead. My name, along with those of the rest of the crew, had been published in the newspapers as missing at sea.

I am not proud of these close calls. A narrow escape from death does not fill you with a sense of satisfaction and accomplishment. But that night, after Donald mentioned it, I did wonder what it is that keeps a man alive when all the odds favor his death. And I have wondered about it much more since that night because later in the war, when the Royal Navy and I settled our small differences and when I joined the Commandos, the curious charm that protects my life was really forced to work overtime. There were times, in fact, when it worked so well that it made me eerie and nervous. I would look at myself in a mirror and doubt my mortality. Then I would decide that I was being saved for some extra special type of painful death to make up for some of the extra special sins I have committed in life.

The charm worked, for example, one morning in 1941 when my corvette was in a convoy nearing Malin Head, the northernmost tip of Ireland. When day broke, the water was covered with mist but the sky overhead was clear. I was standing on the monkey bridge of the corvette with both hands on the handrail, hoping to catch sight of land as the mist lifted. A seaman came on the bridge with a mug of coffee and rum for me. As I turned away from the handrail and took a step toward him, reaching for the mug, there was a ripping noise and a German plane swooped so low over our heads that he just missed the masts. He dropped a bomb which luckily fell clear of our stern by five yards. Then I saw another bomb drop and hit one of the ships in the convoy squarely amidships. There was an explosion and the ship went up in flames.

After we had picked up survivors from the sinking ship I went back to the bridge. I noticed that the handrail was damaged and found seven machine-gun bullet holes in it. The bullets had gone clean through the rail. They would have gone clean through me, too, if I had not stepped away from the handrail and reached for the mug of coffee and rum one second before the German plane came out of the mist and strafed us.

Not long after that my ship was laid up for an overhauling that was scheduled to take ten days. Half of my crew was given leave and I had planned on a vacation in England with Lucille. But a commander sent for me and asked if I would forgo my leave to do a special job for him. In the Royal Navy you can't very well say no to a commander.

The naval headquarters at Londonderry in Northern Ireland, to which my corvette was then assigned, had received word that a German mine had washed ashore at Ballycastle. The officer in charge of demolishing mines was away on another assignment at the Isle of Man. The commander wanted to know if I would take a party of men to Ballycastle and examine the mine. From the description he had received, the commander believed it was a new type of enemy mine. He wanted me to dismantle it and bring back as many parts as possible to our research laboratory. If, however, the mine seemed too dangerous to dismantle, I was to patrol the beach and keep the townspeople at a safe distance and send back to headquarters for a motor launch that would tow the mine to sea and explode it there. The commander apparently assumed that I was an expert on mines. All I knew about them I had learned from the Royal Navy's little booklet on mines and that was not much.

I studied a few diagrams that he showed me. As I was leaving his office he said to me, "Orsborne, remember one thing. If the mine begins to make a hissing sound while you're dismantling it, for God's sake get away from it fast."

I started up the coast toward Ballycastle with a petty officer named Harry Hunter and eight enlisted men. When we arrived in Bushmills, the nearest large town to Ballycastle and the home of Bushmills Irish Whisky, the whole population was lined up along the narrow streets to greet us. News of the mine had spread over the whole countryside and we found ourselves being welcomed as the heroic saviors of that part of Ireland. The police inspector and his sergeant shook hands with all of us and told us that they had been waiting for us anxiously since early morning. They led us through the cheering throngs to the local hotel and invited us to order whatever we wanted—on the house. It was obvious that the people of Bushmills expected the mine to destroy us all and they did not want us to die sober or with empty stomachs. From time to time, while we were drinking and eating, various leading citizens would walk into the hotel dining room and look at us admiringly and then would shake hands with each one of us.

When we had finished we climbed back into our truck and the police inspector came up to give us directions. Seven miles up the road we would find a cottage and in it was the man who had reported the mine.

"But surely you'll come along with us to show us the way," I said.

The inspector drew back in horror.

"Not me," he said. "You couldn't get me to go within five miles of one of those things." With that he handed me two bottles of Bushmills Whisky and wished me good luck.

When we reached the cottage an old lady came out and told us that her husband was down on the beach, watching the mine. We drove to a high bluff overlooking the beach. The tide was out and we saw an old man and a little boy sitting on a boulder about ten feet from the mine, which was bobbing up and down lazily in the wash of the tide.

Looking through my binoculars, I saw that it was a plunger mine. A plunger mine has a steel rod fitted into its bottom. When the mine is planted at sea a line is attached to the rod and fastened to the ocean bottom. The line pulls the rod out of its socket and this makes the mine alive. If the mine breaks lose from its mooring, as this one had done, the line releases the rod and the rod slips back into its socket inside the mine. That makes the mine safe and harmless.

But through my binoculars I saw to my dismay that the old man was holding a piece of rope that he had tied to the rod on the bottom of the mine. The rope pulled tightly on the rod, keeping it drawn from its socket and also keeping the mine ready for action. It was likely to explode at any minute.

I waved at the man and yelled at him to drop the rope. He waved calmly back at me and made no move whatsoever.

We went down on the beach and ventured nearer to him. I yelled at him again. He stood up to walk toward us but before he did so he handed the rope to the boy and told him to hold it tightly until he returned.

"For the love of God," I screamed at him, "tell that boy to let go of that rope before we're all blown to kingdom come!"

The old man shook his head calmly.

"We're not letting go of that mine," he said, "until you pay me the three pounds reward for finding it."

We stared at him and then we stared at the mine. A wave came in and lifted it up. We turned away and tried to cover our heads.

"You'll get your three pounds," I said. "You'll get it from the government."

The old man shook his head again.

"I'll get it now," he said, "or you don't get that mine."

I tried to watch the mine and argue with the old man at the same time. It took us fifteen nerve-racking minutes, with the tide coming in and the mine bobbing up and down more rapidly, before we were able to coax him into letting the boy release the rope. I had to write a statement, promising him the three pounds.

Hunter, the petty officer, and I and two men approached the mine gingerly. We found that the rope had wound around the rod and kept it from sliding back into the mine to safeguard it. The mine was about four and a half feet high and just as big in width. We stood knee-deep in the water and began to work on it.

I put a man on either side of it to keep it from swaying and I took a heavy wrench from Hunter and gripped it on one of the nuts that fastened the top cover. As I gave the wrench a half turn there was a hissing noise. I found myself alone with the wrench in my hands. My three helpers were running up the beach like wild deer.

I was too weak to run. I put my hands on my head and bent over and waited.

Nothing happened. I straightened up and looked. The mine was there and it had stopped hissing.

I staggered out of the water and sat down on the sand. After a while the men gathered around me. They were still pale. My voice was trembling when I said to them, "What the hell did you all run for?"

"You said to run, sir," Hunter said. "You said if there was a hissing sound to get away quick."

"Well, you certainly did," I said. "A Spitfire couldn't have moved faster."

I told Hunter to open one of the bottles of whisky and we all had a drink and considered the situation. The whisky didn't seem to do me much good. But we summoned up enough courage to take another stab at the mine. This time when I twisted another one of the nuts the hissing was louder than it had been before. And this time I was the first one out of the water and up on the beach.

We got out the whisky bottle and had another drink. I suggested one more try.

"Not me, sir," one of the seamen said. "I don't care if you shoot me. I won't go near that thing again." Another seaman said his legs could not stand all the running.

"How about you?" I asked Hunter.

"If you persist, sir, I'll go with you," he said. "But I really think you should call for a launch and have it towed to sea."

I thought about it for a few moments. I had drunk almost a half bottle of whisky by myself but I still could not feel it. Under normal conditions I would have been cockeyed. I proposed finishing the bottle and then making one last attempt to dismantle the mine. This time, I promised Hunter, I would keep on unscrewing the nuts even if it did hiss.

Hunter and I waded out to the mine and he watched while I worked on one of the nuts. The hissing began and it grew louder and louder as I loosened the nut. Hunter edged away. There was a sudden "plunk" and the nut flew into the air. I dived under the water and tried to swim away.

A big wave hit me and carried me up on the sand. When I opened my eyes I saw Hunter handing me the second bottle of whisky.

"Here, sir," he said. "And for God's sake, no more. That's all I can stand. We're finished."

I agreed with him. "I'll take one more close look at it," I said, "and then we'll go back to Bushmills and I'll phone a detailed description of the mine to the commander."

I went back to the mine and while I was examining its construction I noticed a wide crack in its side. This, I realized, was the reason for the hissing. When the cracked side rolled above the surface of the water, air entered the inside of the mine. When I loosened the nuts the air came out and hissed.

I started to remove the nuts one by one while the men watched in amazement from a safe distance. Then I called for Hunter to bring the men and a coil of rope. We had another drink of whisky all around and proceeded to remove the insides of the mine: two hundred-pound drums of TNT, the mechanism, and an eighteen-inch detonator. The whisky must have started to take effect because I noticed that all of us were singing while we worked.

We piled the TNT and the mechanical parts in the truck and drove away, with me sitting in the front seat carrying the detonator, wrapped in a piece of sandy burlap sack, on my knee. The people in Bushmills greeted us as though we had won the war. We stayed there, drinking porter and whisky, until after eleven o'clock. When we finally reached Londonderry it was three o'clock in the morning. We put the parts in the mine-clearing shed and I walked into the office with the detonator in my hand to telephone the commander. His voice sounded sleepy.

"It's Orsborne, sir," I said. "I've got the whole lot you sent me for."

"What do you mean, the whole lot?"

"I've got the mine case, the TNT, the mechanical works, and the detonator."

"Where have you got all this stuff?"

"Right here beside me in the mine-clearing shed," I said.

The commander became wide awake in a hurry. I thought he was going to jump through the telephone.

"Good God!" he roared. "In the shed? The detonator? Where have you put the detonator?"

"It's here beside me, on the table," I said.

The commander moaned. "Oh, God!" he said. "Orsborne, for God's sake, don't move. Don't let any of your men move. Don't move that detonator. Don't even touch it. There are nine prepared mines in that shed with you and you're liable to blow up the whole blasted town of Londonderry. Oh, God help us all! Just sit there. I'll be right with you."

I went out to the truck. The men were falling asleep. I explained that we had to remain there until the commander arrived. In a few minutes it seemed as though every high-ranking Navy and Army officer in Londonderry was in the mine-clearing shed. Two officers placed the detonator tenderly on a cushion and carried it to an automobile. They drove ten miles out of town and destroyed it in a quarry. The TNT was taken to a swamp and ignited and left to burn itself out. The only part of the mine that was kept was the mechanism. The commander told me to report to him in the morning.

The combination of a hangover and the realization of the panic I had caused gave me a bad morning. When the commander poured me a glass of whisky my hands were trembling so much that I asked for a cup of tea instead.

"Orsborne," the commander said, "that sack you wrapped the detonator in, it was rather sandy, wasn't it?"

"Yes, sir," I said. "It had been lying on the beach while we were working on the mine."

"I just wanted to point out to you that if the slightest particle of sand had rubbed into that detonator you would not be alive today," the commander said. "That ride back from Ballycastle in the truck last night, didn't it give you rather a bouncing? And you held that detonator on your knee all the way?"

I said that it was and I did.

"Amazing," the commander said. "Why that detonator didn't go off before you reached here I'll never understand. Well, Orsborne, you can have your fourteen days' leave."

I managed to thank him.

"You know, of course," he added as I was leaving, "that I didn't mean for you to bring back the whole mine. We only wanted to have a look at the mechanical parts. Not the TNT, nor the shell, nor the detonator."

"I'll remember that the next time," I said.

But one of my great weaknesses is my inability to remember things the next time. After my experience with the innkeeper's daughter in Norway, you would naturally suppose that I would be careful about exposing myself to stabs in the neck. But I allowed myself to be knifed again in the neck by a German bayonet during the Commando raid on Tobruk in North Africa. I will resist the temptation to make a pun here about sticking my neck out once too often.

Most people think of the British Commandos in connection with the large-scale hit-and-run operations like Tobruk, Dieppe, and Narvik or as first-wave shock troops, like the American Marines. As a matter of fact the Commandos were used during the war mostly for small and highly secret missions that were never publicized in the newspapers. Parties of three or six, or sometimes twelve or twenty, Commandos would slip ashore at Normandy six months before D-Day and spend two days there getting information on German coastal defenses or taking soundings to check the depth of the water along the beaches. Or they might go into enemy territory to take a quisling leader from the underground people and bring him back to England. Another typical Commando assignment was the job I did with three other men at Blankenberghe on the Belgian coast on Christmas Eve, 1943. If ever my life was charmed, it undoubtedly was that night and that next day.

There was an important factory at Blankenberghe that supplied the Germans with aircraft parts. We planned to bomb it from the air but the high command wanted to make sure that the bombs found their mark. The Commandos were asked to land four men by rubber boats on the beach at Blankenberghe. Each man was to plant a flare at each of the four corners of the factory building a few minutes before the Royal Air Force bombers came overhead. The flares would outline the target for the bombardiers. After the factory was bombed, of course, the four Commandos were to get back to the beach and out to sea again—if they could. The high command wished them the best of luck.

A motor torpedo boat dropped us a few miles offshore. There were two of us in each rubber boat. The bombing was scheduled for three o'clock that morning and we were supposed to plant our flares and light them at two minutes before three. It took us longer than we expected to get ashore and bury the deflated rubber boats in the sand and strike inland to the factory. We had studied aerial photographs, maps, and prewar snapshots and picture post cards of the area until we felt we could find the factory blindfolded. But the place was alive with German sentries and anti-aircraft positions. We could hear the sound of the planes approaching from the North Sea as we lit the flares and the bombs were dropping as we ran from the factory.

The mission had been scheduled for Christmas Eve because we had information that the factory would be closed that night for the holiday. It was expected that it would be easier to place the flares under those circumstances and the lives of the Belgians who were forced by the Germans to work in the factory would be spared. But it seemed to me, as I tried to find my way back to the beach, that the closing of the factory for the night increased the number of people in the roads around it. The neighborhood was as crowded as Piccadilly Circus or Times Square.

The factory was burning brightly and the German anti-aircraft guns were going full blast. I became confused and began to lose my sense of direction. Running down a dark, tree-covered lane, I almost bumped into a German sentry. Luckily his back was turned to me. I drew back and fell to the ground without making any noise and rolled quietly under a hedge. I lay there, listening. The German stood, listening. After a while another sentry walked up the lane from the opposite direction and I heard them talking to each other in low tones. They began to search the bushes with flashlights. I slipped through the hedge and into a field and crawled away.

I hid in the field for an hour or so, waiting to see if the countryside would quiet down. But the bombing of the factory had everybody awake and excited. I did not know where I was so I decided to go back toward the factory until I saw some familiar landmark and then to start again for the beach. The roads were still full of people of all ages, some running and some gathered in groups, talking about the bombing. I was wearing a blue workingman's coveralls over my uniform so I attracted little attention. If I found myself in a close corner, I was to strip off the coveralls and let myself be captured in uniform. This would keep me from being shot as a spy. I felt in my pocket and made sure that I had the small tube of morphine that all Commandos carried in enemy territory. If we were in danger of being captured, we were supposed to jab the needlelike end of the tube into our leg and squeeze the tube itself. This gave an injection of morphine, which would make a man insensible and incoherent for five or six hours. In such a state it was impossible for him to give information to the enemy, even under torture, that might jeopardize the other Commandos who might be in the area. After five hours, when he regained consciousness, such information as he could give would generally be useless.

It was getting light and when I approached the factory it was almost broad daylight. I suddenly decided to get under cover somewhere fast and to wait until evening before trying to work my way back to the beach. I looked around and saw the door of a large building that seemed to be a hotel or a tavern. I went to it and opened the door and walked inside. I found myself in a large room. There was a big, long table in the room and around it, some seated and some standing and talking, were a dozen German Army officers.

My heart rose into my throat. My first thought was that I was finished. I tried to think of some way that I could get out of the workingman's coveralls so that I could show my uniform before they laid hands on me.

Then it gradually dawned on me that the officers were paying no attention to me. One of them glanced at me casually and then turned back to a magazine that he was reading. I noticed other magazines and newspapers and a pack of playing cards on the table, and a wine bottle and salt and pepper shakers and coffee cups. The room was not a headquarters, as I had first assumed. It was an officers' mess. They thought I was one of the servants, who were probably in and out of the room all the time.

I looked around me and saw an electrical fuse box on the wall. I opened it and pretended to examine the fuses and the switches that were inside it. Then I closed the box and walked slowly around the room, looking at the light fixtures in the ceiling.

The bulb in one of the fixtures was burned out. I climbed up on the table and unscrewed it. One of the officers, somewhat annoyed at being disturbed, got up and walked away to make room for me. I spread a magazine on the table to put my feet on. I can still remember vividly the full-page picture that I saw when I opened the magazine. It was a photograph of Churchill and Roosevelt, shaking hands and smiling at each other.

I climbed down from the table with the bulb in my hand and walked to a door on the other side of the room. If it had been the door of a closet I might have lost my poise. But it opened on a stairway. I went down the stairs and into a big kitchen, where I found two women staring at me. They started to ask me excited questions in a Flemish tongue that I did not understand. I was afraid that the Germans upstairs would hear them. I didn't know what to do. Finally I held my finger to my lips.

"*Angleterre!*" I whispered. "*Angleterre!*"

They understood that I was British. The older woman threw her hands up in dismay but she motioned to the other one to be quiet. She pulled me into a dark alcove off the kitchen where there was a large bed and pushed me onto the bed and pulled the covers over me. Then she and the other woman returned to the kitchen and busied themselves cooking breakfast for the officers upstairs. They would fill the plates and put them in a dumbwaiter elevator in the wall and call to a waiter, who would hoist them up and out of sight. After an hour or so the older woman brought me a plate of eggs and a cup of *ersatz* coffee. In sign language I told her that I wanted to get to the beach. Half in sign language and half in French she indicated that it would be best to wait there in the bed until darkness came.

The women worked in the kitchen all morning. Once a tradesman came in to deliver vegetables but he paid no attention to the bed in the alcove. After lunch the two women climbed into the bed with me for a nap. The older one made sure that the younger one did not sleep next to me. About eight o'clock that night the older woman led me out a back door, making sure first that no one was about, and pointed the way to the beach. We kissed each other and she wished me Godspeed.

I found the beach without trouble and then I located the spot where we had buried the rubber boats. I was starting to dig for them when somebody fell on me. I felt an arm strangling my neck and a knife at my back. Then the arm relaxed.

"Blimy," a voice muttered. "I wasn't sure it was you. Where you been?"

It was the little Cockney Commando who had landed with me the night before. I told him what had happened to me and asked him about the two others.

"I've been waiting around here all last night and all today and I've seen no one," he said. "I was just about to give you up and leave by myself alone. The other two must have been done in by the Jerry."

We decided to push off, figuring that if the other two Commandos were still at large they would be able to find their rubber boat, which was still buried in its original hiding place. We took turns on the hand pump, inflating our boat, and managed to get it through the surf and out to sea. After a half mile or so we flashed our blue torchlight once. After a moment we saw a quick answering blink from the waiting motor torpedo boat. In another hour and a half we were aboard her drinking coffee. The motor torpedo boat waited off Blankenberghe another twenty-four hours for the other two Commandos. They never appeared.

I am also inclined to list among the narrowest of my narrow escapes from death a certain romantic interlude that occurred in a town in England where I was attached to a Commando training camp. I became acquainted with a charming and understanding young woman who had a house of her own there and the acquaintanceship blossomed and bloomed for all of six months. I knew that the young woman was married to a naval officer but she didn't tell me who he was or where he was stationed and I never bothered to embarrass her by asking. I did notice once or twice, when I took her to London and met other naval officers, that they seemed rather cool and uneasy in her presence. I attributed it to their puritanical upbringing and thought no more about it.

One evening, however, the lady and I were drinking with an Army officer, who was a close friend of mine, and when it came time for him to go back to his quarters he was in no condition to move. We carried him to the lady's house.

"Put him in that spare bedroom near the kitchen," she said. "You'll find a pair of pajamas in the lower drawer of the clothes chest."

I opened the wrong drawer and the first thing I saw was an admiral's full-dress hat. I wore it back to the living room and jokingly announced that I had been promoted. The lady laughed and I laughed. Then the laugh froze on my face.

"By any chance," I said, "is this your husband's hat?"

"Yes," the lady said casually, "it is."

The first thing I did the next morning was to call upon my commanding officer. I told him nervously that I seemed to be in a bit of a jam.

"Yes," he said. "I've been waiting patiently for you to become aware of it. In fact the whole Royal Navy has been waiting patiently for you to become aware of it. Didn't you know who her husband is?"

"No, I didn't know," I said. "All I know now is that he's an admiral. Which admiral is it?"

My commander named one of the most important and most powerful admirals in the Navy.

"What do you suggest, sir?" I asked in a tired voice.

"I suggest a change of station for you and a tearful farewell for her."

That very day I received orders to another Commando training unit in another part of the country. The lady and I said our tearful farewell and I denounced the heartless government for separating us. I took care after that never to see her again.

A year and a half later, when I had forgotten the whole incident, I was reassigned to a combat command overseas for duty in a forthcoming invasion as a beachmaster. When I arrived at my new headquarters to report for duty I was told to wait a few minutes so that the commanding admiral could see me. I didn't understand why such an important and busy man as the commanding admiral wanted to see me personally. While I waited I asked a clerk what was the admiral's name. He told me. It was the lady's husband.

My palms and my forehead broke into a sweat. I looked around for the nearest exit. There was only one thing to do: make a run for it.

Perhaps I could get rid of my uniform, change my name, and get a berth on a merchant ship in the harbor as a seaman. But just then the clerk announced that the admiral was waiting to see me. In a daze I walked into his office.

The admiral smiled and stood up as I entered and stretched out his hand to me.

"Orsborne, by Jove, sir, I am delighted to see you!" he exclaimed. "Perhaps you don't remember me but I talked with you a few times at the Admiralty back there several years ago, just before you made that remarkable voyage in that small boat with the false smokestacks. The *Girl Pat,* wasn't that the name of her? Well, sir, I wanted to see you today because of my wife. Orsborne, you don't know how much I appreciate the fine way you looked after my wife and entertained her last year while I was away. It was a most kind and most considerate thing for you to do. She wrote me all about you and she is very grateful to you and I am, too, sir. By Jove, won't you sit down?"

And out came the whisky bottle.

As Donald Gillies said, I must have a guardian angel.

CHAPTER 2

ALL MY LIFE I HAVE BEEN RUNNING AWAY TO SOME-place new and usually getting into trouble after I got there. Every week when I was a child in Kirkton, a village in the Scottish highlands, I would come riding home on the back of the bicycle that was pedaled by Rummy Nose McBain, the county policeman, who seemed to enjoy the job of handing me back to my mother, safe and sound. When the poor woman took me into the house, she would always ask the same question: "Whatever makes ye wander, laddie?" And I would always make the same reply: "I don't know, Mums. I just wanted to go somewhere."

After we moved to Aberdeen, to be nearer my father, who joined the Navy at the outbreak of the first World War, I ran away with two other children one day and visited an art gallery. I grasped the hand of one of the statues and, to my terror, it broke off at the wrist. I noticed another statue near by which showed Hercules kneeling on one knee. I placed the hand between Hercules' buttocks. I was certain that it would never be discovered.

One of my companions, a little rat named Kelly, told on me and I was summoned to court. My mother was mortified. All the way to the courthouse she boxed my ear and kept saying, "Your dad is at war and you have to disgrace his good name." At the courthouse we met a gentleman who was either a lawyer or a social worker, and he was nice enough to offer to plead for me.

"My lord," he said to the judge, "this boy was never in trouble before. We cannot blame the curiosity of youth for an unfortunate accident. He merely wanted to find out what the statue was made of.

My lord, we must remember that the youth of today is different from the youth of yesterday. He does not rely on statements. He seeks facts. He is taught to think and to investigate for himself, not to accept the investigations of others. This innocent boy was merely following his teachings."

The old judge looked at the man over his glasses.

"I can understand all that," he observed. "But still it was a peculiar place to hide the hand."

I never did have an adolescence. I topped off my running away by running to the Navy and signing up as a seaman in 1917, after my father was reported missing at Gallipoli. I was fourteen years old at the time. I told the recruiting officer that I was sixteen and he said the Navy would take me if my mother signed the papers. I gave my tartan plaid kilts to a waterfront hag who signed the papers for me and pawned the kilts to buy a bottle of liquor.

Before I was fifteen I was on a submarine chaser in the Dover Patrol and before I was sixteen I was wounded at the Battle of Zeebrugge. According to the history books, every man at Zeebrugge was a volunteer. It is true that the men who sailed the ships into the entrance of the Zeebrugge canal and sank them there were volunteers. But the rest of us who fought in the battle volunteered for it in the following novel manner:

The day before the battle a high-ranking officer boarded each vessel and spoke to the assembled men. "Men," he said, "soon we shall be in action against our common enemy. Each one of you knows the tradition of the British Navy. What is expected of you is the same as what was expected in the days of Nelson. If any one of you has any doubts as to his courage to see it through, he may step forward two paces." There was a moment of silence. "Dismiss," the officer said.

That was how we volunteered. As one of the men on my ship, a fellow called Cockney Joe, remarked afterward, "It would have taken more guts to step forward than it would to die twice with a jar of rum in each hand."

My commanding officer received the Victoria Cross for taking his ship into the enemy shore and picking up survivors from the scuttled vessels. He visited me in the hospital later and asked how old I was. I lied as usual and said I was eighteen. He handed me a newspaper clipping. When I opened it I found a picture of myself and my brother with a caption that gave my real age, fifteen, and said I was missing from home. He did not reveal my age to the Navy but he ordered me to write to my mother and he wrote to her too. On the first of July 1918, I went home for sick leave and on July 4 I celebrated my sixteenth birthday there. It was the last birthday I ever spent with my family.

After I was honorably discharged from the Navy at the end of the war I shipped aboard several Scotch and British merchant ships as a seaman. One of them was the *Kirton,* a three-hundred-tonner that ran between Aberdeen and the Firth of Forth. The *Kirton* was a family affair. The skipper was a potbellied man known as Stucco Willie. His son, Young Willie, was the mate and every member of the crew, except me, was related to him either through blood or by marriage. One day in Aberdeen when I was on my way to board the *Kirton,* I met a fellow who had been particularly cruel to me during my first few days in the Navy. I had always wanted to pay him back and I did not intend to pass up this opportunity. The third time I knocked him down he struck his head against the side of a brick building. I thought he was dead.

I ran for the ship. When I went aboard, Stucco Willie informed me that the sailing would be delayed for a day because the fireman had not appeared. I was willing to do anything to get out of Aberdeen immediately so I volunteered to do the firing myself. When we reached Dundee, I left the ship and joined the crew of one of the last great American sailing vessels, the *San Francisco.* The next morning I was on my way to Genoa, where we loaded with saltpetre and headed for South Africa. I spent my seventeenth birthday on a beautiful, azure-blue calm sea off the Canary Islands. The trip south was slow. We zigzagged over the equator, trying to catch on our sails the slightest breeze, and we watched several days pass without a ripple on the water. The sun blistered the decks. We did not sight the Cape of Good Hope until the eighth of September, five weeks after we had left the Cape Verde Islands.

We stayed at Durban for three days. When the *San Francisco* sailed across the Indian Ocean to Cochin in southern India, I was the bosun. Then we sailed back to Durban, stopping en route at Madagascar, and across the South Atlantic and around Cape Horn, where I saw icebergs for the first time in my life. It was a rough trip, marked by storm after storm. The big sailing ships like the *San Francisco* were things of beauty but hard work to maintain. Coming across the South Atlantic, the aftermast was dismasted and had to be spliced and the sails were continually being torn away and ripped to ribbons. When we rounded Cape Horn we headed north in the Pacific, making tacks that lasted for weeks. We docked at San Francisco, the ship's home port. The owners were about to sell her so the entire crew was paid off and discharged.

Knowing nothing about San Francisco, I asked a sailor in a waterfront café where I could find lodgings for two or three days. He suggested a place that was owned and operated by a Chinaman named Chang. The front of it downstairs was a store where Chang sold coffee and soft drinks and sandwiches. There was a back room where he served a terrible prohibition moonshine that the sailors called snake juice. Upstairs there were two rooms filled with cots. I was assigned to one of the cots. The first night I slept there somebody stole my wallet. That left me with only three silver dollars which I had put in one of my pants pockets.

When I told the policeman on the corner about it he said I should have known better than to sleep in such a dive. Feeling sorry for myself, I went to a restaurant and ordered a cup of coffee. I was sitting at a table staring at the cup of coffee when an attractive girl, about eighteen, sat down opposite me and smiled at me shyly. I asked her if she wanted some coffee and she nodded and we began to talk. I described my voyage from Scotland and told her how my wallet had been stolen. She sympathized with me. She seemed to me to be a refined and well-mannered girl and I wondered what she was doing alone in a waterfront restaurant. Then she asked me if I wanted to go home with her. I thought she was inviting me to meet her father and mother and I was delighted.

After we had walked a few blocks she turned to me and asked how much money I had with me.

"I told you my wallet was stolen," I said. "I only have two dollars."

"Let's see," she said.

I took the two silver dollars out of my pocket and showed them to her. She took them out of my hand and began to scream at me.

"You cheap limey!" she yelled. "What do you mean by insulting me? You know I don't work for less than five dollars!"

24

The people on the street were beginning to stop and look at us. I had enough trouble as it was so I got away from there fast. That left me with only fifty cents. I walked the streets all day and sat up all night on a pile of logs on the docks, hoping that I might find a berth on an outgoing ship in the morning. That was when I met Scoush.

He was walking down the gangplank of a ship. I called to him and asked him if they needed any new men in the crew.

"Hell, matey," he said, "I don't belong to this ship. I just used it to sleep in last night." Then he looked me over. "Had your breakfast yet? No? Well, come on with me."

Scoush led me back up the gangplank and took me into the galley and introduced me to the cook. "Meet a very close personal friend of mine," he said. "We went to different schools together. A very high type fellow with a lot of connections on Wall Street. Fix him one of your delicious table de hoot à la carte blue-plate special breakfasts and maybe he'll put in a good word for you the next time you want a loan from J. P. Morgan."

The cook laughed. "Any friend of Mr. Scoush doesn't have to go hungry here," he said, winking at me.

As soon as the cook served me a cup of coffee with rolls and bacon the world seemed brighter. Scoush sat down and talked to me while I ate. I told him about my wallet and the girl. "You are lucky she didn't take your socks too," he said. Scoush was from St. John's, Newfoundland, where he had been a cod fisherman. It had taken him two years to get to San Francisco. He had stopped along the way to work as a cowpuncher and a farmer and a dock hand. For some reason he was very anxious to go to South America but he did not tell me why. We made a bargain; we would both look for berths on the outgoing ships. If I found one on a ship headed for South America, I would turn it over to him. If he found one on a ship that was not going to South America, he would turn it over to me. For the next two days we inquired everywhere but we found nothing. In the meantime we ate well on various ships that were tied up at the docks and at night we slept on them. We paid for nothing. Scoush seemed to know everyone on the San Francisco waterfront, and everyone seemed to know him. "Let me see," he would say. "Shall we eat dinner on that Canadian freighter? No, I think we'll take pot luck on the fruit boat where we had breakfast yesterday. Frank, the cook on the fruit boat, generally turns out a better dessert."

On the second day we were together Scoush broke down and told me why he wanted to go to South America. His father, before his death, had been a bosun on a sailing vessel. On one voyage he had gone ashore at Patagonia, on the southern coast of Argentina, to get fresh-water kegs filled at an inlet. The bed of the fresh-water stream was covered with mussel shells and Scoush's father gathered a pail of them to cook when he returned to his ship. While he was eating the mussels he found six pearls in them. He said nothing to the rest of the crew about his discovery but when his ship docked in Boston he took them to a jeweler to be appraised. The jeweler told him the pearls were of no value because he had damaged them by cooking them.

Scoush's father was sure that a fortune in pearls was to be found in the bed of that fresh-water stream. If he had found six in a single pail of mussel shells, he reasoned, it should be easy to find thousands of them. He always intended to return to the place where his ship had anchored but he died before he was able to make the voyage. During his last illness he told Scoush the story and drew a map for him which showed the outline of the coast in that area and the shape of the bay that led to the mouth of the stream. Scoush showed me the map. It was a small drawing in blue pencil, with the position of his father's ship marked by a red anchor. The only trouble with the map was that it did not indicate where on the coast of Argentina this particular bay was located. The coast of Argentina, especially in that southeastern section, was full of such bays and such fresh-water streams. To Scoush's way of thinking, this was a very minor difficulty. He was sure that he could find the right bay.

"I've been planning this trip for two years," Scoush said. "I've saved up more than three hundred dollars and I've got it all here in this money belt around my waist. Why don't you come with me? I figure we can get a ship to Buenos Aires and maybe work our way on down the coast and then buy a small boat for seventy-five bucks and start looking for that bay and that creek or that river or whatever it is. We'll get rich. What do you say?"

He didn't have to ask me twice. I was just as excited by the idea as he was.

A few days later we saw a commotion on one of the piers where

26

a French ship, the *Paul Vernier,* was docked. There had been a drunken brawl and a stabbing aboard and the police were removing three members of the crew. We found out that the ship was scheduled to sail that day for the Cayenne River with a load of machinery for a sugar plantation. It was not Buenos Aires but it was South America and that was good enough for us. The mate said he needed no seamen but the chief engineer was looking for two firemen. We signed on and he told us to report for work in two hours.

Scoush and I rushed to Chang's place, where my kit bag had been checked at the rate of ten cents a day. Scoush carried all his belongings in his pocket. His belongings consisted of two sets of crown and anchor dice. The kerchief he wore around his neck was marked so that crown and anchor could be played on it. When he found somebody with money to lose, he produced the dice and spread the kerchief on a table or the floor and he was ready for action.

Firing the ship's furnace on that hot voyage through the Panama Canal nearly killed us both. With the help of his dice, however, Scoush ran his bank roll up to five hundred dollars before we reached French Guiana. At Cayenne we found that the *Vernier* was moving south to Buenos Aires so we eagerly volunteered to stay on in the boiler room. In Buenos Aires we left the *Vernier* and spent a few days on the waterfront running crown and anchor games, until we managed to get on a powered schooner named the *Venado Cuarto* that traded as far south on the Argentine coast, as Deseado. We offered our services to the skipper for food only. He said that we were crazy. When I saw the bleak, cold land that we were venturing into I began to think that perhaps he was right. We said good-by to him at Deseado, a town that reminded me of the dreary little villages in the Shetland Islands, north of Scotland. There were a few shops where you could buy anything from a loaf of bread to a coffin. A few small fishing boats lay in the natural harbor and the countryside was usually blanketed in the morning with a heavy mist that rose slowly when the sun climbed high. The natives were an easygoing, friendly lot with no interest in work. They loved to sit and exchange stories with us by the hour.

After bargaining a half hour we bought a boat from one of them for ninety dollars. It was a thirty-year-old fishing craft, twenty-seven feet over all with a half-covered deck, two masts, and lug sails. We loaded it with enough provisions to last us for three months and set off to sea one morning in a drizzling rain. We had showed Scoush's map to the natives at Deseado but they merely shrugged their shoulders. They said that the coast was full of bays that looked exactly like that one.

For five days we held the boat well out to sea. It leaked like a wicker basket and we had to bail continuously. There was always a foot of water sloshing around our feet and our clothes were always wet. Our bodies ached and it seemed as though we were always shivering. When the weather became wetter and colder we decided to find a place ashore where we could build a fire and dry ourselves. As we closed on the coast we found great black rocks rising out of the water, devoid even of bird life, and the land behind them was barren, without a tree or a shrub. Finally we found an inlet and Scoush headed the boat for the middle of it between two treacherous reefs, rounding a headland into a smooth bay and running the bow up onto a shingle beach.

As we went ashore the sea birds on the beach stared at us resentfully and refused to get out of our way when we walked near them, as though the land was their private property. The place was absolutely still except for the lazy wash of the little waves. We gathered turf and seaweed and lit a fire and drank the first coffee we had had since leaving Deseado. Then we covered a spot near the fire with dry turf and stretched out on it and tried to sleep.

But we stayed awake, shivering with the cold and wondering if we might be attacked by Indians. We took turns stirring the fire and then after a few hours we took one of the sails from the boat, wrapped ourselves in it and finally, through sheer exhaustion, fell asleep. We stayed there for two days and explored the inlet, sailing two or three miles inland without seeing any sign of life except birds.

Then we continued down the coast, stopping in every bay and cove that even faintly resembled the one on our map. There were plenty of them, all somewhat similar to the one we were seeking. The mussel shells were plentiful, too, and we opened them until our hands were torn and sore. When the weather grew even colder and the nights seemed longer and more miserable, Scoush began to get discouraged. "Let's go back, Dod," he said, "and get another boat, at least one that we can sleep in." I could not see any sense in turning back now that we had gotten this far.

We must have covered five hundred miles when we found ourselves one day passing a rocky headland and running into a long waterway that wound back to the right between high and bare hills. Then for the first time we saw smoke. The thought of talking to human beings again excited us.

We expected to find a village. But when we rounded a bend in the river we saw that it was only a small group of Indians, standing around a fire on a sandy beach. We shouted and waved to them but they stood like statues and stared at us without making a sign of recognition. They were dark-skinned, with long, matted hair, and we could not tell whether they were men or women. Obviously we were not welcome so we decided to wait awhile before approaching any nearer.

We lowered the sails and threw the anchor over the side. The water was very clear and when I looked down into it I saw that we were directly over the green, slimy timbers of a sunken ship. As the tide dropped, the ribs of it arose on each side of us like a huge fence. We scraped some of the barnacles off one of the timbers and tied alongside it. We found it was thick, black oak. Then we recognized the structure as that of an old galleon ship that must have been there for hundreds of years. Scoush and I were so excited about the ship that we forgot about the Indians. When we looked again at the beach we found that they had vanished, leaving the smoldering fire behind them.

We edged our boat ashore. I armed myself with the iron stock of the anchor and Scoush put a small hatchet in his belt. But the Indians were nowhere to be seen. There were hundreds of mussel shells on the rocks and beside the ashes of the fire. Up until then, the mussel shells had been small and black. These were large and brown, about six inches long, and they were lined with smooth mother-of-pearl. We built a new fire and cooked our supper, feeling enthusiastic for the first time since we started the voyage. We felt that we were finally getting near to Scoush's father's promised land.

We slept that night on the boat offshore. In the morning we found that the tide had gone far out to sea, exposing boulders on the small beach that were covered with mussel shells. I tore several of them open, hoping to find pearls, but each one was a disappointment. While we ate breakfast we decided to stay there and really spend some time working on the mussel shells. We built a semicircular lean-to with rocks and the sails for protection against the cold wind. While I was gathering rocks I found four human skeletons, dry and dusty with age, under a pile of stones at the top of the high ground behind the beach. I picked up one of the skulls and I was surprised to hear Scoush, whom I had always regarded as a hard-boiled and worldly character, begging me not to disturb it. "You know what they say, Dod," he said nervously. "To lie near the dead is to join them. Put those stones back and let's get away from here." I decided that there was some connection between the skeletons and the galleon that was lying in the river. Perhaps the ship had put into the inlet to bury her dead and had been attacked by Indians and sunk.

To satisfy Scoush's fear of the skeletons, we broke camp and moved farther into the inlet. Around another bend we found the mouths of several fresh-water streams that ran down from a valley. We selected one of them and sailed up it until our boat scraped on the bottom. The rocks on either side of this creek were covered with mussel shells.

While we were making a new camp there, on a dry beach protected by a steep wall of rock, I thought I smelled smoke. I walked farther along the edge of the stream. The smell became stronger. I peered over some rocks and saw some Indians sitting around a fire. They would throw mussel shells on the fire, wait until they were cooked, and then rake them out with a stick, tear the inside from the shell, and eat it and toss the empty shell over their shoulders.

As I watched them I heard Scoush's voice behind me. "Dod!" he yelled. It echoed all over the valley. The Indians jumped to their feet.

I turned around and ran back down the creek. I saw Scoush jumping up and down and shouting at the top of his lungs.

"I've found them!" he shouted. "I've found them!"

He held out his cap to me. In it were seven pearls, ranging in size from a pinhead to that of a small pea.

I had a hard time trying to tell him about the Indians. Finally I managed to make him listen and I told him that they were near by and had heard him shouting and that we had better get ready to take to the boat and pull out in a hurry. We waited for them to make an appearance. Then we crept cautiously back to the rocks where I had seen them. The fire was still there. So were the empty mussel shells. Again, the Indians were gone.

We never saw them again. How they ever lived in that desolate country with no vegetation and no livestock I don't know. Apparently they were more afraid of us than we were of them.

Scoush was beside himself about his discovery of the pearls. We slept well that night with the steep cliff sheltering us from the wind and in the morning we began the job of gathering and opening mussel shells. The tide was low and I began to dig them out of the mud in the bed of the creek.

"Why get your feet wet?" Scoush said. "There are plenty to be had on the sides of these rocks."

That seemed to make sense so, like him, I spent the rest of the morning tearing them from the rocks. We would take them to the fire and sit there, opening them. Sometimes we would find one pearl in a hundred shells, sometimes one in thirty shells. Then I noticed that every shell with a pearl in it had a certain distinguishing disfiguration on the outside of its belly. From then on we opened only that type of shell and we found pearls in nine out of every ten of them.

We continued to open shells for the next three days before we realized that our food was running low. We had underestimated our appetites in that cold climate. We felt that we had accumulated a fortune in pearls already so we decided to start back to Deseado the next day. Before we left I went back to the bed of the stream and dug up a few more shells there and added them to what we had in the boat. Our supply of pearls filled four matchboxes. They were of all colors and shapes and sizes.

The trip back to Deseado was an ordeal. Food was scarce and we ran into snow and rough weather. The boat leaked worse than ever. We reached Deseado exactly two months from the day we had left it. The natives gave us a warm welcome. We didn't tell them about finding the pearls. We became known in the town as the two *loco hombres* who sailed south for nothing and came back with nothing. The next schooner from the north was not scheduled to arrive in Deseado until Christmas so we pulled our boat out of the water and the natives helped us to patch it up. We set sail again and followed the coast north into the Gulf of San Jorge. We made good progress in the clear frosty wind but by the time we reached Rawson the boat was ready to sink. We waited in Rawson two weeks and made a deal with the captain of a fishing schooner who took us all the way to Bahía Blanca for five dollars each. After what we had been through, the journey from there to Buenos Aires seemed like a pleasure cruise.

In Buenos Aires we showed the pearls to a jeweler who told us that they were worthless. The majority of them, he said, were immature seed pearls and the others were not perfect enough to be of value. But he tried very hard to find out from us where we had found them. We walked out of the store, telling him nothing.

The next appraiser we took them to spent a whole day examining them. He selected twenty-five out of the whole lot and offered us two hundred and seventy dollars for them. We were bitterly disappointed and discouraged.

Scoush went into the interior of Argentina to take a job in a granary and I found a berth on a ship that was returning to England. I took a matchbox full of the rejected pearls with me. A few months later, after I became nineteen, I entered nautical school to study for a mate's certificate. The principal of the school was interested in the pearls and he asked me to show them to a friend of his, a member of the Fishery Board, who had made a study of pearl-collecting methods. This man told me that Scoush and I made a grave mistake when we selected the shells on the rocks instead of the ones in the bed of the stream.

When the tide recedes during the summer months the mussels that cling to the rock are exposed to the sun and air. The heat opens the shells and disturbs the secretory process that forms the pearl. Valuable pearls are usually found in shells that are constantly covered by water. I am sure that the twenty-five pearls that were bought in Buenos Aires came from the shells that I dug out of the bed of the stream. I have often thought of returning to that inlet and making another search for a fortune in pearls. But this time I won't worry about getting my feet wet.

My old enemy from the Navy did not die when he hit his head against the building in Aberdeen. A few years later when I was the captain of a whaling vessel I met him on the street in Grimsby and we shook hands and had a drink together. He was down and out so I signed him on my ship as cook. He turned out to be the best cook I ever had.

CHAPTER 3

*B*EFORE THE WAR THERE WAS A COMBINE OF THIRTY-five trawlers from the British port of Hull, called the Gamecock Fleet, that fished without interruption in the North Sea for more than ten years. Every week a boat came out to pick up the catch and take it to the fish market in London. And every week two ships from the fleet returned to Hull. They would load up with a supply of coal and provisions and their men would have a week of liberty ashore. At the end of a week these two ships would return to the fleet at sea and two other ships would replace them in port. Each ship spent thirteen weeks at sea before it received its turn to spend a week ashore.

In 1939, when England declared war on Germany, the government ordered all British fishing boats to return to their ports. And so for the first time in more than ten years the entire Gamecock Fleet came into Hull together. It was discovered that one woman in Hull had been happily and peacefully married for a number of years to five different men in that one fleet.

If it hadn't been for Hitler and Chamberlain and the invasion of Poland, her harmonious design for living might never have been disturbed. The five men were from five different ships. No two of them were ever in town at the same time. All five men gave her their pay allotment books. All five of them were paying her for the rent and the groceries.

This is the only woman I ever heard of who married into the maritime profession and got the best end of the deal. Almost without exception, the wives of seafaring men find life lonely and frustrating. I remember one night in Grimsby carrying home a skipper pal of mine who had had too much to drink. It was close to midnight and his ship was scheduled to sail at five in the morning. "Put him on the couch in the parlor," his wife said wearily. "It's no good undressing him. I'll have to rouse him in a few hours when the automobile comes to drive him to the docks." Then she turned to me in desperation. "Ever since we were married it's been like this. He comes ashore and he heads for the pub. He comes home sleepy and falls on that couch and stays there until it's time to go to the ship. And then he's gone for another month or two months. I never get to talk with him, let alone love him. I can't stand it." I knew another girl in a seaport town who was married and widowed three times before she was twenty-eight. Each husband was lost at sea. I have always felt, seriously, that out of fairness and respect for womankind a man of the sea should never marry.

But there comes a time when your convictions weaken. This resolution of mine started to waver one morning in Liverpool when I was standing outside the office of the shipping company that owned the *Tusken,* waiting for the *Tusken's* captain, Brick Melvin. I was then almost twenty years old and I had just completed my third voyage as Melvin's first mate, a feat that was considered miraculous by seamen from the river Mersey. Melvin was not an easy skipper to sail under and he usually hired a completely new crew at the end of each trip. This time I had got into some trouble at Oslo. I had caught the bosun of the *Tusken* in the act of stealing and carrying ashore some coils of rope from the ship's stores. He was drunk and he started to tell me in rather indelicate language how he had drunk more salt water than I had seen and how I should be still tied to my mother's apron strings. I lost my temper and knocked him down and he rushed at me with an uplifted coal shovel and I managed to get a hold on one of his arms and broke the bone in it across my bended knee. The captain was now reporting the affair to the shipowners. I expected to be fined five pounds sterling for striking the bosun and I expected to be fired by the company. But I didn't much care. While I was thinking about my troubles I heard a girl's voice behind me saying, "Excuse me. Are you Mr. Orsborne, the mate of the *Tusken?*"

I turned around and looked. I was no Errol Flynn but I had known a number of women, enough to be able to talk to them without digging my toe in the ground and twisting my cap into a knot. But this one made me weak in the knees and speechless. I saw smooth dark hair and a cameolike complexion and brown eyes that did things to me. I managed to answer her question with a frightened nod.

"They were talking about you in the office," she said.

"Oh," I said.

"I heard Captain Melvin say he had been looking for an officer like you for years," she said.

"Oh."

"And my grandpa said the firm would pay your fine."

"Oh."

"Sometime I'd like you to tell me why you broke that man's arm. Will you?"

"Oh," I said. "Oh yes!"

She smiled and walked away, stopping before she reached the corner of the street and looking back and smiling again. After she was gone I realized that I did not know her name or where she lived. I gathered that she was the granddaughter of the shipowner. Then I became aware of Captain Melvin standing beside me. He was telling me that everything was straightened out and we were sailing in three days for Denmark. I got into a cab to go back to the hotel with him. He talked about various things and after a while he looked at me and said, "You're very quiet, Mr. Mate."

For the next two days I spent as much time as possible loitering in the street around the shipowner's office, pretending to look into shopwindows. I practiced carefully the expression of surprise that I would put on my face when I met her again and tried to think of the right things to say. But I did not see her.

I was thinking of her constantly when we started for Denmark. After one day at sea, something went wrong with the engines and we turned back to Liverpool for a overhauling job that would take a month or six weeks. Melvin went on a vacation and left me in charge of the ship. One Sunday morning in June I decided to get away from it for a few hours. I boarded a ferryboat with the Sunday newspapers under my arm, hoping to find a pleasant spot across the river in New Brighton where I could stretch out on the grass and read them.

When I walked onto the ferry she was the first person I saw. I forgot to use the surprised look. She said, "Good morning," and we began to talk. When the ferry reached the other bank we walked together until she stopped and said, "I don't think you ought to come any farther. I live there beside the park."

We looked at each other.

"You still haven't told me why you broke that man's arm," she said.

"Any time you wish," I said.

"My name is Lucille," she said.

"Mine's George," I said. "But they call me Dod. That's a Scottish name."

"I've never heard it before but I like it. Would you care to see me this evening?"

"Very much."

"Walk along the river edge until you come to the end of a wall. Wait there and I'll try to be there at seven-thirty. Wait until eight o'clock. If we have company for dinner I'll try to sneak out."

That night she met me. After I told her the story about the bosun I had a hard time trying to talk. We sat under a beech tree and I carved our initials on the trunk. She always spoke of it afterward as "our tree." When I kissed her we both blushed and I said, "I hope you are not angry."

"I wanted you to, Dod," she said. "I'm not angry."

We saw each other from then on whenever we could. Sometimes we sat under the tree and other evenings we went to a cinema and held hands. She even came to the ship's dock a few times and I went down the gangplank and talked with her. I wondered now and then if her wealthy grandfather would permit a penniless first mate to marry her but we still made plans. Then, one Monday night, Lucille did not keep a date she had made with me. The next morning I was asked to report at the owner's office.

Her grandfather kept me waiting for almost an hour. Then he saw me in his office. He sat down at a large desk and left me standing in the middle of the room. He stared at me for several minutes without a word and then he asked me how much of a bank account I had. I told him that I had no bank account.

"And what sort of a home do you expect to have when you get married, Orsborne?" he asked.

This took me by surprise. I said I didn't know.

"And what have you to offer my granddaughter? Nothing. Absolutely nothing. And you have the nerve to see her."

I said nothing. That seemed to make him angrier.

"I would rather see her married to the devil himself than married to you or to any man of the sea. She will never see you again. I have sent her abroad until she gets over you. Now get out of here. See the cashier and get your money. And don't come near this office again."

I walked out slowly. I thought of various things I might have said but it was too late to say them now. For a few days I watched the neighborhood near her house, hoping at least to be able to say good-by to her. But I did not find her.

I went to other shipping offices looking for another berth. I was the youngest first mate in Liverpool at the time and I had a good reputation there. Now I found that nobody would hire me. Owners who had been eager before to have me on their ships would shake their heads before I opened my mouth to ask for a job. After a few weeks I happened to meet on the street the cashier who had paid me off, a nice man named Phillips. He asked me how I was making out. I said I was doing well but I saw that I wasn't fooling him.

"Take a bit of advice, lad," he said. "Don't waste your time here. You won't find a ship in the whole of Liverpool, if you know what I mean."

I knew what he meant. I had been blacklisted.

"Thanks, Mr. Phillips," I said. "Just tell me one thing. Has Miss Lucille gone away?"

"Yes, lad. She's gone to the south of France with her aunt."

"Thanks a lot," I said. "And so long."

I went across England to the rough and tough port of Grimsby on the river Humber, where I found a place as mate of a trawler that fished in the Arctic. It was hard and dangerous work but it paid well and after a year of it I had saved enough money to go ashore and study at Grimsby Nautical College. I planned to attend the college for six or eight months in preparation for the Board of Trade examination for a master's certificate which I might be able to tackle in a year or so.

But after I had studied at the college for three months the principal urged me to make an attempt at the next examination for captains' tickets, which was scheduled to be held in only six weeks. This seemed to me to be absurd. The examination was very difficult and needed long preparation. I didn't see how I would be ready for it in six weeks.

But the principal felt it was worth the gamble. He pointed out that I was the only mate he had ever known who had seven full years of sea experience at the age of twenty-one, as I was then. If I passed the examination I would be the youngest certified master in England. That, of course, would reflect credit on him and on the college. Finally he persuaded me and I filed the application.

I was living in Grimsby with the mother of one of my old shipmates. She and her daughter, a pleasant and well-educated young widow, a few years older than I, kept a lodging and boarding house. When I came back from my interview with the principal and announced that I was going to sit for the skippers' examination, the daughter volunteered to help me with my studies.

Every night after supper we sat together and went over my books until the small hours of the morning. She was a bright girl and she was a great help to me with the task of cramming on navigation, the Rules of the Road, and the Laws of the Sea. Then we began to put the books aside at midnight and do other things.

When the morning of the examination day arrived the landlady and her daughter and five other boarders gathered at the door to wish me good luck. Without thinking, I said, "If I pass, we can get married." A cheer went up.

I really did not expect to pass. There were twenty-six other mates taking the test and they were all much more experienced than I was. The next man to me in age was twenty-eight. The examination lasted for several days and only six out of the twenty-six candidates were awarded the master mariner certificates. I was one of them. I left the building walking on air.

I was still in a dream world when I came back to the boardinghouse. "I passed!" I yelled in the front hallway. Everybody turned out to shake my hand. Then I heard somebody saying, "And now we will have a wedding." That pulled me up short. I had completely forgotten the rash promise I had made when I left to take the examination.

But I didn't see any way to back out of it. We were married at three o'clock one afternoon and at three o'clock the following morning I was sailing from Grimsby in command of my first ship. I regret to say that I got more of a thrill out of being in command of the ship than I did in being married. I am still married to the same girl and we are the best of friends. But I haven't spent much time with her since our wedding day. I have been too busy with other things.

Finding yourself at sea in charge of your own ship for the first time is a moving and memorable experience. As I sailed down the Humber and into the North Sea that morning I repeated to myself the master's rules of the sea:

> *To keep cool, calm and collected at all times.*
> *To think first of all lives under my care or command.*
> *To think secondly of all property under my care and command.*
> *And lastly to think of myself.*

The responsibility of a sea captain in the British mercantile marine is a terribly heavy one. If he makes one single mistake he never lives it down. A classmate of mine at the nautical college, a steady and industrious fellow whom I shall refer to here as John Smith, became a captain after four unsuccessful tries at the examination. On his fifth voyage as a skipper he took an old steamship to Iceland and ran it ashore in the fog on the southeast coast of that island. The sea was calm and Smith lowered a boat to have soundings taken around the ship. The boat slipped and fell into the water while it was being lowered and dipped its stern, letting water into it. Smith cursed the men who were handling it as clumsy fools and lowered himself into the boat and bailed it out, a thing he never should have done. Then he called to his first officer, "Mr. Mate, throw me the lead. As long as I'm here, I may as well take the soundings myself."

The fog was so thick that Smith lost sight of his ship when his boat moved a few feet away from it. Then the boat, too, stuck its nose in the mud and it took Smith and the men who were with him fifteen minutes to pry it loose. They could find no trace of the ship after that. It was February and there are only a few hours of daylight in that northern latitude at that time of year. Darkness fell and Smith and his men rowed for several hours. Twenty-four hours later they landed in the surf on a clay beach, where the boat was smashed. Daylight came again and the fog lifted. They scanned the sea for miles around but found no trace of the ship. Six days later they stumbled into a lighthouse, frostbitten and starved, with their clothing frozen as stiff as boards.

When he recovered, Smith was brought back to England and put on trial for abandoning his ship. At the trial the mate testified that a few hours after the captain had pulled away in the boat to take soundings he found that the ship was afloat and drifting into deep water. He rang for the engines to be turned on and steamed south for twenty minutes to get clear of the shallow water. Then he kept the ship in the area for twenty-four hours, sounding the foghorn, in hope of locating the captain's small boat. When the boat failed to appear the mate decided that it had been lost at sea. He headed for the nearest port, eighty miles away, and reported the incident. An Icelandic gunboat searched the coast for the boat without success.

The Board of Trade inquiry showed that the ship had run aground at low tide at the mouth of a small river. If Smith had merely anchored the ship and waited, it would have refloated in a few hours, as indeed it did.

The prosecuting attorney leveled a damning blast at Smith for leaving his ship and getting into a lifeboat when it was in misfortune. His master's certificate was suspended indefinitely and he was ordered not to sail as an officer of any rating for a period of two years.

But even harsher than the sentence of the inquiry board was the sentence passed on him by other men of the sea who did not understand the circumstances of the case. Captains and mates who were his friends passed him on the street without a nod. The town gossips pointed to his wife as the woman who was married to a man who had deserted his ship. Two years later Smith fell from a ship in the river Humber where he was working as a deck hand and was drowned. A lot of us felt that he committed suicide. His young widow told me that on the very day he died he received a letter from the Board of Trade reinstating his mate's certificate.

For five years after I became a captain I did a little bit of everything, including rumrunning, whaling, and more deep-sea trawling in the Arctic waters. Then I began to get bored. I wanted something new. After one trip I tied up at the home port and went to the company office and told the distinguished and titled owner of my ship that I was through. He was astonished.

"Where are you going?" he asked.

"I don't know," I said. "I haven't made my mind up yet."

"Anything wrong with your ship? Anything upsetting you?"

"No, sir," I said. "Nothing wrong. I'm just fed up."

The owner became indignant. "You're an idiot," he said. "You know we're in the midst of a shipping slump. Masters are standing ashore at ten for a penny. Do you expect us to give you another ship the moment you come crawling back here asking for one?"

That was all I needed. I told him where he could put his ship. And I walked out.

I went back to Liverpool. The office of Lucille's grandfather was closed and the firm was apparently out of business. Her house was empty and there was a "For Sale" sign on it. I walked to our tree and found our initials on its trunk, already almost invisible with age. And then, in town, I bumped into Phillips, the old cashier. He told me that the shipping company had merged with another concern that had its office in London. Phillips introduced me to a man who offered me a job in the West Indies. He represented an importer of molasses, who needed a master to run a small boat among the out-of-the-way islands, picking up molasses shipments and taking them to the large ships that would carry them to England. I took the job.

After the grim and gray Arctic, the West Indies seemed wonderful. I worked on the molasses boat for nine months. Then I bought for nine hundred dollars a schooner named the *Hermosa* that had been lying at Grenada in the Windward Islands since the first World War. Her timbers were covered with barnacles and weeds and there were four feet of stagnant water in her hull but that did not discourage me. After a great deal of work and a new suit of canvas and several gallons of tar, she looked perfect. I went into free-lance trading, carrying cargo between Trinidad, Barbados, Martinique, and the various Windward Islands.

It was a really superb life. Looking back on it, I wonder why I was ever foolish enough to leave it. I was my own boss. I went only where I wanted to go and when I wanted to go. I took orders from no one. I had an excellent crew of blacks who did all the work on the schooner and supervised the loading and unloading of cargo. I would land in one of those throbbing, colorful West Indian towns and spend two days and two nights drinking the best rum and enjoying the entertaining company. On the morning of the third day I would crawl back to the boat, exhausted and weak. The boat would be loaded and ready to go. After four days at sea, sleeping all morning and all afternoon in a pair of shorts on the sun-drenched deck and eating fresh fruit and drinking coconut milk, I would step off the boat at the next port, feeling as fit and as strong as a tiger. And then two more days of drinking and carousing. And four or five more days of pleasant convalescence on the bright blue ocean. To make things even more delightful, this carefree existence was also prosperous. I was collecting fat fees for transporting cargo and the money was coming in much faster than I could spend it. I actually had in Port of Spain a large bank balance.

One day before lunch I was sitting on a veranda in Trinidad, drinking rum swizzles with two very good-looking Portuguese girls and an American named Ryan, who called himself Major Ryan. The major, a sharp character if there ever was one, was discussing an expedition he was planning to lead into the South American jungles along the border between British Guiana and Brazil in search of Redfern, the missing aviator who was believed to have crashed there. Word had come out of the jungle that Redfern was alive and being cared for by primitive Indian tribesmen. Ryan wanted me to go with the expedition as its navigator and map man. He had me sold on the idea when a small boy approached our table and told me that a lady wanted to meet me at the hotel. I knew practically all the ladies in Port of Spain and none of them was better-looking than the Portuguese girl who was sitting beside me. I told the boy to go away.

I resumed the conversation with Ryan. A few minutes later I happened to notice the same boy again. He was standing in the doorway, pointing me out to a woman who obviously was not a Trinidad woman. I looked at her again. And then I stood up. It was Lucille.

Everybody on the veranda stopped talking and looked for the next few minutes.

After we relaxed and separated she said, "I found you. At last I found you, Dod."

When we went back to her hotel she told me how she had met Phillips and he had told her about my going to the West Indies and she had taken the next boat. After we had lunch I asked her when she was planning to go back to England. She laughed.

"I'm not going back to England," she said. "I came here to marry you. I told everybody on the ship that I was coming out here to marry you."

I did not get up enough courage to tell her I was already married until late that night.

"Never mind," she said. "I loved you first and you loved me first and I know you always loved me. Tell me you did."

I did and it wasn't just words. She had always been with me.

We spent several days together. I told her about Ryan's expedition. The time for it to get under way was drawing near. At first she wanted me to take her with me but I would not do it. I didn't know whether to break my promise to Ryan. I was ready to go back to England with Lucille and try to lead a normal life. Or at least a fairly normal life.

She made up my mind for me. One evening when we were sitting in the hotel garden she told me that she was leaving for England the next day.

"You're different from other people, Dod," she said. "Maybe that's why I love you. If I made you give up this kind of life you'd resent me later when you began to miss it."

The next day we said good-by in her hotel room. She asked me not to come to the dock.

"Now listen to me," she said. "If you ever need me I'll come to the other side of the world for you. And there'll never be anybody else. I'll be waiting for you. When do you think you'll come to England?"

I told her it might not be for a year.

"Whenever it is, come to me as soon as your ship docks," she said. "That's the only thing I ask of you."

CHAPTER 4

*M*AJOR RYAN'S EXPEDITION ASSEMBLED AT GEORGE-
town in British Guiana, a place that has always seemed to me to be the
most backward and mismanaged of all the British colonies. The people
there would steal the sugar out of your tea. There is more voodooism
in the colony than there is in Africa. The government offices were
headquarters for thieves and grafters and the British officials regarded
themselves as personages more important than dukes or earls. In any
other part of the world they would have been unable to achieve the
prestige of a traffic cop.

It did not take me long to see that Major Ryan had neither the
technical training nor the practical knowledge necessary in a leader of
an expedition such as this one, which planned to move into an uncharted jungle wilderness. I wondered how he had ever rounded up the
financial backing and scientific endorsement for his ambitious under-
taking. However, he was full of guile and he had a clever tongue. No
doubt he had talked some wealthy people in the United States into
believing that he was a modern Daniel Boone who could find Redfern,
the missing flier, just as dramatically as Stanley had found Livingstone.
I don't think that he had ever seen before a countryside that was not
illuminated by street lights.

We found that we were wasting our time trying to organize the expedition in Georgetown. The natives there wanted no part of us. They
were lazy and afraid of the jungle. We moved down to Paramaribo in
Dutch Guiana, or Surinam as it is now called, and there we engaged
some Djuka bushmen as guides and a number of creole natives from
the town to serve as cooks and carriers. When we started our journey in

six canoes there were twenty men in the party. This included, in addition to Ryan and myself, a young man from New Orleans named Dick Lamely, who was to be Ryan's assistant and medical officer, and a Venezuelan named Tony, who had charge of the carriers and cooks. We went up the coast and then inland on the Courantyne River, where the mosquitoes and flies were so thick that if you opened your mouth to talk dozens of them would find their way into your throat. The smell from rotten vegetation along the riverbank was nauseating. After two days of this Ryan began to talk about turning back.

Our first stop was at a native village thirty miles beyond Orealla. We found that the father of the tribe there was a missionary from Wales who had come to South America to convert the heathen and ended up instead as the husband of five wives and the father of fourteen children. He refused to talk with us. We continued on up the river, despite the swift current that tried to push us back, until we reached the fork where the Courantyne meets the New River and the Coeroeni River. We camped there and met a Dutch trader who advised us to follow the New River, which came in from the right. He had heard from the natives that a white man, who might be Redfern, was living with one of the tribes near the headwaters of that stream.

For some reason that we couldn't make out, the Djuka guides did not like the idea of venturing into that territory. Ryan had to bargain with them and offer them more money before they consented to go on. After two days we reached a rapids that blocked our way. We decided to cut a trail along the bank of the river that led to the smoother water up ahead. Leaving the canoes, we began to cut a path through the bush that grew like a thick wall. It took us three days to make the trail. Finishing it, we returned to the starting point and prepared our canoes and supplies so that they could be carried over the freshly cleared trail the following morning. Ryan suggested that we split up for the night, one group sleeping beside the canoes and the other group staying with the supplies, about a hundred yards away. Ryan said he would guard the canoes. Lamely, Tony, and I stayed with the supplies. We were exhausted from working on the trail and we fell into a deep sleep.

In the morning when I awoke I discovered that Ryan was gone. So were all the canoes, most of the supplies, and the Djuka guides, the only ones in the expedition who knew the country.

Lamely was staggering around the camp, with a dazed look in his eyes, muttering to himself. At first I thought he was merely shocked

because Ryan had deserted us. Then I noticed that he was soaked with sweat, although the sun was not yet above the trees, and the words he was muttering were declensions of Latin nouns. He was delirious with fever.

Tony was sitting and staring at the river with a vacant, hopeless expression on his face. The native cooks and carriers were blaming each other for not staying awake and watching Ryan and the guides. Their petty quarreling and bickering at such a time made me furious. I picked up a stick and began to beat them. They backed away from me and stopped their noise.

I finally succeeded in making Lamely lie down in the shade. I was covering him with a mosquito net and putting Dover tablets down his throat when I heard a thundering sound, like the hoofbeats of a herd of wild horses. The carriers started to scramble up the trunks of the palm trees, yelling, *"Bru! Bru!"* Tony jumped to his feet and shouted at me.

"Pigs!"

I stood beside Lamely and drew my hatchet from my belt. Down our newly made trail, heading straight at us, came hundreds of the ugliest animals I had ever seen, huge, grizzled wild boars. They charged with their heads close to the ground, screaming and grunting, tearing at the vegetation while they ran with yellowed, sharp tusks. I stood as though I was hypnotized and stared at them and as they came to me they separated and rushed by on either side of me. The last one, lagging behind the rest, was a fat old sow, followed by a litter of her young. She stopped and glared at me with her wicked little eyes and then ran across Lamely's chest and into the bushes.

While my heart was still thumping from the fright, the sky darkened and there was a long peal of thunder. The rain came down in torrents and completely soaked everything we had. Then it stopped and the sun came out. I looked at Lamely and saw a stream of red ants passing underneath him. I turned him over and found thousands of ants eating into the flesh in his back. Tony and I stripped him naked and covered his body with turpentine that I found in the medicine chest and stretched him on a hammock that we hung between two trees. He was unconscious.

Tony and I could not decide what to do. It was impossible to move in any direction without a canoe or boat and we had neither. Tony felt that perhaps Ryan would return with the canoes and the guides but I knew that we would never see him again. He did not have the courage to go on with the expedition. And he did not want his financial backers to know that he had turned coward and failed to finish the job. So he fixed it so that Lamely and Tony and I, the witnesses to his failure, would be left in the jungle to die.

We made a fire and took turns watching it that night. I was afraid to sleep. I felt that the native carriers, hating me for the beating I had given them that morning, might attempt to murder me if I closed my eyes.

When daylight came I saw a small canoe in the river, only a few yards away from us. Sitting in it were two delicately built Indians with spears resting across their knees. I waved to them to come ashore but they paddled farther away from the bank and stopped and stared at us. Tony tried a few bush languages on them but they gave no sign of recognition. I saw them eying the small hatchet that hung from my belt. I took off the hatchet and cut a bamboo stalk with one stroke and held the hatchet toward them with the handle extended. That made them come ashore.

Through sign language I got them to understand that I wanted to trade the hatchet for their canoe, which they were glad to do. I asked Tony to select two of the most trustworthy carriers and put them in the canoe with Lamely. I told them to take him down the river to Orealla, which they might be able to reach in three days with the current behind them, and to ask the police there to send help for the rest of us.

When the canoe disappeared around the bend of the river Tony told the two Indians in sign language that we wanted to go to their tribal village. We filled our haversacks with trading material. Only a few yards from our camp the Indians pushed aside some foliage and we found ourselves on a winding jungle path. It led into a clearing full of tall, yellow grass and then we reached a village. About forty Indians came out to meet us. They were ugly and emaciated. They could not understand us and we found it impossible to follow their conversation.

Both the men and the women carried blowguns and darts. I had heard that the Indians in that part of the interior of South America fired these darts, dipped in snake venom, at any stranger but these people were friendly and took pains to make us comfortable. They led us to their chief, a wrinkled old man with white matted hair and sparse chin whiskers. He motioned to us to sit by the fire and eat with them. Two women appeared, carrying four bush turkeys with arrows still sticking through them. The women held the birds over the fire until most of the feathers were burned off and then dropped them, entrails and all, into a pot to boil. We sat for an hour while the turkeys cooked. No one said a word. Then the turkeys were removed from the pot and passed to the chief. He tore them apart and handed pieces of them to each of us and to each of the Indians.

Afterward I looked around the village and I noticed two long spears leaning against a tree. They were tipped with a smooth metal. I saw that it was the kind of aluminum that is used in aircraft construction.

I showed it to Tony and we tried to ask the chief about it. At first he stared at us. I gave him one of the hatchets that we had brought as trading material and I drew with a stick on the ground the shape of an airplane. I also fashioned a model plane from pieces of wood.

The chief stood up and flapped his arms like a bird and made a noise like an airplane motor. This went on for at least ten minutes. Then he sat down and stared at me again. I took out a small pocket knife and handed it to him. He examined it carefully and stood up again and made more flapping motions and more motor noises for another ten minutes. He sat down and stared again. I gave him a can opener. He stood up once more and went into the same act. I was beginning to wonder if I was being taken for a sucker when he stopped and pointed at the fire and spread himself flat on the ground with his arms outstretched. Then he pointed at the fire again and made gestures, indicating a big blaze, and pointed toward the hills beyond the clearing.

Evidently that was the answer to the problem that the expedition had set out to solve. A plane crash in the hills, followed by a fire.

"Well, Tony," I said, "if you ever run into Ryan, you can tell him that after he left we found out what happened to Redfern."

We left the Indian village and went back to our camp by the river and waited another day and another night for help to come from Orealla. Then we wondered if perhaps the canoe with Lamely in it had failed to get through to that town. Tony and I decided to try building a raft.

We cut down four palm trees and lashed them together in the form of a square and laid across them bundles of bamboo poles. It made a raft that did not balance well but after three more days of waiting we decided to take a chance with it. We put our remaining supply of food on it and pushed off into the river.

The raft navigated rather smoothly in midstream but it was hard to manage when it struck one of the banks. We were afraid to use it at night. If we fell off it, we wouldn't have been able to see the riverbanks. The stream was full of all varieties of reptiles, insects, bats, and crocodiles. We saw forty-foot pythons curled in the mud at the water's edge. My body was covered with festered sores from thorn and branch scratches that did not heal in the steaming jungle heat.

We managed somehow to get to a place on the river that we estimated as being thirty or forty miles from Orealla. While we were camped there overnight the river, swollen by the unusually heavy rains, rose suddenly to a few feet of where we were sleeping and carried away the raft. The native carriers became panic-stricken. They told Tony that I was an evil man who had brought misfortune to them. They blamed me for the disappearance of Ryan. There were five of them against Tony and me. I decided that it was no time to show any sign of fear or weakness.

"Tony," I said, "translate this for them. Tell them that they are right. I am a very evil man."

While Tony put this into their language I took my hatchet from my belt and ran my finger along its edge.

"And now tell them that I can read what is in their minds. Tell them if there is any killing done here, I will do the killing."

When this news was broken to them I could tell from the guilty expressions on their faces that I had made the right tactical move. They might believe that I was some sort of a devil who couldn't be trifled with.

It was hopeless to think of building another raft. The river was too fast and rough. There was only one way left for us. That was to hack our way through the pathless, tangled jungle, staying as close to the river as possible. We let each carrier take as much as he wanted from the stores. I took only a pound of rice and a bottle of quinine and my hatchet. It was slow and hot going. I was getting dizzy spells and chills. I felt sure that it was the beginning of malaria but I did not want the natives to know it. Even though I was quite weak, I would call orders in a commanding voice to make an impression on them.

A creek full of hungry crocodiles forced us to detour away from the river and I came across a trail that headed north, the direction we were following. Rather than zigzag back to the river and cover extra mileage, we decided to stay on the trail. Besides, it had the added advantage of being fairly clear of obstructing foliage. We followed the trail all that day. Late in the afternoon, when the sun was getting low, I took over the leading position in the procession. After a few miles I turned around and saw no one on the trail behind me.

I walked back and stood and listened. But I heard nobody approaching.

"Tony!" I yelled.

There was no answer. I waited a few moments and yelled again.

"Tony!"

A monkey in a nearby tree screamed at me. I ran back down the trail for more than a half mile but I saw no one and heard nothing. Tony and the five natives had vanished completely.

I was bewildered and frightened. I was alone and darkness was falling fast upon the jungle. I tried to calm myself and figure out what to do. Perhaps Tony and the natives had branched off onto another path. If that was the case it would be best for me to stay where I was and wait for them to discover their mistake and retrace their steps and catch up with me. But I realized that it was more likely that the natives had grabbed Tony from behind and had killed him noiselessly while I walked innocently away from them. We were on the British Guiana side of the river. They would have gone back to the river and crossed it to the Dutch Guiana side and made their way to the coast.

The rain began to fall and in a moment I was soaked to the skin. I sat down on a boulder, feeling lost and miserable and sick. The rice in my knapsack, wet with rain, swelled and I ate a few handfuls of it. It was getting darker by the minute. I had no means of lighting a fire.

I sat on that boulder in the pouring rain all night long. I was unable to move in the pitch-black darkness. Except for the noise of the falling rain and swish of the rivulets of water that ran past my feet, I did not hear a sound. The only time I could see anything was when there would be an occasional flash of lightning. It was the longest and the most terrifying night I have ever spent in my whole life. Once or twice before daylight finally appeared in the east I thought I was going out of my mind. Why I did not lose my sanity I don't know.

Toward morning the rain slackened off and when I stood up I found my limbs so stiff and sore that I could hardly walk. I carried my hatchet in my hand for a while, so that it would be ready if I had to use it. But I did not have the strength to carry it. I put it back into my belt and staggered on. The straps of the haversack were unbearable on my shoulders. I took it off and threw it away. My boots were full of water and seemed a ton weight but I knew that if I took them off my feet would swell and I would never be able to put them on again. Finally, however, I was forced to take them off and cut off the leather above the ankle. My legs were chafed raw. I threw away my socks and put on my boots and resumed walking. The rain stopped and the jungle noises became alive again.

After a few miles I noticed that the trail was getting wider and smoother. Then I saw a tree with a piece of white cloth tied around it. I ran toward it, yelling, "Tony! Tony!" I was sure that he had come back to the trail again and he had left the cloth as a marker to show me that he was ahead of me.

But then I heard an answer in perfect English. "Hello, there," a voice said.

I ran in the direction of the voice. I came upon four men sitting in a dinghy that was moored at the edge of the river. They were Negroes, dressed in European clothes and wearing sun helmets. When they saw me they were startled. I must have looked like a wild man. They would not let me come near the boat until they questioned me and until I threw away my hatchet.

They were balata tree markers who had come up the river from Orealla, which was only three miles away. They told me that they had heard about two Dutch Guiana natives putting ashore a white man at Orealla but everybody in the town had presumed that the white man, Lamely, was an escaped convict from Devil's Island. They said he had died on the way down the river. The man who did the talking for the group was an African Negro named Van Cotten who worked for a rubber firm in Georgetown. He had charge of the crews of tree markers in that area. He was kind enough to dress my sores and he took me to his home and fed me. That night he let me sleep in his bed. Because I was a white man, his wife and his seven children slept outside the wooden house.

The next day I went to Georgetown, where I was immediately

arrested and put into Brickdam Prison and questioned by the police, who wanted to know how I had escaped from Devil's Island. Five different newspaper reporters came into my cell and offered me money if I would give them the full details of my escape from the penal colony at French Guiana. The police promised not to send me back to Devil's Island if I gave them the story exclusively. When I told them that I had never been imprisoned at Devil's Island they laughed at me. They pointed to the sores on my legs and insisted that they were caused by chains that I had worn in solitary confinement.

Two British officials called on me to threaten me with a thrashing unless I talked. I lost my head and started to attack them but I checked myself and managed to convince them that I was entitled to see a lawyer. They finally did send me a Negro lawyer and I gave him the entire story of what had happened on the expedition. He talked with the commissioner of police and I was released from prison. I took a room at the Tower Hotel and wired my bank in Trinidad for money. The same newspaper reporters called on me again and offered me two hundred dollars if I would tell them what I knew about Redfern's fatal crash. I told them what they could do in blunt, indelicate terms.

I made inquiries and found that no searching party had ever been sent out to look for us, although the natives who brought Lamely's body to Orealla must have described our predicament. I never was able to find a trace of Tony. The natives must have killed him. He would never have left me of his own choice.

A few years ago somebody told me that Major Ryan was in Brazil. With the money that he had raised for the expedition he opened a hotel for tourists there and he was doing very well.

CHAPTER 5

WHEN PEOPLE FIND OUT THAT YOU HAVE TRAVELED rather extensively, they always ask what part of the world you like best and where, if you had the choice, you would prefer to spend the rest of your life. My answer today to both questions is India. I like the country and I love the people. There is less affectation there than anywhere else.

But nineteen years ago I felt that the best place on the face of this earth was the Barawi Islands in the Arabian Sea, where I once spent seven of the happiest weeks I have ever known. The ancient mariners called the Barawis the Paradise Islands and to me they were Paradise. I hated to leave them. I always wanted to go back there and live as one of the natives until one evening in London ten years later when I met again a man I had known there. He told me how the Barawis were later spoiled, like so many other places, by the arrival of civilization. I will never go back now. I want to remember them as I knew them.

After the collapse of Ryan's expedition I went to Trinidad and made a deal to sail my schooner to British West Africa and sell it there. And then I got mixed up with a character in West Africa who hired me to supervise gangs of natives that were clearing and reclaiming tracts of jungle land. When I discovered that my employer was selling these plots of uncultivated land to innocent victims in England as thriving peanut plantations, I decided to check out and get away before the roof fell in. I returned to England and celebrated a reunion with Lucille for a month. Then I began to get restless again and signed up to take a deep-sea trawler to Bombay. It had been bought in England by an Australian company. In Bombay I was to turn the ship over to a skipper from her new company who would take her the rest of the way to Sydney.

In Bombay I collected my pay and an allowance of fifty pounds to cover my fare back to England but I was in no great hurry to start the return trip. Jack Francis, a friend of mine, found me a room in the Seagreen Hotel on Marine Drive and we spent several nights together. In ten days my pay and the expense money were gone. I told Jack that he had better find me a job quick. He was in charge of the sailors' and firemen's union in Bombay. He took me to a European named King who managed the Malabar St. Coromandel Company. They needed a skipper for an old trading schooner. King explained the situation to me.

"We trade in the Laccadive Islands, Captain," he said. "Now north of the Laccadives there's a group of islands known as the Barawis. The people on the Barawis have been taking their goods for trading purposes to the Indian mainland, mostly to Mangalore, which is more than four hundred miles away. We want to send this schooner to the Barawis to establish a trading station there in the islands themselves. The British government wants to send a doctor there, for scientific reasons. He'll be your only passenger. Our company representative will be aboard, of course. We expect you to assist him with the work of getting the trade agreements made with those people."

King pointed to the islands on a chart that was spread on the table. They were like pinheads and there was no land anywhere near them. Near their position, the chart was marked CR and PD, which means coral reef, position doubtful. It was a lovely assignment in navigation. Really charming.

"Not much to go by, is there?" I said to King.

He shook his head.

"How long is the job and how much?" I asked.

"Three hundred rupees per month for three months, increasing by fifty rupees a month up to five hundred rupees. If the trade is good, you'll get more."

I took it. A week later I found myself in command of the ugliest hulk I had ever seen. It was an eighty-foot schooner, thirty years old, named *Essmero*. It had a dilapidated and ancient paraffin-driven engine and five sheets of patched canvas, a crew of eight coolies and a cook. The cargo consisted of a few bundles of various small wares, several rolls of cotton dress material, jars of Indian rum, and several chests that belonged to the doctor. The doctor, an Englishman named Maxwell, was all right. The company representative, an Indian who called himself Mr. Blimero, was a skunk.

We chugged out of Bombay with the coolie engineer kneeling beside the engine and pouring oil over it continually from a milk tin while it croaked and sputtered. I decided to take a chance and try to hit the Barawis directly from Bombay, instead of going first to the Laccadives and then turning back north from there. Dr. Maxwell and I spent the first five days sitting in the sun, discussing the world and mankind. On the fifth day the engine broke down and Mr. Blimero and I became enemies.

I felt sorry for the coolie engineer and spent several hours sweating in the hot cubbyhole astern that we called the engine room, trying to repair the engine. When we came on deck to get a breath of air Mr. Blimero began to shout at the engineer in Hindustani, apparently blaming him for the breakdown, and then picked up a bamboo stick and hit him. My temper was short and that released it completely. I took the stick away from Mr. Blimero and hit him at least three times. The doctor pulled me away from him and he ran away.

"What's he trying to do?" I fumed. "Run the crew? He's only a passenger on this ship."

"Calm down," Dr. Maxwell said. "He thought he was doing the right thing. He shipped the crew. Now you've made a bad error."

"Why?"

"You can't strike an Indian like that. You've lowered him in the eyes of the coolies."

The next day the engine started and stopped six times but the day after that our luck changed. The engine began to operate smoothly and we found a breeze from the northwest that ran our speed up to eight knots. On the thirteenth day I began to zigzag so that I would be able to see more water and toward dusk we spotted white surf far to the west northwest. We sailed in that direction for an hour but darkness fell. In the morning we found that the surf was breaking on a reef that had no land near it. We turned south again and in the afternoon we sighted land. It was a beautiful, long island with stately palm trees but it was surrounded by dangerous reefs. I stayed three miles from it, taking soundings and wondering what to do next. Then I heard shouts from the crew. Several canoes were coming toward us.

The people in the canoes were light-colored with straight noses. They wore silver and gold bracelets and arm bands and some of them had earrings but they wore no clothing whatsoever. Even though more than half of them were women, they clambered aboard the ship without fear or suspicion or hesitation. And also without an invitation. They acted as though we were old friends and they welcomed us cheerfully and with no formality.

One of them told Dr. Maxwell that this was the Barawi Islands but we could not land on that one. We had to go around its eastern end to a larger island three miles away. We sailed in that direction and found ourselves in a stretch of water, three to four miles wide and strewn with coral reefs. We stopped the engine, clewed up the sails, and left ourselves in the hands of the natives, who actually towed us with their canoes, dipping and straining against their paddles in unison with a chant that they sang. They pulled the ship all afternoon, finally bringing her into a narrow channel lined on both sides with palm trees that I could have touched from the deck with a boathook. The channel led into a beautiful basin-shaped lagoon, where we dropped anchor within twenty yards of a red sand beach. This was the largest of the seven Barawi Islands.

The natives led us ashore to meet an aged French missionary named Father Yanam. He had lived there for thirty-two years and we were the first visitors from the mainland that he had seen in fourteen years. He invited us to dine with him on the veranda of his bungalow. We ate delicious chicken, turtle meat, curried eggs, rice, fish, and sweetmeats that were served to us in small heaps on fresh banana leaves. Thinking that I was being polite, I would finish every scrap on each leaf only to find the native serving girl replacing it with a full leaf. I whispered to Dr. Maxwell that the food was coming out of my eyes. "When you've had enough, leave a little on the leaf," he said. "Otherwise they'll keep on serving it to you."

That night I slept under the stars with a cool fresh breeze, faintly scented with jasmine, fanning my brow. There were no mosquitoes and none of the bad smells of India.

Mr. Blimero began to negotiate with the leading natives and Father Yanam. A disagreement broke out between the company representative and the priest the next day when we started to unload the ship. Father Yanam did not want the rum to be brought ashore. Mr. Blimero wanted to use it for trading material. Dr. Maxwell acted as the mediator and they argued for several hours in an Indian dialect that I did not understand. I sat and drank orange juice and smoked cigarettes, saying nothing. Finally Dr. Maxwell turned to me and said, "It's for you to decide, Captain." He explained the situation.

The people on the islands were originally Christians and they still have a strong strain of Caucasian blood. Three quarters of the population are females because the men go to the Indian mainland three times a year to trade and the young men, getting their first taste of sin and wine there, often stay and never return. There was no money on the island. Father Yanam felt that the importation of rum and money would corrupt the people and cause jealousy, quarrels, and unhappiness. He was willing to let the company pay for the turtle shell that it wanted with harmless goods. But he did not want them to pay for it with money or rum. If the company did not have enough goods to barter for the turtle shell, money could be entrusted to him and he would use it to build the natives a church. He wanted to keep the islands free from greed.

The priest's request sounded reasonable to me and I said so. I said that there were enough other goods on the ship besides the rum to use in trading and the rum could go back on board.

Mr. Blimero was furious. He remarked that the whole affair was none of my concern and that it was for him to make decisions for the company. He said that I was the master of the ship but not the master of the islands.

"I'll give you your choice," I said to him. "You and the rum can stay here and I'll sail back to Bombay tomorrow. Or the rum goes back on board and we stay and trade according to the father's terms."

We stayed. And I have never enjoyed anything so much as the life I lived for the next seven weeks. It was a perfect existence. The people were completely natural. They worked cheerfully without a whistle to tell them when to begin work and when to stop it. They ate when they were hungry and slept when they were tired. There were no political arguments, no dishonesty, no ambition, no selfishness. One evening I saw some men staggering under enormous loads of wet copra that they carried in nets on their shoulders. I said to Father Yanam, "Why do they carry so much weight at one time?" He stopped one of the men and asked him. The man, smiling, said, "What you wish to do tomorrow, do today and what you wish to do today, do now."

And to make my stay perfect, I fell in love with the most beautiful girl I have ever seen. Her name was Kanakamm and she had golden skin with long black hair and lovely brown eyes. The day we left I made sure she was not in one of the canoes that towed us out of the lagoon. If she had been, I would have taken her to Bombay.

Naturally, when Mr. Blimero turned in his report, the company saw to it that I was discharged immediately.

One December evening in London nine years later I went looking for Donald Gillies at his flat in Chelsea and, finding no one there, I dropped a note in his letter box which said that I would be having a beer or two for the next hour in the Three Bells pub around the corner in Kings Road.

When I sat down in the pub and ordered a beer and opened my newspaper I noticed an elderly, pasty-faced man at a nearby table. I could feel him staring at me and it annoyed me. Finally I stared back at him indignantly. He smiled and stood up and walked over to me, holding out his hand.

"Hello, Dod," he said.

"Hello," I said. I tried hard to place him. He was not a sailor.

"The *Essmero*," he said. "The Barawi Islands."

It was Dr. Maxwell. He had served two years in jail for a narcotics charge and he had lost his medical license. He said he was selling radios.

He said that Father Yanam died a year after I visited the islands. Mr. Blimero brought in a cargo of liquor two months later and began to operate a monthly steamship schedule between the Barawis and the Laccadives. The Barawis became overrun with immigrant coolies from the Laccadives and when Dr. Maxwell left the islands, disease and famine were beginning to break out there.

A few years later I heard another story about the Barawis from a friend of mine who is a British newspaper editor. One of the paper's feature writers, on a tour of India, heard about an Englishman who had made his home on one of the Barawis. He was the only European on the islands. The writer felt that the Englishman's retirement from the civilized world might make an interesting story. He decided to pay him a visit.

The Englishman received the writer cordially and invited him to stay for a week. He introduced his wife and his daughter. Both of them were astonishingly beautiful. The writer had a hard time telling at first which was the wife and which was the daughter. They were tall and dark-haired, with dark and rather slanted eyes that seemed to suggest a trace of Asiatic ancestry. But they had been educated in Europe and they were familiar with the best places in Paris, London, Switzerland, and the Riviera. The whole family was intelligent, witty, and, apparently, happy. The father and the daughter were painters of talent. The walls of their attractive and comfortable bungalow were lined with their work.

The situation baffled the writer. Why were such civilized and charming people avoiding the society of the world? He decided to ask no questions for a few days. He would try to find out the answer by himself.

They sat up quite late talking the first evening. After he said good night and retired to his room the writer began to undress. The room was dimly lighted by one candle. While he was removing his shirt the candle went out. As he fumbled for a match to relight it he found that there was a woman in the room. He could not see her clearly in the moonlight that came in the window but he saw enough from the vague outline of her face and figure to know that it was either the mother or the daughter. He could not tell for sure which it was. The woman indicated with a finger to his lips and a shake of her head that he was to remain silent. She lifted the mosquito netting and went into his bed. Sometime later in the night while he was asleep she left the room and when he awoke in the worning he found himself alone.

The mother and the daughter both greeted him politely on the veranda when he sat down with them for breakfast. While he was eating he studied their faces secretly, searching for some sign or some expression that would tell him which one it was that had been with him the night before. But he saw nothing. He expected that during the day one of them might say something to him. But he was alone once or twice with the mother and later he went out to walk with the daughter and both women were polite, friendly, but impersonal.

That night when he went to bed the woman was there in the dark again. He tried to question her but she forced him to be quiet and remained silent herself. Again she left him before daylight.

And so it went for the whole week. Every night she came to him. Every day the mother and the daughter with their looks and their words and gestures told him nothing.

On the morning of the day that he was leaving the writer sat down to talk with the Englishman. He finally asked him why he and his family had chosen to live on the remote island.

"Your wife and your daughter are beautiful and charming," the writer said. "They must crave the company of old friends and new acquaintances. How can they be happy here?"

The Englishman looked out at the water and shook his head. "You don't understand what keeps us here," he said. "I have another daughter, even prettier than this one. You didn't see her. She's living a half mile down the beach. She has leprosy."

The editor who was telling me this paused at that point and took a sip from his drink.

"The story could end there," he said, "but it doesn't. The writer came back to London and told me what had happened. But he never wrote the article because two days later he committed suicide."

"Why did he commit suicide? Did he leave a note or anything?"

"No. He left no explanation. I presume it was one of two things. Perhaps he discovered that he was hopelessly in love with the girl. Or perhaps he thought he was doomed to become a leper himself. If it was fear of leprosy, his fear was groundless. Several doctors have told me that leprosy is rarely contracted through sexual intercourse."

"Why don't you write the story yourself?" I asked. "Wouldn't it make a good plot for a piece of fiction?"

"It isn't worth a damn," the editor said. "Nobody would believe it. As the Americans say, it would sound too corny."

CHAPTER 6

A FEW MONTHS LATER I FOUND MYSELF STILL IN INDIA. I had been hired by the government to survey the uncharted portions of the Godavari River which flows almost entirely across the southern part of India, winding through Hyderabad and emptying into the Bay of Bengal at the northeastern tip of the Madras Province. I established a residence in the forest officers' bungalow at Cocanada, a primitive and smelly town near the swamplands of the Godavari's delta. The filthy drainage from the swamps runs through the center of the town and acts as a sewage disposal stream for a quarter of a million people. It is common to see the putrid and half-burned corpse from a Hindu cremation floating on the muddy water. The summer heat in Cocanada is usually 120 degrees in the shade and the town is full of noise at all hours of the day and night. The shouts of merchants and bullock drivers. The barking of dogs and jackals. And the everlasting sound of music and drums, celebrating a dance for one of the many Indian gods or a birth or a marriage or a death. But after a time you get accustomed to it.

I worked on the surveying project with a British engineer named Denton. We spent three or four days a week on the river and two or three days in Cocanada, drawing charts or resting. We became very friendly with two Indians who had been educated in England. One of them, Raja Derayya, was a landowner and exporter. The other, Danraj Naidu, was the superintendent of police in the district.

One evening we were sitting with them on the veranda of our bungalow, drinking and discussing the possibilities of building a harbor in Cocanada, when a red-turbaned and barefooted Mohammedan policeman came to the bungalow and handed Naidu a report. He read it and then showed it to each one of us in turn.

The report came from the inspector of police in Rampashedavram and it said that the tiger named Appalswama had killed a fifteen-year-old boy in the interior village of Kekkular three days ago.

"Appalswama?" I said. "Do you people have names for each tiger in the jungle?"

"This is a special tiger," Naidu said. "There is a story behind his name."

There seemed to be a story behind everything in India.

It seems that there had been a man named Appalswama in a small native village in the Badulas district who was a great hunter. Somehow he had gained possession of a single-barreled shotgun. Every few days he would come in from the jungle with a wild animal that he had slain and he would chop the carcass up in the village square and sell the meat. The skin he would present to whatever woman had taken his fancy. He was a great hunter of the human female as well as the beast of the jungle. Although the men in the district respected his ability with the shotgun, they hated him for his ability to capture the ladies.

One evening Appalswama visited the nearby village of Kekkular, where the people were celebrating a market-day festival. A strong native wine, made from the sap of the palmyra tree, was flowing freely. In the middle of the party somebody noticed Appalswama entering the hut of the headman of the village. Appalswama was leading by the hand the new young wife of the headman. At last he had been caught in the act.

The men of Kekkular armed themselves with spears, bows, and knives and surrounded the hut. They called for Appalswama to come out. He knew that he would never be able to reason with them in their wine-lit excitement. He appeared at the door with his gun and when they started to throw spears and knives he shot and killed one of the villagers. The siege went on for several hours and during that time Appalswama killed four more men. The villagers saw that the shotgun was hard to beat so they made an agreement with him. They would let him leave the village alive, provided that he took the unfaithful wife with him and never returned again. To show his good faith, he was to let the woman carry the gun when they came out of the hut.

Appalswama agreed to these terms. But the drunken villagers did not keep their word. Before he reached the edge of the village they seized him and tied him to a bed and carried him to the village square, where they chopped off his arms and legs and threw them to the village dogs. Before sunrise they carried the trunk of his body to the jungle and left it for the wild animals.

But the men who carried it there heard the roar of a tiger before they returned to the village. And in the three months that followed Appalswama's killing, one man, three women, and two boys had been carried away from the village in broad daylight by a tiger. The remains of their bodies had been left where the villagers had thrown Appalswama's body. The people in Kekkular were convinced that Appalswama's soul had entered the tiger and he was punishing them for breaking the terms of the truce that they had made with him. That was why the tiger was now known as Appalswama.

I turned to Naidu when he finished the tale and said, "But surely you don't believe it."

"What do you mean?" he said. "This is the seventh report of a killing that I've received from Kekkular."

"Oh, I don't mean the killings," I said. "No doubt there is a man-eating tiger on the prowl up there. But do you believe that it possesses a man's soul?"

Naidu shrugged his shoulders.

"I've been educated in England but I am still a Hindu," he said. "I feel that there is something unnatural about this beast. Three of the best tiger hunters in Madras have gone after him and I went with them. They were unable to set eyes on him, although there is no doubt of his existence. His tracks showed that he was stalking us as we hunted him. We tied a bullock in the jungle and sat all night waiting for him to come and kill it. Instead he killed that night in a village five miles away. We went there and waited beside the half-eaten bullock for his return. Tigers always come back and finish their victim. While we waited he went to a village we had left the previous day and killed a woman. I swear he knew every move we made. As I said, this is no ordinary tiger. The Raja here and the governor of Madras have both offered five-hundred-rupee rewards for his killing."

Denton and I both spoke at once. "If I had a few days to spare I'd like to take a crack at him," I said. Denton said the same thing.

"You would need more than a few days," Naidu said. "You would have to play hide-and-seek for a week or two weeks before you tracked him down."

I had forgotten the tiger the next morning when I went away for three days to take soundings on the river. Denton stayed in the bungalow to work on some maps. When I returned I found him missing. My servant boy said that he had gone hunting and had left word that he would be back in a few days.

The next morning I received a telegram from Rajahmundry, a town forty miles up the river. "Come at once," it said. "Denton mauled by tiger." It was signed by Naidu.

I left at once in our truck but when I reached Rajahmundry I found Denton's body already lying in the police station with a sheet over it. The left arm was torn off at the elbow and the right arm was twisted and broken. His body, from his chest downward, was crushed into pulp.

"We don't know exactly what happened," Naidu said. "He turned up here four days ago and left for Kekkular with two rangers. He was up in a tree, twenty feet above the ground, waiting for the tiger to visit a freshly killed bullock. A few hours later the natives heard a shot and a cry for help. They approached the tree, beating drums to scare the tiger away, but they found him still there, standing over Denton. When he saw the natives the tiger roared and leaped into the jungle. The rangers took Denton downstream in a canoe that night but he died on the way here."

Denton and I had hunted leopards together and we had both received instruction from the best native hunters. I knew that he was a crack shot and very careful. I wondered how the tiger had got him.

A week later, against the advice of everybody I knew, I loaded the truck with supplies, called for Naidu and Derayya, and started for Kekkular. It took us thirty-six hours to get within a mile of the village. At one point forty men had to pull the truck with rope over a rutted track for three miles. When I offered the headman a few rupees for their help he backed away in horror. Naidu explained that I had insulted him. A white man was considered divine in those parts and it was deemed an honor to be of service to him.

"Touch him or shake his hand," Naidu said. "Show him you are friendly."

I shook his hand and gave him a pair of shorts. He left his tribe and stayed with me for the rest of the trip.

When the sun went down we were still ten miles from Kekkular. Riding over that rough ground was like being at sea in a rowboat. Naidu said we would have been more comfortable on the back of a bullock but the earth seemed firm, despite the rocks and the tall grass, so we decided to keep going. Just before it became really dark Naidu grasped my arm and something flashed in front of our headlights.

"Tiger!" Naidu said.

I stopped the truck and reached for my gun and stepped out.

"What are you going to do?" Naidu said.

"Shoot if I can see the damned thing."

"Don't be a fool, Captain. Please come back. Come back."

I saw that he was begging urgently so I got back behind the wheel.

"That tiger is standing right there behind that bamboo clump," Naidu whispered. "You weren't five yards from him. Even if you shot him, he would still get you. We're too close to him. Give me the gun and I'll cover you. Now drive past that clump as fast as possible."

When we were safely past the tiger Naidu let out a sigh of relief.

"I know you've hunted leopards, Captain," he said. "But, believe me, tigers are different. The tiger springs at you even when he is dying and, if he merely touches you, you can be crushed to death."

A mile from the village we were stopped completely by rocks and boulders. The villagers, knowing of our approach by their tom-tom communications system, came out with flaming torches to scare away the animals and carry our luggage for us. I found them looking at me with awe. Naidu told me that they had already heard that I was a powerful white man who had come to avenge the killing of Appalswama's white victim.

That night they fed me peacock and wild pig with rice until I was uncomfortable. I went to sleep on a charpoy covered with mosquito netting inside a bamboo enclosure. In the morning we set off for the jungle, accompanied by six villagers and my faithful headman, who was wearing my shorts and feeling very proud of them. His name was Mumgunankuam but that was too much for me. I called him John.

We went back to the place on the road where we had seen the tiger the previous night. Just as Naidu had said, he had stood behind the clump of bamboo. We saw his paw marks there. We followed his tracks back to the road—he had followed the truck for several hundred yards—and then we lost them. They went into the jungle.

We decided to tie a live bullock to a tree not far from where the tracks went into the jungle. In another tree we built a small bamboo platform twenty feet above the ground, camouflaging it with a screen of green foliage and leaving an opening through which I could observe the bullock. The platform seemed to me weak enough to collapse at a sneeze. We left it when it was completed and returned at four that afternoon, leading the bullock. Six natives tied him to the tree with a rope, placing him so that my gun could cover him. Naidu advised me to make no move until after the tiger had finished killing the bullock and had started to eat it. Then I was to shoot. He and Derayya shook hands with me and wished me luck. I climbed to my perch in the tree and they and the natives went back to the village, making a great deal of noise in their departure so that the tiger would think that every one of us was withdrawing from the jungle.

When darkness fell, I attached a five-cell flashlight to the double barrel of my high-velocity rifle. The jungle was noisy as the night wore on. There were a thousand insects buzzing around my head constantly and I was also serenaded by croaking bullfrogs, squealing small animals, and screaming monkeys. After trying to free itself, the bullock lay down and went to sleep. Now and then it would awake suddenly and jump to its feet as though it sensed danger. I would get tense and wait for the appearance of the tiger. But then the bullock would relax and go back to sleep. My body became cramped and stiff. I was afraid to move it for fear of making noise.

At last daylight came and with it arrived Naidu and Durayya and the natives. I dropped down to the ground and we untied the bullock and led it back to the village with us. The bullock and I returned to the same spot that afternoon and spent the next night there. Still there was no sign of the tiger. I stayed in the tree for a third and a fourth successive night with no result and I began to get disheartened. I wanted to try tracking him down in daylight. Naidu would not hear of it.

"You must wait for him," he said. "He is too wise to pursue. You must wait until he comes to you. No doubt he has been watching us since we've been here and he is probably well aware that he is being hunted."

When I came down from the platform in the tree I would sleep until after lunchtime. On the morning after my fourth night of watching I was awakened by a commotion in the village. A group of natives had come from another village four miles away, bringing the news that Appalswama had killed a woman there that morning as she was drawing water from a well. Men who were leading cattle to the well saw the tiger carrying the woman into the jungle. They chased the tiger, trying to frighten him into dropping the woman's body from his mouth, but they found her badly torn and dead.

We walked to their village that afternoon in the heat of 120 degrees. The scorching sun was exhausting. We looked at the remains of the woman. A few children stood near it with sticks in their hands to keep away the village dogs.

The natives carried the woman's body back to the spot where it had been found. We built another platform in a nearby tree and I climbed to it and settled down for another night of waiting. This night was darker than the previous ones. The corpse below me smelled badly.

After several hours I heard the insects around the corpse rise suddenly with a loud buzzing, as though somebody was disturbing them. Then the corpse moved.

I fired excitedly and turned on my flashlight. I saw that the body was still there. I could see nothing but insects around it. In a few minutes the jungle was full of torch-bearing natives and Naidu was at the bottom of the tree, asking me what had happened. I told him that I thought I had seen the corpse move.

"Come down," he said. "The tiger won't come here tonight. If he was anywhere near, the shot would have scared him off."

We found no tiger tracks in the area the next morning and we decided that the corpse might have been moved by one of the village dogs. Ants were eating the body right down to the bones. We returned to Kekkular, leaving instructions for the natives to tie a live bullock near the watering place where the woman had been attacked. If the tiger killed the bullock, they were not to touch it but they would inform us. We also tied a bullock at my previous place down the road near Kekkular. But instead of watching from the tree, I waited in Kekkular for news that one of the bullocks had been slain.

It came the next morning from the other village. The bullock at the watering place had been killed by Appalswama. Some tribesmen who had been hunting wild boar saw the tiger leaving the bullock and disappearing into the underbrush.

We dashed off for the village, hoping to get there while the tiger was feeding. When we arrived the whole bullock was gone. We found only the rope that had been used to tie it to a tree. We followed a bloody trail into the jungle and along a sandy, dried bed of a stream. In a clearing where the grass was short we came upon the dead bullock. It was torn open but only a few of the entrails were eaten.

I wanted to hide on the ground near by and wait for the tiger's return but Naidu would not hear of it. He insisted upon calling the natives and erecting another platform in a tree. This took us a few hours. When the platform was finished late in the afternoon I climbed into it and covered myself with green branches. This time I felt sure that the tiger would appear.

That night the moon was bright and visibility was perfect. But it takes infinite patience to stay still in a tree and after five nights of it my patience was wearing thin. When my watch told me that it was ten o'clock I was restless. I decided to give it another hour but no more. At eleven o'clock I climbed down from the tree and slung my rifle over my shoulder and walked to the dried stream bed. I had not gone far when I saw something standing directly in front of me. It was the tiger.

The moonlight was bright in the sandy stream bed and we could see each other almost as distinctly as if the sun was out. He was not more than fifteen feet away from me.

I became paralyzed with fear. I could feel the hair on the back of my neck standing upright and my whole body turned cold.

The tiger stared at me and groaned softly, baring his teeth and lifting one paw and feinting at me with it. He crouched slowly and then lunged a few inches, pretending to spring at me, and bared his teeth again. He was like a cat playing with a mouse. He was trying to make me move.

I was incapable of making any movement. I had no control over my muscles. I stood there, helpless and frozen with terror, and watched him make three more feints at me.

Then I began to feel the warmth coming back into my legs and my stomach. Gradually the warmth came up into my chest and my arms and neck and I inhaled and felt my heart start beating again. The rifle was still hanging on its sling behind my right shoulder. I thought about it for the first time and wondered how I might be able to get it into my hands before the tiger jumped on me.

The tiger relaxed and slowly turned his huge head away from me, as if he was disgusted with me. I worked my shoulder around in a circle and the rifle sling slid from it and slipped down my arm, bringing the rifle into my hands. I tried desperately to push the safety catch forward. Then I remembered that it was not on.

When I lifted the rifle the tiger's head was still turned away. I fired. He leaped, twisting himself sideways, and landed in the undergrowth at the top of the seven-foot-high bank of the dried stream and then roared. The birds and the monkeys for miles around began to scream and chatter. I ran forward to the edge of the bank. I felt sure that I had hit him.

Then I heard a crashing from the underbrush and the thudding sound of a body landing and I turned and saw the tiger behind me. He had leaped from the brush into the dried stream bed again and he was now standing in the same spot that I had been when I fired at him.

Without aiming, I fired the remaining cartridge at him point-blank. He crouched in the sand, glaring at me, and snarled.

I heard voices in the distance but I stood there with the empty rifle in my hands and stared at the tiger, feeling helpless. Without taking my eyes off him, I dug with my hand into my pocket and pulled out two cartridges and clumsily reloaded the gun. He still crouched and glared at me. This time he was about ten yards from me.

I heard Naidu's voice somewhere behind me. Still keeping my eyes on the tiger, I shouted, "Don't come near. I think I've wounded him."

Naidu and the natives circled around me and came out into the stream bed behind the tiger. The natives stopped and Naidu approached the tiger alone with his rifle raised. Then he bent down and picked up a stone and threw it at the tiger. The beast did not move.

"He's dead," Naidu called to me.

Later we found the tracks that showed that the tiger had evidently paced up and down in the sand of the stream bed earlier that night, ignoring the bullock and waiting for me to come down from the tree.

Nobody slept in Kekkular that night. Six strapping natives carried the tiger to the village. The flesh was shared by everyone, even the children. The natives believe that tiger meat gives great strength and that it inoculates the eater against the danger of tiger attacks. The tiger's head was placed on an anthill so that its skull would be picked clean. The skin was cured and the head mounted for me later in Madras. And I became a hero in that part of India. The people in Cocanada already knew about the tiger when I came out of the jungle and everywhere I went I was congratulated. Nobody would have believed me if I had told them that fear had saved my life and killed the tiger. But I know that's how it was. If I had not been too terrified to move, the tiger would have leaped on me before I brought the rifle down from my shoulder.

CHAPTER 7

*T*O REPEAT A WELL-WORN PLATITUDE, IT IS THE LITTLE things that can change the whole course of your life. You miss a train and go into the station restaurant for coffee and meet a man who talks you into quitting your job at the bank and moving to Canada. In Canada you meet another man who talks you into going on the stage and you end up in Hollywood as a much-divorced movie star. Perhaps you would have been better off if you had not missed the train.

If I had not met Donald Gillies, I would not have worked for Scotland Yard on the narcotic smugglers, and if I had not worked for Scotland Yard, I would not have been recommended to Naval Intelligence, and if I had not been recommended to Naval Intelligence, I would never have been mixed up with the Italians and the Spanish in the Mediterranean and I wouldn't have sailed the *Girl Pat* across the Atlantic. And if I hadn't sailed the *Girl Pat,* I wouldn't have had to serve a prison sentence in Wormwood Scrubbs.

I am glad I met Donald Gillies because being a convict in Wormwood Scrubbs was a wonderful experience. I wouldn't have missed it for anything.

I met him on the North Sea one gray morning after a bad three-day storm. I happened to be there because I was running some whisky up the coast for a friend. We saw a vessel in trouble and it turned out to be a gentleman's yacht, badly smashed by the storm and helpless. I put my ship alongside her to tow her but she was so damaged that a towline attached to her bow would have pulled her apart. I had a bright idea. We attached life buoys and life belts to a twelve-inch rope and dropped its end on the sea in front of the yacht. Then I raced

71

our ship around the yacht's stern in a circle, letting out rope as we went, came back and picked up the end and passed the line through its eye. With the winch we tightened the rope around the yacht like a lasso. Don't ask me how we did this in the heavy sea but we did and thus we towed the yacht safely to shelter in the Bay of Dogs.

The yachtsmen were very grateful. They had run into the storm while returning from the Bergen races in Norway and they had given themselves up. Donald was one of the men on the yacht and he and I became fast friends. We discovered that we had been born near each other in Scotland. He had been in charge of J. Walter Thompson's advertising office in London and now he was in the advertising business for himself. He was a brilliant man, a confidant and adviser of government leaders. It got so that whenever I was in London after that I spent a lot of my time with him.

One evening in 1934 I had a dinner date with Donald at the Café Royal on Regent Street and when I got there I found him sitting with a man whom he introduced to me as Inspector Leyland of Scotland Yard. Donald said that Leyland wanted to meet me because he hoped to be able to get some information from me.

"What sort of information?" I asked. "I don't think I've murdered anybody recently."

The inspector smiled as if he had to listen to that sort of devastating wit every day in the week. He explained that he would like me to come to his apartment after dinner to meet the chief of customs. We went there and found the customs man, a fellow named Drake, awaiting us. Leyland did the talking. He began by asking me about my knowledge of the coast, which I assured him was adequate.

"You know quite a lot about smuggling methods, don't you?"

"I do," I said. "Don't ask me how I learned about them, though."

The inspector explained that a narcotic ring was smuggling dope into England in large quantities. It was coming from the Continent but so far the police had not been able to discover where and how it was being brought into the country. They had only one lead. Two men had been picked up in two different cities recently, each of them carrying a small amount of belladonna. They had both traveled from Yorkshire a few days before they were arrested. The inspector added that all arriving ships were being carefully watched but so far they had revealed nothing.

"Have you watched the ships as they passed up a waterway like the Humber, for instance?" I asked. "A piece of timber or an old fend-off could be dropped into the water with anything attached to it. And somebody in a small boat could row out from the shore after the ship passed and pick it up."

"That's an idea," Leyland said.

"Furthermore, if the stuff is coming into Yorkshire, it must be landing somewhere between Middlesbrough on the north and the Humber on the south. There are no ports between those points so it might be a coastal job, involving small boats that don't need a deep harbor. That strip of coast is only eighty or ninety miles long. It shouldn't be hard to watch."

"Have you a motorcar?" Leyland asked me.

"No," I said, "but my girl has."

"How about spending a month's holiday on a tour of the Yorkshire coast? At our expense. You could sort of keep your eyes open and let us know if you see any place where smugglers might be at work."

It sounded pleasant and Lucille was delighted with the idea. We started at Bridlington Bay and drove slowly up the coast, stopping and spending a day here and there. It was May and the spring weather was fine. There were only a few visitors at Bridlington, most of them yachtsmen painting their boats in preparation for the summer. We stayed three days in Scarborough, a beautiful town by the water's edge. There, too, the vacationers had not yet arrived. I made the rounds of the local pubs and talked with the fishermen. I could see nothing that looked out of the way. A few miles south was the village of Filey, practically hidden by high cliffs and protected by a dangerous reef. There was a strong coastwise current there that made the landing of small boats in the dark a risky business so I crossed Filey off my list. We saw nothing in Robin Hood Bay and I tramped the beaches and looked over every inlet and point all the way north to Redcar without noticing anything that seemed suspicious. In Redcar I met one of Leyland's men. I told him what I had seen and he advised me to forget the whole thing and to return to London as soon as I felt like doing so. Lucille and I had enjoyed Scarborough so much that we decided to stay there a few more days on our way south.

As we were driving into the town I noticed two Danish fishing smacks tied to a jetty in the harbor. This was odd. The best market for fish was Grimsby and that was where the Scandinavians usually brought their catches. A resort town like Scarborough was no place for them.

After we registered at the hotel I strolled down to the harbor and looked the two ships over. They were registered from Esbjerg. I struck up a conversation with some of the crew. They spoke English well. They said they usually stopped in Scarborough for two or three days once a month, on their way back to the fishing banks from Grimsby. One of the men was engaged to an English girl there and, to give him a chance to see her, they used Scarborough as a place to rest and to work on the ships.

I met some of them again that night in a local pub. I found that the Danes were well known and well liked in Scarborough. They spent money freely there; a little too freely, I thought. But their ships were always inspected thoroughly by the customs officials.

I thought about them again that night after I went to bed. If they went into Grimsby after fishing for ten or fourteen days, the Danish ships would spend two days unloading their catch there. It would take them another day to sail from Grimsby to Scarborough. And they said that they usually spent two or three days in Scarborough. The trip to Scarborough also took them a long way off the course from Grimsby to the Dogger Bank, where they would be most likely to fish. It did not add up. They were wasting too much time on the Yorkshire coast, just to accommodate the courting of one crew member. Fishermen do not waste time. Then it dawned on me. Perhaps they were not landing fish at Grimsby at all. I looked at my watch and saw that it was one o'clock in the morning. But I reached for the phone and woke up Leyland in London.

"I think I have something," I told him.

"After waking me at this hour, you'd jolly well better have something," he said.

He arrived the next day with two men and we talked first with the local customs officer. The Danish fishing boats had been stopping there regularly since the previous summer but there was no evidence of smuggling. Then we checked the harbor authorities at Grimsby and found that those particular ships had not landed at Grimsby in more than a year. My hunch was correct.

But it had taken us three days to get that information from the record books at Grimsby and during that time the Danish boats had left Scarborough. We alerted the coast guard and lighthouse keepers to watch for their return and to take note of where they might be landing the contraband. We waited two weeks for their reappearance but saw no sign of them.

One evening before the sun went down I drove Lucille down the shore to the south of the town and parked the car on the top of a high headland overlooking the sea. We noticed two lobster boats about a mile and a half out from the shore, setting lobster pots. I looked at them through my binoculars and noted their registration numbers, SH32 and SH12. They seemed quite far at sea for lobster fishing. And it was the wrong time of the year for it, too. We continued to watch them until they finished setting the pots and headed off toward Scarborough Harbor.

I drove to a nearby coast guard station and asked the man on watch if he had noticed the boats.

"Yes," he said. "They laid those pots yesterday about this time and they'll be back out there tomorrow again to pick up today's pots and to put others down. That's how they work."

"Let me see your charts," I said.

I took a bearing on the position of the pots and located it on the chart. The water was too deep for lobster pots there.

We drove back to the hotel. Leyland had returned to London but the other two Scotland Yard men were there.

"Pack your things," I said to them. "We're moving down the coast to Bridlington. I'll explain why on the way."

After we checked into the hotel at Bridlington I hired a motor launch. It took us three hours to get back up the coast to where the pots were tied. We could have done it much easier by getting a boat in Scarborough but I didn't want the townspeople there to know what we were up to.

It was hard work pulling the pots up by hand. In the first one we found an empty watertight canister, something like a thermos bottle. There was a canister inside each pot. We dropped the pots again and went back to Bridlington.

The next day we watched from the headland while the fishermen raised the pots and replaced them. That night we went out in our launch and raised the pots but the canisters were still empty. This game of hide-and-seek went on for three more nights. Always the canisters were empty. On the fourth night the coast guard on the headland called us on the telephone. He had heard a Diesel engine offshore in the darkness. He was certain that it was one of the Danish fishing smacks.

We put out from Bridlington and when we came near the pots we shut off our engine and drifted. There was a mist over the water and a light rain was falling. We made out the dim, black shape of a fishing smack near the pots and we heard voices. When daylight came a few hours later we saw one smack lying three miles offshore and the other one coming down from the north to join it. We waited until they both headed for Scarborough and we approached the pots and hauled them. One of the canisters was filled with vials of opium. The others held various narcotics and glass tubes of the very valuable and highly taxable essence of perfume. We replaced them in the canisters and lowered the pots.

We had to wait several hours for the fishermen to arrive on the scene and we made coffee on the stove in our motor launch. I found a good-sized pot under the stove. I filled it with sea-water and put it on to boil and then pulled up one of the lobster pots. I took a lobster from the pot and boiled it until it had changed its color from dark green to bright red. Then I replaced it in the fishermen's trap and lowered it toward the bottom of the sea.

The fishermen did not come on the scene until five o'clock that evening. They ignored us and began to haul up the pots. We started our motor and came near them.

"Hi!" I called to them. "Any chance of getting a lobster?"

One of them straightened up and glanced at us.

"Wait till we've hauled the pots," he said.

We stayed next to them and said nothing. We had a hard time keeping our faces straight when one youngster pulled up the pot with the boiled lobster in it. The men stared at the bright red shell and their mouths hung open in amazement.

Before they had a chance to figure it out we jumped into the nearest boat. "We're the police," I said. "Keep hauling the pots. We know what's in them."

The fishermen told us enough to break up a big smuggling ring that was operating in Yorkshire under the direction of a man named Godfrey, who stopped frequently at the hotel in Scarborough under the guise of a traveling salesman. He maintained a headquarters in Pall Mall, London, with a large secretarial and bookkeeping staff. The other Danish boat was leaving narcotics in lobster pots five miles north of Scarborough. The fishermen were being duped by the smugglers. They received a ridiculously small sum of money for picking up the canisters and they claimed that they did not know the canisters contained narcotics. Twenty-two smugglers went to jail.

That summer I went on another voyage to the Arctic and I stayed with the ship all the next fall. I will always remember the ship for her Christmas pudding. We ate it off Iceland and it was a fine pudding with a thick white frosting on its top. The frosting amazed me because I knew that our stores were short of confectionary materials. I asked the cook how he had made it.

"Did you really like it?" he said.

"The frosting was delicious," I said. "How did you do it?"

"To tell you the truth," he said, "I made it out of whitewash."

When I came back from the Arctic I loafed for a month and then took a new trading ship on her maiden voyage from Liverpool. When I brought her back I found a telegram from Inspector Leyland awaiting me. He wanted me to have lunch with him in London the following day.

After we exchanged pleasantries he told me that he wanted me to talk with a man named Hall about a job. The whole thing sounded very mysterious.

"I don't know exactly what it is but I think you'll like it," Leyland said. "Now here's what you do. Tomorrow morning at eleven o'clock go to this address and ask the man at the desk in the hallway to show you to this room number. You must not write down the room number now. We don't want you to be carrying it about on your person. Memorize it. Tell the man at the desk the room number and your name. Then you'll be taken care of."

The next morning I located the building. There was a man at a desk inside the door, as Leyland had said. He recorded in a large book my name and the number of the room I was to visit. After I waited for a few moments a young man led me upstairs and pointed at a door.

"Don't knock," he said. "Walk right in."

I opened the door and walked in. The door slammed shut behind me very quickly and firmly, as though it was operated by a mechanical device. I found myself, not in a business office as I had expected, but in an oak-paneled room that seemed to be the study of an expensive apartment. A pleasant-looking white-haired man stood up from a large desk and greeted me.

"Orsborne, I'm Hall," he said. "I am pleased to meet you."

He offered me a comfortable chair and a cigar and poured scotch and soda. I found myself talking familiarly with him about nothing in particular and everything in general. I was astonished to find out that he seemed to know all about me. He talked about various places I had been and knew the names of ships that I had sailed on.

"Orsborne, I don't know if you've guessed yet who I am," he said finally. I hadn't. "I represent the Royal Navy's Intelligence service. We are considering you for a rather important and confidential bit of work and we must know first a great many things about your personal life. I must ask you a question and I don't want you to be offended by it, Captain. This woman who writes to you constantly when you're abroad and with whom you live when you're in London—is she your wife?"

"Must I answer that?"

"Certainly not," Hall said. "But we are talking in strict confidence."

"She's not my legal wife. We live together and love each other but we are not married."

"Do you mind telling me her full name?"

I told him Lucille's name.

"Fine," Hall said. "I knew it and I also knew that she was not married. I was merely testing you. You see, Orsborne, I owe you an apology. I have seen letters that you and the lady have written to each other."

I toyed with the idea of standing up and belting him on the chin. But I did nothing because I was too interested in what he said next.

"This office is concerned with getting information of all kinds from all over the world. If I was asked tomorrow how many people in Odessa take Epsom salts, I could assign investigators to find out and report a reasonably exact figure. The task I have in mind for you is not that of an investigator. We need a courier and a contact for our investigators in the Mediterranean, someone who can pick up information from our agents and forward it to our headquarters. I understand that you are a good navigator and that you know small boats and you know the Mediterranean. Leyland also tells me that you are a good judge of character."

I said nothing.

"This job we're offering you is an extremely dangerous one and a thankless one. There is no glory in it. You will be performing a valuable service for your country but the country will never know about it. You'll have to act better than someone on the stage because if you don't act convincingly you may pay for it with your life. We haven't the plan worked out in detail yet but we thought of sending you to the Mediterranean disguised as the captain of a small fishing boat. Think it over. Come back tomorrow and tell me your decision. I hope you accept."

As I stood up and shook hands with him Hall handed me a slip of paper.

"Give this to the man at the door," he said. "Otherwise they won't let you out of the building."

I went directly to a pub in Chelsea and had a drink. Then I had another drink slowly while I thought it over. I rang Leyland but he was not in his office. I went down into the tube and went to Lucille's house and that evening she and I went to the Metropolitan Theatre where the featured act was a troupe of German girl roller skaters. I paid no attention to them. Afterward Lucille and I had a few drinks with some of her friends. I did not hear a word that anybody said.

The next morning I stopped in to see Donald at his office. When we were alone he said to me, "Well, are you going to take it?"

"What?" I said. "Take what?"

"You know what," Donald said. "But it is best that we don't talk about it. But you'll take it. You couldn't turn down a thing like that. Not you."

I was astounded to see that Donald knew about the offer from Hall. Then I remembered that Donald was closely associated unofficially with the Admiralty and I realized that he probably had as much to do with my being selected for the interview as Leyland did.

I left Donald and went to Hall's office, being admitted after the required ritual. We shook hands again and then we sat down and he looked at me and I looked at him.

"Well?" he said.

"I'll take a basinful of it," I said.

He was puzzled and he lifted his eyebrows politely. "What was that you said?" he asked.

"I said I'll take a basinful of it," I said. "Colloquial expression. It means that I have decided to accept your proposition."

"Oh," Hall said. "That's splendid. Basinful, eh? I must remember that one."

A few minutes later he interrupted something that he was telling me and said, "By the way, Orsborne, what are your politics?"

"I haven't any, sir," I said.

"What do you think of politicians?"

"I think of politicians as men who make promises to people and then get fat forgetting their promises," I said.

Hall laughed. "Very sound point of view," he said.

I spent the next two months studying Diesel engines and taking inoculations and injections for tropical diseases. I also studied Naval Intelligence procedure. I was to become a laundry mark. The agents with whom I was dealing were known only by the numbers of their laundry marks, which were on all their clothing. My laundry mark was 45. Agents would recognize me if I mentioned laundry to them and used the word "forty-five" somewhere in the conversation.

I spent several weeks working with naval camouflage experts on the design of the boat that I was to take to the Mediterranean. She was a seventy-five-foot, Diesel-powered fishing boat but she was constructed so that her appearance could be changed radically whenever we felt that it needed to be changed.

There were two masts that could be raised or lowered quickly. There was a dummy smoke funnel that could disappear into the engine room. We could make her look like a sailing vessel with the masts and sails up and the funnel out of sight. Or we could keep up the masts and put up the funnel. Or drop the masts and leave the funnel in view. Or drop both the masts and the funnel and present the silhouette of a Diesel-driven fishing craft. The Admiralty later adopted this design and used many boats of this type in the war. It was known as the MFV or Motor Fishing Vessel.

We carried no radio or wireless, for that would have seemed suspicious. Our guns were hidden behind a wall panel in the bridge and there was a compartment in the fishing net storage hold in the bow for hiding secret messages and documents. The documents were kept between thin covers that were weighted with lead. If we threw them overboard in an emergency or if the boat sank, they would not float to the surface of the water.

The boat had a speed of fourteen knots and a cruising range of two thousand miles. I called her *Mon Amour* and Donald's advertising firm, Graham and Gillies, was listed as her owner. But I made arrangements to change her name and her registry as often as I changed her appearance.

Lucille had no idea of where I was going. I dropped out of sight without saying good-by to her because I could not explain about my lack of a mailing address. Donald told her that I had been called away unexpectedly and that I would write to her soon, which of course I never did.

I had an excellent crew of four men, all of them carefully selected by the Admiralty. Allen was a tall, husky Cornwall fisherman who had served five years in the Navy, and Jarvis, the mechanic, was a red-headed Yorkshireman. There was also an extremely tough and extremely valuable little Cockney from the barges of the Thames. We called him Spud. The youngest member of the crew was Coats, a thin, pale boy from southern Ireland, who would have been an officer in the Navy except for his weak eyes. He came from a wealthy family and he had studied at Cambridge. At first he did not swear, smoke, or drink but under our bad influence that soon changed. He was only nineteen.

The men in the crew were not officially told of the purpose of the voyage and they asked no questions. But it didn't take them long to discover that I was interested in other things besides fish.

We sailed from England early in June and passed Cape Finisterre in Spain as a Spanish fishing trawler with the masts up and the imitation funnel realistically belching smoke from the small smokebox inside it. Off Portugal we became a schooner with the sails up and we arrived in Gibraltar as a motor fishing boat.

I had been told in London to contact Agent 11 in Gibraltar. He was the manager of a marine engineering firm there, a quiet man in his fifties who looked like anything but the chief of all British Naval Intelligence investigators between Gibraltar and Suez. I went to his shop with an excuse about needing repairs for one of the boat's bottom ends. We talked about it and then he asked me if I needed anything else.

"Some fuel," I said. "And I want to see about getting some laundry done."

"The laundry is apt to get mixed up," he said. "You'd better have it marked."

"It is marked. I use forty-five as a laundry mark."

He nodded.

"Why don't you have dinner with me at my home tonight?" he asked. "Meet me here about five-thirty."

That night he told me that I could expect to stay in Gibraltar for about a week and gave me a briefing about the situation in the Mediterranean, which was then fomenting. Mussolini was starting to invade Abyssinia and Franco was preparing in North Africa for the revolution in Spain. The British wanted information about Mussolini's arms and troops and they wanted to stop him from supplying Franco with munitions, guns, and aircraft, as they were certain he was doing.

Before we left Gibraltar at the end of June, Agent 11 added a Frenchman to our crew. He was to act as the skipper when we were in French and Italian ports. He was a young fellow, easy to get along with and quick-witted. I didn't question him about his past but it was obvious that he was an experienced and capable secret agent.

We changed the boat's name to *Regester* and flew the French flag and fished our way slowly northward on the Mediterranean to La Seyne, near Toulon on the French coast. The fishermen there swarmed over our boat, looking at its construction curiously. Our Frenchman explained that it was a new boat, built for experimental fishing in the Mediterranean, and, if it worked well, a French boat builder whom he mentioned by name would construct more like it. Everyone was very much impressed. We sold our catch and divided the money among the crew.

From there we went to Genoa, where the Frenchman led me into a ship chandler's shop. While we sat drinking white wine in the rear of the shop with the proprietor we were joined by an Italian who spoke perfect English. After a few moments we were exchanging laundry numbers with him. He gave us two eight-liter wine jugs to carry back to the boat and he advised us to go south to Naples as fast as possible. The agent in Naples had an urgent message for us.

The Frenchman and I went to the boat, each of us carrying a wine jug. I could tell that my jug had no wine in it. When we were clear of the harbor I took it below where none of the men could see me and broke it open. I found inside a folder of blueprints and a sheet of paper with coded writing on it. I placed them between the lead-weighted covers that resembled the covers of a loose-leaf notebook and hid them behind the joints in the net store.

I came up on deck. The first thing I saw was an Italian destroyer, heading straight at us.

I became panic-stricken. My first thought was that somebody ashore had betrayed us. I was on the verge of running below and dropping the blueprints and the coded message overboard when the destroyer turned, looked us over casually, and went away.

We went down the Italian coast, staying well out at sea, and in the Gulf of Salerno, south of Capri, we shot our nets and fished. If we had really been depending upon fish for a living we would not have had such luck. The boys in the crew were delighted. They liked to fish because the entire profits of each catch were handed to them. With our hold full, we put into Pozzuoli, a fishing town five miles from Naples.

The customs officers there were suspicious. Our name had been changed again to *Aveyron* and we showed a registration from St. Raphaël. The Frenchman was very convincing. He told the customs officers that our new type of net had caught our entire haul of fish in three hours. Actually, we had been fishing for thirty-six hours. The customs officers were so astonished by this revelation that they forgot about their suspicions. One of them wanted to know where his uncle could buy a boat like it. The Frenchman calmly gave them the name and address of a shipbuilder in Marseille.

We collected five hundred lira from the fish market for our catch and our marvelous net became the talk of the town. The local newspaper published a story about it the next day.

But this wasn't getting us in touch with the agent in Naples. He was the owner of a hotel there. It was up to me to contact him alone because the Frenchman had to stay with the boat in case the authorities came around to ask more questions. I didn't know a word of Italian and I had never been in Naples.

The dock was filled with curious sight-seers all day after the newspaper story appeared. I found two of them who spoke a little English and invited them aboard for a drink. After the fourth or fifth drink I told them that I wanted to go to Naples and have fun. They offered to go with me. We reached the city about seven-thirty that night. It seemed to be full of music and people. My companions warned me against speaking English in crowded places. They said that there was a strong feeling in Italy against the British and the Americans. I didn't talk at all.

By ten o'clock my friends seemed quite drunk and I took the chance of showing them a slip of paper on which I had written the name of the agent's hotel. They said it was too expensive for us. I persuaded them finally to show me what it looked like. They took me to it and after I noted its location I agreed with them that it did indeed seem too swanky and too subdued for three simple fisherfolk.

We went to another café, where I tried to pull the hazy drunk act and wandered out the door. I had to get rid of my two drinking partners. But they followed me and led me solicitously back to the bar. I looked at the clock and saw that it was nearly midnight. I began to get desperate. I staggered out to the street again with the two Italians at my heels. This time I put up an argument and flatly refused to go back to the café. I walked down the street between them with my arms around their shoulders. When I was trying to think of an excuse that might enable me to get away from them, I felt one of them slipping his hand into the pocket of my trousers where my money was kept.

We were passing a dimly lit archway. I straightened up suddenly, grasped a neck in each hand, and brought their two heads together. One of them went down. The other started to fight. I brought my knee up into his stomach and he went down too.

I ran down the street and turned the corner into a main thoroughfare, where I slowed down to a walk. The hotel was only a few blocks away. It was an elaborate place and I was reluctant to walk into the lobby in my fisherman's clothes. I was standing under a tree near the entrance to the driveway when a car turned in and stopped at the door. Two bellboys came out to get the luggage and I walked forward and beckoned to one of them. He seemed to be frightened by me. I gave him the Fascist salute and held my finger to my lips and handed him a slip of paper on which I had written the name of the proprietor of the hotel. I pointed upstairs questioningly and the bellboy nodded.

Still frightened, he took me around the hotel to a dim hallway inside a side entrance. I took a pencil from my pocket and wrote on the back of the slip of paper, "There's 45 pieces of laundry waiting to be picked up." I gave it to the bellboy and pointed upstairs. He nodded quickly and hurried away. He must have thought I was one of Mussolini's strong-arm men.

I waited a long time in the hallway. I wondered what I would do if anybody came to me and started to ask me questions in Italian.

At last the bellboy came back and signaled for me to follow him. We went outside and around to the rear of the hotel and in another door and up a flight of stairs. At the head of the stairs we went into a room where a short, fat man in a red dressing gown was waiting for us.

The fat man began to roar at me in Italian. I don't know what he said but I knew it sounded abusive. The bellboy left the room looking at me as though he was sorry for me.

When the door closed behind him the fat man took me into another room. His manner changed and he smiled at me. It was a soft, fat smile. Everything about him was soft and fat.

"Why didn't you come in the daytime?" he said.

"I can't speak Italian," I said. "I wanted to be seen as little as possible."

"You can't speak Italian?" he said very softly. "But there are many people in Naples who cannot speak Italian."

He was beginning to irritate me. I couldn't see any point in wasting so much time with polite talk. I wanted him to give me whatever he had to give me and then I wanted to get back to the boat.

"Very well," I said. "There are many people in Naples who cannot speak Italian. But it so happens that I was advised not to speak English. I was told that the people here wouldn't like it."

The fat man broke into a wide smile and moved his head slowly from side to side in mock astonishment.

"Now whoever told you a ridiculous thing like that?" he chuckled. "The Italians don't like the English? Ridiculous. My dear man, Italy is not at war against England."

This did not sound to me like a man who was supposed to be a British agent. I stared at him, wondering if I was in the wrong hotel. Perhaps the two Italians had misdirected me. Or perhaps the Italians had discovered that the proprietor of the hotel was a foreign agent and had removed him to prison. This might be one of Mussolini's men that I was talking to. I jumped to my feet.

"What nationality are you?" I said.

"Nationality? Me? I was born in Corsica, just like Napoleon, you know. But what difference does that—oh, I see!"

He began to laugh uproariously without making a sound. His eyes squeezed together into fat slits and his shoulders shook. The fat of his enormous stomach quivered under the silk of the red dressing gown. It took him quite a while to calm himself and then he sat for a few minutes, breathing hard and wiping his wet eyes.

"My dear man," he said finally, "you are tired and unstrung. Get some sleep and we'll talk again in the morning."

"Morning?" I said. "I must leave now. Tonight. I've got to get back to my boat."

The fat man smiled again and shook his head.

"My dear man, the streets are empty. You are a stranger in the city. You will be picked up and questioned. Sleep here tonight. In the morning I'll arrange for you to get back to your ship safely."

I tried to protest but it was no use. I didn't sleep much that night. I was sure that the fat man was an impostor in the pay of the Italian government. In the morning I would be arrested as a spy. Or perhaps I would be followed back to the ship so that the whole lot of us could be captured. In any event I was certain that the fat man could not be trusted. I thought about trying to slip out of the hotel and I got out of bed and went to the door to see if anybody was in the hallway outside. The door was locked. I didn't know what to do.

CHAPTER 8

*I*N THE MORNING I WAS STILL NERVOUS. WHEN I AWOKE I dressed quickly. I looked out the window, wondering if I could get to the ground from it without hurting myself. I was still wondering when the door was unlocked and a waiter came in, carrying my breakfast on a tray. While I was eating, the fat man entered the room. Instead of the red dressing gown he was wearing an immaculate white linen suit with a pale yellow silk shirt and a brown-and-yellow flowered tie. He took an envelope from his coat pocket and handed it to me.

"When you've finished breakfast you can ride back to your boat in my marketing van," he said. "And now, my dear man, would you mind if I gave you a few words of well-meant advice?"

I felt relieved but I noticed that he was smiling again. I did not like his smile.

"Last night you thought I was not a British Intelligence agent," he said. "Now tell the truth. Didn't you?"

"I didn't like the way you talked," I said. "I went to a lot of trouble and risk to come here. I felt I was entitled to a different sort of welcome."

"How long have you worn your laundry mark?"

"Three months," I said.

"Three months," the fat man said. "My dear man, I've worn my mark for fifteen years. Let me tell you something. You are too tense and too nervous. In this work you must be simple and carefree. Never enter a hotel by the back door in the dark of night. Stroll in through the main entrance at the cocktail hour with an expensive cigar in your mouth and an expensive countess on your arm. Look at me. Would you take me for a spy?"

I looked at him. He seemed like anything else but. I shook my head.

"Neither would anyone else, my dear man. That is why I have been able to serve your government for fifteen years. This is one of the finest hotels in Italy and I am a very popular host. Mussolini's trusted men love to come here. Do I peer at them from behind a potted palm? No, I slap them on the shoulder and joke with them and tell them the latest gossip and serve them the finest wine. My dear man, that is the way to handle yourself in this work. Remember it and you'll live much longer."

I invited the fat man to have coffee with me and by the time I left the hotel we were friends. I left with a market basket over my arm and climbed into his truck, which drove me to Pozzuoli. The trip attracted no attention because the truck often went to the fish markets there.

The crew was eating breakfast when I went aboard the boat. They were none too happy when I announced that we were leaving immediately.

"This is Saturday, Skipper," Spud, the Cockney, said. "I did well with a signorina last night and I had expected to really knock her over tonight."

When we started to move out two harbor officials ran along the pier shouting at us. The Frenchman yelled back at them.

"You forgot the harbor dues and clearance papers," he told me. "But I said we were only going out for an hour to test the motor."

When we were out of sight of land I raised the masts and the sails and the men repainted the white hull black. We renamed the boat *Mon Amour.* Whenever we came near a ship I eased the motor and let the sails fill out to give the impression that we were a lazy schooner. When darkness came we lowered the masts and opened her up with all the power that she had. On July 2 we arrived in Gibraltar safely under the name of *Morning Star.*

I handed over the material to Agent 11. He told me that German and Italian Fascist agents were arriving in Spain in great numbers and Moorish tribesmen, under German and Italian officers, were massing in Libya. A clever and dangerous Spaniard named Juan March, working for Franco with German money behind him, was operating a vast espionage system with secret agents all over the Mediterranean. His men were the ones we had to watch.

At the end of July my boat pulled out of Gibraltar with sixteen extra crew members aboard. We dropped them one at a time in Spain, Morocco, the Balearic Islands, Algeria, and Libya. They were British agents. In August we set out along the North African coast, disguised as the *Leonora* and ostensibly headed for Port Said to fish for the British naval vessels there. Actually we were aiming at Zuara, a little town on the Libyan coast, eighty miles west of Tripoli. There were two hundred planes in crates at Zuara, waiting to be flown by Italians and Germans to Morocco, where they would be used in Franco's planned attack on Spain. We thought it might be well if they never left Zuara. Aboard my ship were fifteen sticks of high explosives that could be used to prevent their departure.

When we sighted Zuara we faked a breakdown offshore and flew distress signals. No one paid any attention to them. I edged nearer and nearer to the old broken-down breakwater and finally a few native boats came out to look at us. I yelled at them for help. They took our ropes and pulled us to within a few yards of the breakwater, where I dropped anchor.

Two Italian officials came out and boarded the boat. I explained that we were British fishermen en route to Port Said and showed them a run on two bearings. One of them spoke English quite well. He said that the bearings would have to be repaired in Tripoli and offered to take me to a merchant in town who might be able to help in the matter. I gave them both cigarettes and English pound notes, which they accepted readily. From then, the best was none too good for me as far as they were concerned.

Zuara turned out to be a collection of huts scattered along the road that leads from Tripoli to Tunisia. There was also a barracks, occupied by white and black Italian troops, and a few modern buildings. Camels were always lying in the road, chewing their cuds. All around the town was the desert.

I wondered where the planes were being stored and assembled. For three evenings I stayed in town, either at the barracks or at the merchant's shop where wine was sold, but I heard nothing. Then I noticed that three trucks full of Italian workmen drove in from the desert every night at seven-thirty and unloaded at the barracks. Obviously these men were uncrating and assembling the planes. I made a few more discreet inquiries and found out that they worked at a group of warehouses in the desert two miles from the town.

The two Italian officials who were my great and good friends made things difficult for me. One of them was the commissioner of police. He saw that I was entertained at all times while I was ashore and he ordered his men to accompany me to the boat every night at ten o'clock so that I would not be molested. Nevertheless I planned to visit the aircraft assembly plant alone late at night.

The fifteen sticks of high explosive were soft and pliable and I kneaded them together, five at a time, into three large lumps that looked like dough. I did not want a revolver because it would be too noisy. I cut two feet of handle from a broom, hollowed it, and filled it with lead. It was heavy enough to stop a bull. I covered myself with a mixture of black oil and soot from the galley stove. I wrapped thirty feet of slow-burning fuse around my waist and tenderly put three detonator caps, each one wrapped in velvet, into three different pockets. I wrapped myself in a blanket so that I would look like an Arab. I put the round lumps of explosive into a black silk muffler and hung the muffler from the lead-filled broomstick, which I carried across my shoulder. I was all set. And then I started my long walk into the desert.

The town of Zuara was asleep. I almost ran through the desert in the direction of the assembly plant and when I first saw its buildings in the moonlight I started to tremble with excitement. I found that the buildings were surrounded by barbed wire. As I knelt by the wire, trying to figure a way of getting through it, I heard voices. I crawled back into the desert.

Then I saw the dark outline of two sentries with rifles slung over their shoulders. I crawled farther away from the sentries and the barbed wire and unwound the fuse wire from my waist. It was in three sections, each ten feet in length. I fastened a detonator at the end of each strip of fuse, fastening the fuse into place by biting it with my teeth. Playing with detonators in that desert sand where friction could easily explode was not my idea of healthy sport but I had no choice in the matter. When the fuses were attached, I buried the detonators in the three lumps of doughy high explosive.

Leaving the three prepared bombs on the sand, I stood up and walked toward the two guards with one hand full of sand and the other hand grasping the broomstick. I saw that they were both Moors. One of them turned toward me and said something as I approached them.

I threw the sand in his face. At the same time I swung the stick at the other soldier, hitting him across the chest. As he doubled up, I brought the stick down on his head and he went down and out cold. Then I swung at the first one. He dropped as though he had been hit by a sledge hammer.

I didn't know whether I had made any noise. I listened to see if I could hear any other guards approaching but I heard nothing.

I threw both their rifles over the barbed-wire fence and ran to the unguarded gate. But it was locked. I went back and looked at the guards. They were both still limp. I dragged one of them to the gate and propped him with his back against it, in a sitting position. Then I ran back to where I had left the explosives and picked them up. Using the sitting guard for support, I climbed over the gate.

When I was inside the fence I ran to the nearest plane assembly shed and, dropping on my knees beside it, I dug in the sand quickly like a dog burying a bone. I put one of the lumps of explosive in the hole and ran to another shed and dug another shallow hole and buried the second bomb. Then I planted the third bomb against the wall of a third shed. I ran back to the first bomb and lit the fuse with my flint-glow cigarette lighter. Then I dashed to the other two and lit them and ran for the fence. The fuse would burn at about two and a half minutes for each foot so I had about twenty-five minutes to get away.

I opened the gate and took a quick glance at the two guards. They were still out. I started to run down the road to town. After about a half mile I looked back and thought I saw automobile headlights turning into the assembly plant area. I ran faster.

I was just reaching the edge of town when I heard two quick explosions. The ground shuddered beneath me. I found myself in the middle of a running crowd of excited camels, donkeys, and people. Then there were three or four more blasts and the sky lit up. A few ammunition dumps apparently went up along with my bombs.

I didn't stop running. When I reached the ship the crew was on deck. They stared at the black oil and soot on my face. I jumped aboard and ran for the engine room.

"Christ!" Jarvis yelled at me. "What happened?"

"Fireworks," I said over my shoulder. I practically fell down the stairs to the engine room and locked the door behind me. I tore off my clothes and rubbed myself down from head to foot with Diesel engine oil. Then I scrubbed myself white with soap and water.

When I strolled back on deck I found a crowd of panic-stricken natives clamoring to get on the boat. Apparently they thought that the end of the world had come and they felt that they would be safer on the boat than on land. I told the crew to let them aboard. Then Spud nudged me and pointed. The chief of police and the other official from town were approaching the boat.

"Lord, Skip," Spud muttered, "why didn't you let us in on what you were doing? We could have been all ready to move out."

For some reason or other I felt very confident and pleased with myself. I glanced at Spud with mock amazement.

"Why should we move out?" I said. "We've done nothing."

When the police chief climbed aboard I greeted him cordially and said, "What happened?"

He couldn't talk. There were too many excited natives shouting in his ears and jostling him. I turned to the crew and pointed at the natives.

"Make some tea for these poor people," I said. "Maybe they've lost their homes."

The police chief looked at me carefully for a moment.

"They have lost nothing," he said calmly. He waved his stick at them and ordered them ashore. Then he asked me if any of the crew had been ashore during the past few hours.

"No, sir," I said. "I was the only one ashore last night. And I was mostly in your company."

He explained rather apologetically that the military authorities wanted to search my boat. I extended a cordial invitation for them to send their men aboard. I made a speech about how grateful we were for the hospitality that the town had given us and how we would do anything in our power to help during the emergency. I also explained that it was impossible for us to leave because of the repairs that were being done to the boat. So there was no need of guarding us.

When a half-dozen Italian soldiers had searched the boat I asked the police chief to have tea with me. "But tell me, Commandant," I asked, "what happened? Was the town blown up or what?"

"Not the town, signor," he said. "But much valuable machinery."

"I am deeply hurt to think that I or any member of my crew should be suspected of wrongdoing."

"Ah, it is not I, signor," he said. "It is the military. But you have nothing to fear."

However, the military authorities placed two guards on the boat and ordered them to stay there, day and night, until the inquiry of the explosion was completed. That day I visited the merchant who had sent the damaged bearing to Tripoli. He said it would not be repaired for at least two more days. That, of course, was not actually detaining us. We had another bearing to use in place of it. But we could not leave without suspicion until the repair job was finished. When I left the merchant I paid a call upon the police chief. He kept me waiting before he would see me. He said that my boat would have to remain in port until further orders.

"Even after my repairs are completed?" I asked.

"I'm sure the whole matter will be cleared up before then," he said.

I could see that he was not as friendly as he had been before the explosion.

I went back to the boat and pondered the problem. I decided that I was only courting disaster by remaining within reaching distance of Mussolini's lieutenants. They changed the guards at eight o'clock that night. The new guards were friendly Italians who spoke no English. They sat in the cabin, smoking our cigarettes and drinking our coffee while my men played cards. They kept their rifles between their knees but they did not object to my leaving the cabin and strolling about the deck.

Around eleven o'clock I went on the deck and noticed that there was a stiff breeze blowing from the shore. Sand from the desert was blowing against the bridge like light rain. I realized that if I could pull up the anchor the boat would drift away from the breakwater and out to sea without making a sound.

I went on the bridge and turned on the power switch on the windlass. When it had taken in two fathoms of cable attached to the anchor I switched off the power and went back to the cabin. The soldiers did not appear to have noticed the noise. I sat and watched

93

the card game for twenty minutes. Then I told the men in English to talk and shout about the card game for a while. When they raised their voices I went back to the bridge and threw on the switch again. Six more fathoms of anchor cable came in. I shut off the switch and went back to the cabin again. The Italians had still failed to notice anything. I went on deck and saw that the boat was drifting broadside out to sea. I thought once that she was going to bump against a stone quay and give the show away. I strolled into the cabin, whistling, and yelled jovially at the men to make less noise. I told them that we were drifting out of port. Then I smiled at the Italian guards. The Italian guards smiled back at me. The boat was beginning to roll slightly.

I told the men to pretend to go to sleep and to lie down on their bunks as though nothing was happening.

"What if these Dagos start shooting?" Spud said.

"They won't," I said. "If they do, just act surprised."

While the men climbed into their bunks I went casually up to the deck, closing and locking the companion hatch behind me. The Italians did not even notice that I had locked them in the cabin with the crew. I went to the bridge, threw in the air pressure valve and started the motor, and headed her at full speed straight out to sea. She began to dance on the choppy waves. I could picture the two guards below being tossed around in the swaying cabin.

When daylight broke I was out of sight of land. I headed easterly toward Cape Bon in Tunis. Then I took a Webley .38 revolver from the hiding place behind the panels in the bridge and walked aft and opened the hatch.

"All hands on deck," I shouted.

Only the crew emerged. I asked them where the Italians were. The men laughed.

"They're lying on the cabin floor seasick."

The two soldiers were too ill to give a damn whether I took their rifles away or threw them overboard. When I offered them food they shook their heads mournfully. We rounded Cape Bon that night. Gibraltar was eight hundred miles away. I decided to hug the Tunisian coast and to change the name of the boat and pose as a schooner in the daytime. For the next five days I crept along Algeria and Morocco. East of Oran we anchored at dusk and rowed the two soldiers ashore in the dinghy. They were so overjoyed at being released alive that they wanted to kiss us. Then we dashed for Gibraltar.

Agent 11 had already heard from his agents that the Italians were convinced that I had sabotaged the plane assembly plant in Zuara. They had been searching for me with a destroyer and a submarine. Because I was now a marked man, Agent 11 was not anxious to use me in the Mediterranean for the next few months.

"It's a pity you aren't at Aden," he said. "With this Abyssinian war on, Agent 21 could use you. His job in Aden corresponds to mine in Gibraltar. He has charge of our agents in the Red Sea, Arabia, Eritrea, and Somaliland. And Abyssinia. He must have more work than he can handle these days."

"I could go to Aden," I said.

"Too far. It would take you two or three months to go south on the Atlantic and all the way around Africa. Besides, the Italians would get you before you went twenty miles. I can't very well give you a naval vessel as an escort. It would seem extremely strange for a naval vessel to escort a fishing boat."

"I don't need an escort," I said. "And I don't need to go around Africa. I'm willing to chance it across the Mediterranean to Port Said. After I get through Suez, I won't be known. I'm not worried about the Italians."

"But you'd better be worried about Juan March. His agents are everywhere. And after that Zuara job they'll be watching for you. Those planes you blew up were meant for Franco. And that puts you on March's black list."

"I'll take a shot at getting to Port Said."

Agent 11 thought I was out of my mind.

"Oh well," he said finally, "it's your funeral, not mine."

The boat was then painted a lovely white. We pulled out of Gibraltar on the fourth of September just as darkness was falling and twenty miles up the Spanish coast we painted the hull black and changed the name to *Romany Rose*. At daybreak we raised the masts and the sails and headed for the Algerian coast. After six days we pulled into Bizerte without having sighted an Italian ship.

In Bizerte I met a Frenchman who offered me five thousand francs to deliver two hundred British Enfield rifles and four thousand rounds of ammunition to Tangiers. I told him at first that I was on my way back to England and I was not interested. But he kept on talking and raised the price to six thousand francs, three thousand down and three more thousand on delivery of the guns. I knew that the rifles were intended for Spanish Fascist revolutionaries. I felt that it would be amusing to take them and dump them into the sea so that Franco would never get them. So I made a deal with the Frenchman. This was a mistake on my part, as I found out later. The rifles caused me too much trouble.

We loaded the rifles on the boat before we left Bizerte the next morning. We used them for target practice on floating oil drums and driftwood for a few days and then tossed them overboard. On the way to Port Said we passed a flotilla of Italian destroyers but they never suspected our ugly little black schooner. The people who gave me the most trouble on that trip to Aden were the British. They raised hell with me at Port Said.

First, they were indignant because I entered the harbor without flying a quarantine flag. Then they were not satisfied with my papers. My story about wanting to fish for British naval vessels in the Red Sea and the Gulf of Aden made no sense to them. Why didn't I do my fishing near England instead of mucking about the Suez Canal? To their way of thinking, the whole business was most decidedly irregular.

We tied up at a dock in Port Said while I attended to medical clearances and harbor dues and passage fees for the canal and pilot charges and all the other things the British authorities ordered me to sign and pay for. When I went ashore the first morning we were there I noticed two Arabs walking behind me. I went into the building where the medical officer was located. When I came out on the street again twenty minutes later the same two Arabs were leaning against a building in the next block. They followed me back to the dock.

That afternoon I went to the customhouse. The two Arabs were behind me when I walked to the customhouse and they were looking into a shopwindow across the street when I came out of it. Juan March, the chief of Franco's Gestapo, had apparently caught up with me. I told the men in the crew that they could not go ashore after dark.

Port Said was full of Italian soldiers in high spirits and the Suez Canal was full of Italian troopships headed for Eritrea and Abyssinia. I noted quietly that the Italian troopships went into the canal with much less hindrance from the British authorities than I encountered. When we left the canal and moved into the Red Sea, I stayed close to the Arabian shore. That trip down the Red Sea was probably the most boring fourteen hundred miles I have ever covered in my whole life-time. The heat was unbearable. The sand from the desert was often two or three inches deep on the deck. It stung our eyes, matted our hair, and got into our food and water. We were glad to get to Aden.

A few minutes after we tied up at Aden a young Arabian in a white linen business suit came aboard and asked to see the captain. He handed me a business card. It gave the name and address of an ex-porting firm. I turned it over. On the back was written the number 21.

"Thank you," I said. "If I decide to drop into your office while I'm here, whom should I ask for?"

"Our manager's name is Wallace," the Arabian said.

That afternoon I went to the office of the exporting firm and asked to see Mr. Wallace. "I've come in regard to some stores for my schooner," I told the secretary, handing her the card. She conferred with Mr. Wallace and then reappeared, announcing that Mr. Wallace would see me immediately.

Mr. Wallace was Agent 21. He was very British, very precise, with a quiet, cultured voice and a calm manner. He ordered fruit juice and we sat in his office and sipped it while we talked. His duties as head of the exporting firm seemed to keep him busy. His telephone rang constantly and his secretary and assistants were in and out of the room frequently with questions to be answered and letters and statements to be signed. I wondered how he found the time to control the activities of all the British agents in that important and busy Intelligence sector.

He was not surprised to see me.

"I heard you were coming seven days before you left Gibraltar," he said. "Eleven sent me word through an agent who was passing this way. I also had word from Port Said when you went through there. And I know all about you. I regret to say, however, that the Italians and the French know a great deal about you too. In fact you have built up in a very short time a rather unsavory reputation among the Italians and the French."

"The French?" I said. "What have I done to the French?"

"Well," said Agent 21, "there seems to be a slight misunderstanding about some rifles."

I told him about the man in Bizerte and how we dumped the guns and ammunition overboard to keep them from getting into Franco's hands.

"That is not the way it was told to me," he said. "Let me tell you what they are saying about you. Not only the French and the Italians but also the British. The British out here have no idea that you are working for us, you know."

From the reports that Agent 21 had heard, I was a dangerous pirate and smuggler, ready to work for anybody who paid the most money. The Italians said that I had been responsible for the explosion at Zuara and that I had broken out of prison and fled from there, kidnaping two Italian guards. And I had murdered the two guards. The French said I had stolen four hundred rifles from their garrison in Algiers. The French, never ones to go halfway, had even bestowed a nickname on me which was also being used by the Italians and the British. They called me "Le Capitaine Solitaire." This was rather odd because years before in the West Indies when I was operating a free-lance trading schooner the natives in Trinidad and the Windward Islands called me "Solo" and "Solitaire." I worked for no company and went only where I wanted to go and when I wanted to go. I wondered how the nickname had caught up with me again in the Mediterranean.

Agent 21 wanted me to work with his agent in Djibouti, the port in French Somaliland through which everything and everybody connected with the Abyssinian war had to pass. Djibouti was the coastal terminal of the only railroad that ran out of Addis Ababa and consequently in that October of 1935 it was the refuge for the weird assortment of people who were fleeing from Haile Selassie's quivering empire and it was the rendezvous point and jumping-off spot for the even stranger collection of characters who wanted to get into Abyssinia. It was full of baffled war correspondents, loaded down with binoculars, insect lotion, cooking equipment, collapsible rubber canoes, bottles of Vichy water, and tins of pâté, and it was full of retired British and French colonels who were sure that they could become field marshals in the Abyssinian army if they could only get a few minutes to speak with the Emperor. It was also full of munitions salesmen, Communist agitators, pimps, free-lance aviators, inventors of unmanufactured armored cars and anti-tank guns, black marketeers, moneylenders, and adventurers who would do anything for easy money or just for a little excitement. And it was packed with spies. There were spies from France, Germany, England, Japan, Russia, Poland, Greece, the Netherlands, Sweden, Denmark, Arabia, Italy, Spain, and Austria, not to mention the ones from places like Finland and Liberia. With this sort of intrigue and cosmopolitan atmosphere, Djibouti could have been an exciting town. But it was too dirty and uncomfortable to permit anyone to enjoy anything about it.

Our agent in Djibouti was a half-caste Indian who ran a waterfront café. He was a remarkable fellow, charming and popular and fluent in a dozen languages. He seemed to know everything about everybody in that part of the world. I approached him with care. I knew that the town was full of spies and I was afraid that I might contact the wrong one and end up working for the Germans or the Rumanians instead of the British.

After we landed in Djibouti, I located his place from the directions that Agent 21 had given me before I left Aden. I went in and ordered a drink from him. While he was pouring it I asked him if he knew where I could get some laundry done.

"How much laundry?" he asked.

"Oh, about forty-five pieces."

He took the glass of liquor away and poured another one from a different bottle.

"This will be less likely to paralyze you," he said. "How long have you been in this part of Africa? Last I heard of you, you were stealing rifles in Algeria."

We talked and he gave me the latest rumors and the latest established facts from Abyssinia. He was the first one to talk to me about the Italian soldiers as we all talked about them later. The joke about every wounded Italian sleeping on his stomach because of the bandages on his backside was then sweeping Djibouti. The stories about Mussolini's bombers attacking native mud-hut villages were not so funny. Graziani's forces were behaving like barbarians. Our agent was receiving information from both the Abyssinian and Italian forces. Among the material that he gave me to take back to Aden two days later were photographs showing a native buried in the ground with only his head above the surface. The head was covered with molasses and there were three trails of molasses leading from the head to three separate anthills. Italian officers were shown in the photos gambling on which army of ants would reach the agonized face of the native first.

During November and December I carried messages back and forth from Djibouti to Aden. I lived on my boat in Djibouti and visited the agent daily. Every two or three days I left his café with a packet of information under my shirt which I delivered to Agent 21 in Aden. Then I would return immediately to Djibouti and await the next packet. In December we received reports that the Italians were using gas. It was German gas, a new chemical that Hitler had given to Mussolini so that German military observers could check on its efficiency under combat conditions in Abyssinia. Getting a sample of that gas for British military chemists to study became a top priority assignment for all our Intelligence agents. Late in December our agent in Djibouti received the big news from Addis Ababa that our assistant military attaché in the Abyssinian capital was sending to the border of French Somaliland an unexploded gas bomb that had been dropped from an Italian plane.

Somebody had to go to the border to bring it back to Djibouti and then to Aden. It was a journey of seventy miles through desert wilderness. I was assigned to the job and I set out to do it, disguised as an Arab and accompanied by ten Danakil tribesmen. Fortunately we traveled the first twenty miles by motor truck. Then we reached the desert and made the rest of the trip on camels. You could never get me on another camel. Every step was a prolonged sway, ending in a bone-shattering jerk. I would prefer to ride a raft in a hurricane.

We finally reached the appointed meeting place, a border village which consisted of twelve mud huts. The natives did not know what money was. I offered them cigarettes. They examined the cigarettes carefully and then put them in their mouths and ate them.

After we waited for a day and a night the party with the bomb arrived from Addis Ababa. It was a troop of twenty well-trained and well-equipped natives under the command of a British officer. He was a soldier of fortune, an Oxford graduate with impeccable manners who had served for four years in the Abyssinian forces. I could not help comparing him to T. E. Lawrence.

"And what sort of profession do you follow when you are not picking up these sorts of parcels?" he asked me.

I said I was a sea captain.

"My word!" he said. "That is something I could never do. I get seasick."

Before we parted company the British officer gave my tribesmen a stern lecture in their own language about taking precautions to get the bomb safely to Djibouti. On the way back they kept two guards up ahead of our caravan and two others well in the rear while we were moving in the daylight. At night while we camped they took turns staying awake to do sentry duty. The sentries did not stand on their feet and watch for intruders. They stretched on their stomachs with their ears pressed against the sand. They could hear hoofbeats on the ground at a distance much farther than they could see.

We reached Djibouti without incident and I packed the bomb, a sixty-pound affair, into a case and took it aboard my boat and delivered it in Aden. It was sent from there to England. I was told later that the study of German gas from Abyssinia enabled British scientists to develop an antidote for it that discouraged the Nazis from attempting to use their gas in the Battle of Britain and in the combat zones of World War II.

The next time I returned to Djibouti the agent was behind the bar of his café when I walked into it.

"Are you, by any chance, the Capitaine Solitaire?" he said.

"I suppose so," I said.

"Know those blokes?" He indicated with a nod four men in Arab dress who were seated at a table near the door. "They've been asking about you for the past four days," he said.

It could mean only one thing. Juan March's agents. This was French territory and I knew that if I didn't get out quick they would report me to the local French authorities as the pirate who stole the rifles.

"It was nice knowing you," I said to the agent. "If you're ever in London, look me up and we'll have a drink."

I shook hands with him and then turned and studied the four men. The temptation to follow a direct approach to action was too strong to resist. Someday I am going to get my head knocked off following a direct approach to action. But so far I have found that the element of surprise in it gives you an advantage, as it did in this case. I walked straight toward the four men and stopped beside their table. They looked up at me.

"Are you looking for the Capitaine Solitaire?" I said.

One of them shrugged his shoulders, as if to say that they did not understand English. He was wearing an Arabian knife at his belt. I reached for the knife and drew it from its scabbard. The four of them sat there and watched me, saying nothing. I knew then that they were not real Arabs. A real Arab will not let his own brother draw his knife from its scabbard.

I kicked the table over. I waved the knife. The four spies fell over each other trying to get out the door. I watched them disappear in four different directions and then I ran for the harbor.

As luck would have it, three of my men were aboard the boat. Spud was in a wineshop not far from the dock. I sent Coats to drag him out of it and in less than a half hour we were on our way back to Aden.

Agent 21 was not upset when I told him of the fracas in the café and explained that my usefulness in Djibouti had come to an end. He had been planning anyway to let me go back to Gibraltar because there was no longer a pressing need for my boat's services in his territory. He gave me a cargo of his firm's leather to take to Port Said in order to get me through the Suez Canal more easily and he wired a clearance for me to the British authorities there.

I left Port Said and headed into the Mediterranean with the feeling of a man who is walking on eggs. I could not make the entire run to Gibraltar without refueling and I was afraid to stop in Italian or French territory. I decided to go by way of Malta. Not far from Port Said I had a bad scare. Coming straight at me were a number of naval vessels and I managed to identify them as Italian. It was foolish to try to escape from them. I had the sails up and I was posing as a schooner named *Crescent Moon*. If I had opened up the Diesel engine it would have made them suspicious.

I sailed toward them and hoped that they would observe the rules of the sea and give a sailing vessel the right of way. And to my intense relief, the leading ship blew one blast on her whistle and the whole flotilla altered its course to leave room for me. As we passed beside them I saluted them cordially by dipping our British ensign. Each Italian warship in turn returned the salute. The knots in my stomach slowly unraveled.

We went into Malta flying the quarantine flag. I wanted to observe all the rules of British port procedure because I was in enough hot water as it was without tangling again with my own people. The port medical officer came alongside in a tender and climbed aboard to examine the men. He was a young blond chap and when I was being examined he told me that he was another Scot. So naturally I brought out a bottle. After the first drink I found out that he was our agent in Malta.

"Lucky thing you came here," he said. "Agent 11 tried to contact you at Port Said to tell you to stop here instead of heading straight back to Gibraltar. But you left before we could get the message to you."

"What's up?" I asked.

"We have a job for you," he said. "In Naples. But you can't take your boat with you. It's too hot. The Italians have a description of it. You'll go alone on a Greek steamer that stops here for passengers three days from now."

And so the boat was tied up and a Maltese watchman was hired to keep an eye on her. The boys moved into a boardinghouse ashore. My beard was trimmed to a Vandyke and I went aboard the Greek ship in business clothes, wearing a necktie and collar for the first time since I had left England. I was posing as a salesman for a scotch whisky firm. The agent in Naples, the fat man, was delighted to see me again.

"Ah, my good man!" he exclaimed. "This time you enter my hotel through the front door, as I advised you to do. This is better, much better. You have the cigar but where is the countess for your arm? Ah, but we can arrange that."

Upstairs in his room he told me why I was in Naples. He had arranged to get a collection of highly confidential messages and documents from the secret files of the German Embassy in Rome. I was to take them from Italy to Malta. But they would not be ready for me for two weeks.

"While you are waiting you must relax," he said. "Have a good time. I have no countess for you but I have something better. A baroness. Did you bring evening clothes?"

I told him that the agent in Malta had loaned me a dinner jacket and he insisted that I wear it that night.

I had a devil of a time squeezing into it because the agent in Malta was much thinner than I was. I sat alone in the hotel dining room that evening until the fat man came to my table and asked me to have coffee with him and an attractive woman with a great pile of auburn hair on top of her head. It was the baroness. I thought she would be bored with me because I do not dance. Instead she seemed rather thrilled. I was the first man she had ever met who didn't dance and I was a refreshing novelty, she said. She told me that she was Dutch by birth and she lived alone in a villa by the sea not far from Naples and she was a sculptress. I said something about how nice it would be to see her sculpture and the next thing I knew she was inviting me to spend three days at the villa. The fat man, of course, thought it was a capital idea. He gave me a broad wink.

The villa was beautiful. It stood on the top of a cliff at the edge of the Bay of Sorrento and it had a dream-world quality about it. It would have been wonderful except for the baroness.

The first morning I awoke there I went down to the sea for a swim, thinking that nobody in the villa was up. When I came back from the beach, wearing nothing but wet bathing trunks, the baroness was waiting for me at the door. She ran her hand solemnly over my shoulders.

"Exquisite," she sighed. "I must do them in clay. Will you sit for me while I sketch them this morning?"

I tried to laugh her out of it but she was determined. After breakfast I had to pose in shorts for two hours in her studio. I tried to see what she had sketched but she clasped the pad to her bosom.

"You mustn't," she said. "Not until it's completed."

That afternoon after another session of sketching I managed to steal a glance at the drawing board. I found that she was making several studies of me; not merely the shoulders, but my whole body. And in each sketch she had omitted the shorts.

Still I managed to keep things fairly platonic until the third night. Then there was a thunderstorm after midnight and she came to my room and said she was frightened. When the thunderstorm was over she stayed in the room. There was more lightning and thunder before daybreak but she slept through it soundly.

The next morning I told her that I had to be getting back to Naples.

She arose from the breakfast table and threw herself on a divan and began to weep. Then she wiped her eyes and stared at me and began to throw the breakfast dishes at me.

"Brute!" she cried. "Beast! Pig!"

She said that if I left her she would throw herself into the sea. I could not go to Naples unless she drove me there and she refused to take the car out of the garage. There wasn't anything I could do but stay. It was horrible. She stayed at my side constantly. If I let a few moments go by without talking to her she said I didn't love her.

"Nobody wants me," she would moan. "Why wasn't I born a man instead of a woman?"

After a week of this I managed to persuade her to have dinner at the fat man's hotel in Naples. I broke away from her for a few minutes in the lobby and begged for help from the fat man.

"But why do you complain?" he said. "She is quite beautiful and she is wealthy. There are many men in Naples who would give anything to be in your place. Stay with her. When the time comes for you to go back to Malta, I will get you out of it. Relax and enjoy yourself, my dear man."

So I stuck it out for another week. Then the fat man invited us both to come to the hotel for his fiftieth birthday party. I never got as far as the dining room that night. When I appeared in the lobby I was whisked upstairs to the fat man's room, where I changed from evening clothes into a tweed suit. There was an automobile waiting at the rear door of the hotel and it drove me one hundred miles south to Agropoli, where I boarded another Greek trading ship as its second mate. According to the prearranged plan, I pretended to be stricken with malaria the first day we were at sea and the port medical officer carried me ashore at Malta in a stretcher. I handed the fat man's documents over to him and he sent them to London.

The boys in the crew of my boat were delighted to see me and anxious to get going to Gibraltar. They had spent a pleasant holiday at Malta but their money was spent and they were eager to get mixed up in more trouble somewhere else. We fueled and stored the boat the first night I was there and took off for Gibraltar at daybreak, reaching it without incident, although we passed close to a spot where two ships from Russia, loaded with munitions and arms for the Spanish Loyalists, were sunk by Italian submarines.

Agent 11 at Gibraltar was not too keen to have me on his hands and I could understand his point of view. I was too well known to Juan March to be valuable that close to Spain and Morocco. He suggested that I return to England for a rest. So we packed up and headed north on the Atlantic for the Bay of Biscay and home. When we passed Portugal and neared Cape Finisterre at the northwest tip of Spain we began to run short of fuel. I decided to refuel at Corcubion, a small town on the south shore of the cape. I never dreamed that my identity would be known there. Even though it was Spain, it was the Atlantic coast of Spain, a long way from the Mediterranean. That was another mistake in judgment that I made. The Spanish authorities in Corcubion were suspicious of us from the very moment we landed.

Six armed policemen and two officials were waiting at the dock when we came into the harbor. They came aboard and demanded the ship's papers. I told them I had come across the Bay of Biscay from England and I was planning to turn about there and go straight back to England. They kept asking questions. I kept telling them that I did not understand Spanish. I showed them English money and explained that I wanted to buy motor fuel. They nodded at last and motioned for me to come ashore with them. I thought they were going to show me where I could make the arrangements to refuel the boat. I left the crew aboard and went with them alone.

Instead of selling me fuel they put me in jail.

And it was a terrible jail. My cell was solid concrete with a dirty and evil-smelling slop bucket and one wooden stool. I gripped the bars of the door and shouted at the top of my lungs, demanding my rights as a British citizen. Now and then the jailer, a mild old man about eighty years old, would appear in the corridor and plead with me patiently to be quiet. He would hold his finger to his lips and say, *"Un momento, señor. Un momento."*

After a few hours I was visited by a Spaniard who wore a uniform like a lion tamer in a circus. It was full of gold braid and tassels. It would have made Goering envious.

"Buenos días, El Capitán Solitario," he said with a smile.

I said nothing.

"You don't speak Spanish or Italian, Mr. Capitán Solitario?" he asked.

"I don't know what you're talking about," I said. "I am a British fisherman."

"Yes, I know," he said. "That's what you told the Italians before you destroyed those planes in Libya."

"I've never been in Libya," I said. "I came here from England on a fishing trip."

"You've never been in the Mediterranean?"

"Never."

He motioned to the jailer to unlock the cell and he led me to the office of the jail where a plate of bread and cheese and a bowl of white wine awaited me.

"Have something to eat," he said. "Now tell me, why did you come to Corcubion?"

"For fuel. I was fishing in the Bay of Biscay and I was blown off my course by the storm. I want fuel so that I can make the return voyage to England."

"Have you been in Spain before?"

"No."

"Gibraltar or Italy or North Africa?"

"No."

"Do you own the boat yourself?"

"No, I'm only her skipper. Come aboard and you can see the papers."

"Very well, Captain," he said. "I'll return here and we'll go to the boat and look at the papers." He stood up and left, calling to the jailer to serve me more wine. In an hour he came back with another local official and we marched to the dock, trailed by four uniformed policemen.

The boys on the boat said, "What's up, Skip?"

"These people don't believe that we came here from England to fish," I said. "I told them we are merely looking for fuel to take us home again."

Spud winked at me. "Shall we cut up rough, Skip, and bolt for it?" he said.

"These two gentlemen understand English," I said quickly. "Everything will be settled peacefully."

But the man in the gaudy uniform informed me after looking at the papers that I would have to return to jail.

"On what charge are you holding me?" I demanded.

"It is merely a matter of identification," he said. "You and your boat correspond to a description we have received from Valencia. We must keep you here until we are satisfied that you are not that person."

"Before you put me in jail I must see the British consul."

"There is no British consul here. Perhaps the French consul will speak with you."

"All right," I said. "He'll be better than nothing."

They sent a guard to the French Consulate. When he arrived the Spaniards and I were still sitting in the cabin of the boat. The French consul was no help. He advised me to do as the Spaniards ordered. When I asked him to send a message to Gibraltar, telling the British that our boat was being held by force in Corcubion, he told the Spaniards about it in Spanish, not knowing that I was able to understand what he was saying. This made them excited and I decided to follow up on what seemed to be a weak point in their armor.

"I am not leaving this ship until her owners in England or the British authorities in Gibraltar are notified that she is being held here," I said. "And furthermore I must have a reply from them that will indicate that you notified them."

But the Spaniards thought of a way to get around that one. They said that the ship would not be held. They would let it return to England. But I would be held until my identity was established. Then they would send me back to England—if I could prove that I was not the pirate and smuggler who was wanted in the Mediterranean.

I could make no comeback to that proposal. I bought four forty-gallon drums of fuel with the money in the boat's safe and put the remaining fifty pounds in my pocket. The men knew enough navigation to get the boat to England safely. I shook hands with each one of them and thanked them for everything and wished them luck.

"Skip," Spud said, "keep your blasted chin up. You've gotten out of worse jams than this one."

"It was good sailing with you," Coats said. "It was more fun than a music-hall show."

There were tears in his eyes and in mine too.

I felt bad standing on that dock in Corcubion and watching the lights of the boat I had loved so well disappearing in the darkness. And I felt completely down and discouraged when I turned away and started to climb the hill to the jail. I was sure that in two or three days I would be positively identified by the Spaniards. The man in the fancy uniform was a count named Don Regardo and I was sure that he was a Franco sympathizer. And no doubt a follower of Juan March.

The French consul was no better. He visited me in jail and tried to make me confess that I had landed British agents in Spain. "Tell me their names," he said, "and I'll see that you are set free. I'll also fix it so that you can get a high-ranking commission in the Spanish Navy."

"And what if I don't give their names?"

"I regret to say that in that case you will be handed over to the Italians and executed for the murder of those two guards that you kidnaped in Libya."

I said that I didn't know what he was talking about.

"Come now, Capitaine," he would say with a sly grin. "Tell me, just how did you kill those stupid guards? Did you drown them or did you shoot them?"

One day he returned to the jail and offered his proposition again. I warned him that I would make trouble for him with the French government as soon as I was released from jail.

"But I am only trying to help you," he protested. "There are two executions scheduled here for tomorrow morning. Political cases. And they may very well shoot you too."

"If they're going to shoot me tomorrow," I said, "tell them to give me a bed to sleep on tonight. I am tired of sleeping on the floor of this dirty cell."

"But Capitaine, the Spanish prisons do not have beds."

"No, and the French Foreign Office does not have good consuls. Get out of here."

The next morning Regardo, the gay caballero in the doorman's uniform, opened my cell door and led me to the jail office where he gave me a bowl of sour white wine. Two guards entered the room with a priest who bowed to me as they brought him past the table where I was sitting and out a door behind me that led apparently to a courtyard behind the jail. I went on drinking my wine and in a few minutes I heard the cracking of rifles. The old jailer beside me lowered his head and mumbled to himself as though he was praying.

Regardo entered the room again and bowed to me ceremoniously.

"And now, Capitán," he said. "This way, please."

The two guards who had taken the priest outside reappeared and led me through the same door and I found myself in a small enclosure with a white stone wall, not much more than six feet high, on one end of it. On the ground in front of the wall was the body of the priest. It was lying in a pool of blood. The guards placed me with my back to the wall about five feet away from the body of the priest. I looked up and saw a squad of eight uniformed riflemen facing me. My heart came up into my throat. It was hard to imagine that they were going to execute me. But here I was with my back to a wall and a firing squad facing me.

Before the soldiers raised their rifles my dear and true friend, the French consul, appeared in the doorway.

"Stop," he cried in Spanish. "I must speak!"

He ran to Regardo and carried on a conversation with theatrical gestures that were obviously meant for my benefit. Regardo dismissed the firing squad. The Frenchman took out a handkerchief and mopped his brow. Then he walked over to me.

"You see?" he cried. "I am your friend. But for me they would have shot you!"

It was a very impressive piece of acting.

When I was returned to my cell I heard Regardo in the office talking about me to the consul. I gathered from what was said that they had hoped that the firing squad would frighten me into admitting that I had put British agents ashore in Spain. But now that the pseudo execution had failed to produce the desired effect Regardo was puzzled about me. He was not so sure that I was the Capitán Solitario and he suspected that if I was the Capitán Solitario he might catch hell from the Spanish government for letting my boat go away.

That night I was told that I would be allowed to leave my cell and sleep on a bed in the jail office. I wondered what had prompted this sudden burst of kindness. Then I began to see the reasoning behind it. When darkness came the door leading from the jail office to the street was left open. They were hoping that I would try to make a run for the street so that the guards outside would have an excuse for shooting me down. That would be a simple solution of their problem. If I was innocent their hands would be clean. If I was guilty they would be congratulated.

I did not stir from my bed all night long. The door remained open and the jailer, who sat near me, dozed with his head on the table. In the morning Regardo dropped in and inquired if I had slept well.

"Of course I slept well," I said. "Why shouldn't I sleep well? The food here is fairly good and I am able to buy wine when I want it. I have enough money to keep me in wine until the British consul comes to get me out of here."

"You seem sure that a British consul is coming."

"Naturally. My crew will report in England that I am being held here without reason."

"But perhaps the English will deport you to Italy for the murder of those guards in Libya."

"Are we back to that again? I'm tired of telling you that I never saw Libya or the sky over it."

Then Regardo had another idea. "How much would your ship-owners pay me if I sent you to England?" he asked.

"Not a penny. I am worth nothing to them if I am not in command of their ship."

That night I slept again on the bed in the jail office. There were two guards stationed outside the door. The old jailer was with me inside the office. When the sun went down a strong wind began to blow. A few hours after it became dark I walked to the door and whispered, *"Caballero! Caballero!"*

The heads of the two guards appeared in the doorway. I held up an empty wine jug and some British money.

"Vino blanco!" I whispered. A hand reached for the jug and the money. A few minutes later I heard a scraping sound and saw the jug being pushed into the doorway. I went to the door and again whispered to the guards. Again the two heads appeared in the doorway. I handed each of them two pesetas. *"Gracias,"* I whispered. The two heads nodded and then pulled back into the darkness.

I gave the jailer some wine and drank some myself. You would have to drink a lot of that white wine before you began to feel it but I was being extra careful. When the jailer was not looking too closely I let a lot of it run down my chin and into the collar of my heavy turtle-necked white sweater. Soon I had the jug emptied. I went back to the door and whispered, *"Caballero!"* When the two heads of the guards appeared I whispered, *"Mucho vino blanco."* I held out the jug and more money.

One of them took the jug and the money and I listened to his foot-steps departing in the direction of the wineshop. Then I whispered again, *"Caballero!"*

As the second guard's face appeared in the doorway I kicked at it. My toe landed squarely on his Adam's apple. As I ran over him my feet tripped on his rifle and I went down on the steps of the jail and rolled into the street. I picked myself up and started to run. I ran in the direction away from the town, past a few houses, and then I turned off the road and ran into a field. I could hear the old jailer's voice shouting hoarsely.

I hurried across the fields in the darkness, now and then stumbling over a rock or the roots of a tree. I came through a woodland and out into a meadow where I saw the lights of a small village. I circled around the village, still keeping away from the roads. I heard something following me. It was a dog. He rushed at me, growling, and I kicked him in the ribs. He ran away from me, yelping and whining with pain. I walked all night and at daybreak I came out of the fields at a crossroads where there was a signpost pointing the way north to La Coruña, which I had visited once when I was on a trawler in the Bay of Biscay. La Coruña was a large port, with about seventy-five thousand people, and I figured that it would be a safe place for me to head for. But the sun was coming up and I decided against traveling in the daylight. I began to look for somewhere to hole up and sleep until night came again.

A short way up the road that led to La Coruña, I saw a footpath leading through a thicket. I followed it to a stone wall and climbed the wall and found myself in a cemetery. In the cemetery there were a number of table-shaped tombstones: flat stones with four supporting legs and an open space underneath between the stone and the ground. I gathered branches and stalks of tall grass and laid them around one of the tombstones to conceal myself and climbed in under the stone and lay down and tried to sleep. I dozed off and began to dream that Regardo had caught me again and I was awaiting death by the firing squad and then I was awakened by a dull thudding noise. I listened to it and wondered what it was. It seemed close to me.

I peered out from my hiding place and saw two men at the other end of the cemetery digging a grave. Their coats were hung over a tombstone not far from me. I was quite cold so I crawled out and edged along on my hands and knees from stone to stone and reached for both coats and carried them back to the stone wall. I jumped over the wall and crawled into a thick clump of bushes, frightening a rabbit which ran away in terror. I was in luck. There were sandwiches in the pockets of both coats. One of them also had a pipe and a package of tobacco. I ate the sandwiches and tore a piece from the paper that was wrapped around one of them and rolled a cigarette with the tobacco. I smoked and bundled myself in the coats and tried again to sleep. But it was no use. I became wide awake every time a truck or a wagon passed along the nearby road.

I was glad when darkness came and I was able to start walking again. I reached the outskirts of La Coruña around midnight. I knew one place in a town like that where you can always stay with no questions asked, as long as you have money. The whorehouses. I went to one of them near the waterfront. The madam welcomed me and for ten pesetas I had a shave and a bottle of wine and a comfortable bed with a girl in it.

I'll never forget that girl. She was a prostitute but she was one of the finest women I've ever known.

She knew that I had been in trouble but I did not tell her exactly what sort of trouble it was and she asked me no questions. She did not care. She was kind and generous. The next morning she cooked break-fast for me and went out and bought me a new pair of pants and a shirt. She showed me the receipts from the clothing store and counted out the exact change.

"I may be a whore," she said, laughing, "but I am an honest whore."

"Take some of this money for yourself," I said. "You've been a great help to me."

"But why shouldn't I help you?"

She would not take an extra penny. I had five English pounds in my pocket. I wanted to get rid of English money because I was afraid that my description might have been sent out from Corcubion and it would be dangerous to call attention to the fact that I was from England. I talked this over with the girl that day.

"Poof!" she said. "Don't worry. I shall change the pound notes for you."

"But you can't change twenty-five pounds to pesetas," I said. "That much money would seem suspicious."

"But I won't change it all at the same place," she said. "I will take a five-pound note to a café and buy a pack of cigarettes with it. And then do the same thing at another café and so on. Nobody will suspect anything that way. After all, many British seamen come to this house and pay us in British money."

And so the girl walked all over La Coruña and changed a five-pound note at each of five widely separated cafés. I tried to give her ten pesetas when she handed the money back to me in Spanish bills. She wouldn't take it. After we argued she finally said, "Ten pesetas is too much. If it will make you feel better I'll take five."

I stayed with her for two more days and then she went with me to El Ferrol on the ferry and there I caught a train to San Sebastián. I walked across the French border to Biarritz, where I borrowed twenty-five more pounds from the British Consulate and took a train to Paris. Then I crossed over to London.

It was two o'clock in the morning when I walked up the street to Lucille's house. I gave the whistle that she always recognized and she came downstairs in her negligee and opened the door.

"Dod!" she said. "Where in heaven's name have you been all these months?"

I put my arms around her.

"Oh, nowhere special," I said. "Just away on a little job."

CHAPTER 9

I HOPE I HAVEN'T GIVEN YOU THE IMPRESSION THAT I was a great success as an Intelligence agent. A good agent would have handled that sabotage job at Zuara much more quietly. A good agent wouldn't have got involved with those rifles at Bizerte. A good agent wouldn't have been silly enough to make himself known to Juan March's spies in that wineshop at Djibouti. A good agent would never have tried to refuel his boat in a Spanish town like Corcubion. In short, I was much too impulsive and much too inclined to get into trouble and to get well known to ever become a really good agent. Hall pointed this out to me politely when I reported to him at Naval Intelligence headquarters and I agreed with him. But even though I was not cut out to be a really good agent I loved the kind of work I had been doing in the Mediterranean and I wanted more of it. So I waited while Hall analyzed the errors I had made and then I said to him:

"What's the next job?"

Hall looked at me. He would have much preferred me to say that I was leaving him to open a haberdashery shop in the country.

"Well, I can't say really," he muttered. "You're too damned famous to be of much use to us."

"Come on now," I said. "Send me out again."

I coaxed him and pleaded with him. I didn't succeed that day but I came back a few days later and practically got down on my knees and begged. Grudgingly he gave in.

I couldn't use my old boat. The boys had landed her at Southampton and they had gone on to other jobs and other places before I had the opportunity of seeing them again. Hall told me to pick up another boat like it at Grimsby, where it was registered as GY 67 and listed as the property of the Mustag Shipping Company. He also told me to pick my own crew, with each man, of course, subject to approval by the Admiralty.

"You can go down to Gibraltar but take your time getting there," Hall said. "Take care that you stay away from the Spanish, French, and Portuguese shore limit lines all the way down. No landings, please. And stay away from Gibraltar as long as you can. We don't need you there now and the Spanish and Italians will connect you with us if they see you at Gibraltar. Right now they think that you're some sort of freebooter who will work for whatever side pays the most. Let's not disturb that impression. I want you to be near Gibraltar, however, because, as you know, the Spanish civil war is about to begin. When it begins, Agent 11 may need you. But he won't need you until then. Do you understand?"

I said I understood.

"One more thing. You might be useful to us if you got in with the Spaniards. I am going to introduce you to one of our agents here who knows some influential Spaniards in London. You can pose as a sea captain who might be of some use to them—I understand that they are shipping goods from here and from the Continent to Franco's forces in Morocco. They might put you in touch with some people down there that we don't know about."

The agent to whom Hall introduced me managed to have me meet as if by accident two Spaniards attached to the diplomatic service who were then stationed in London. We happened to drop into the bar at their hotel at an hour when they had their daily cocktails.

Before we met them the agent told me about the sort of racket they had been working at an immense profit. Although they were employed by the Spanish Republican government, they had no loyalty either to the Republic or to Franco. They were purchasing airplane parts and munitions on the Continent and holding the loaded ships in port while they bargained to see which Spanish camp would pay the best price for the cargo. Franco was heavily backed financially by the Germans and the Italians while the Communists in the Loyalist government were getting money from Russia. Often Franco could afford to outbid the government and most of the matériel originally ordered for the Spanish government would go to him in Morocco.

Nothing very much came of my meeting with these Spaniards in London. They offered me a job as master of a ship that was going to Morocco and made no bones about the fact that it was carrying supplies for Franco. One of them gave me his card. His name was Obrillo and he held an important post in the diplomatic service. The other one, Montaya, was a purchasing agent for the Spanish government. I heard later that they both got rich on the civil war and never returned to Spain.

I went to Grimsby and picked up the boat. It had the same camouflage facilities as the *Mon Amour*. She was named the *Girl Pat*. I decided to take as my crew Harry Fletcher, Hector Harris, Ginger Stephens and my young brother Jimmie. Fletcher was to be the mate. He was a big strong felow, about thirty, with a face that was badly scarred and disfigured from a motorcycle accident. Perhaps the scars on his face made me misjudge Fletcher. They made him look tough. I found out later that he was not so tough. Harris was a big humorous Yorkshireman with a fondness for drink that I was willing to overlook because he had so many good qualities. Ginger Stephens was only seventeen. He was a Scot with a thirst for adventure. He acted as cook. I say "acted" because he seldom cooked anything without making a mess of it.

We moved down the coast from Grimsby to Dover and at dusk on April Fools' Day, an appropriate date for the start of that voyage, we left Dover and headed for the Bay of Biscay. There was a terrific storm that night and the harbor authorities had forbidden all ships to go out in it. But we slipped away without showing a light. And we took a bad beating from the weather for the next four days. It seemed as though the deck was always under water.

I had been promising myself ever since I had broken out of that jail in Corcubion that I would return someday and pay my respects to Count Regardo for putting me in front of the firing squad. When we sighted Cape Finisterre on the fourth day the temptation to do so right then and there became too strong. I ignored Hall's orders to stay outside the three-mile limit and headed the boat for Corcubion. To ease my conscience, I told myself that the men needed a day's rest ashore after what they had gone through in the storm.

In a café at Corcubion we found out without much trouble that Regardo lived in an elegant mansion five miles out of the town. The townspeople did not have much use for him. In addition to being the commissioner of police, he was also the commandant of that military district. That night the men and I piled into a taxi and drove to Regardo's. I armed each man and myself with a Webley automatic but I did not know exactly why because I did not have an idea of what I was going to do with Regardo after I found him. It wouldn't have been sensible to shoot him or even to muss him up. That would have got us into bad trouble and it was a bit too soon on the voyage for bad trouble. I decided that I would scare him a little, show him that I was still alive and back at work again, and cause him a little trouble that wouldn't be too physical.

There was a long driveway that led from the road to the door of the house. When the taxi stopped I told the men to stay in it.

"If I don't come out in a half hour," I said, "one of you stay here and cover the cab driver and the other three of you come into the house and get me."

"God love you, skipper," Harris whispered. "Not wishing you bad luck but I wouldn't mind if you didn't come out. I'd love to shoot this thing."

There was a pull bell at the door. I pulled it and the hall lights inside came on and a servant opened the door. I pushed him aside and walked in. I spoke to the servant in Spanish, telling him to tell the commissioner that Le Capitaine Solitaire was there and that he wanted to speak to the commissioner immediately. Just so there would be no mistake about my identity, I also told him to tell the commissioner that this Le Capitaine Solitaire was British.

The servant stood in amazement and looked me over.

I snapped my fingers. *"Importante!"* I shouted.

The servant backed away hurriedly, bowing and saying, *"Sí, señor!"*

A few minutes later a door at the end of the hallway opened and Regardo himself appeared. Instead of the fancy uniform he was wearing a gray lounge suit. He looked as though he wasn't sure about whether to speak to me or whether to turn around and run.

I walked toward him smiling, with my hand out.

"Como está usted?" I said.

He smiled weakly. "Your Spanish has improved since we last met, Capitán," he said.

"Yes, but it would be better for me it we spoke English."

He was afraid to look me in the eye.

"What brings you to Spain again?" he asked.

I patted the handle of the Webley that was sticking out of my belt.

"Perhaps I came to kill you," I said.

"Now, now, Capitán," he said. "That unfortunate incident, it was nothing. We merely held you as a matter of form, you know. It was a pity you ran away. Two days more and we would have set you free."

I took out of my pocket the card that Obrillo had given me in London and handed it to him.

"I've come to Spain looking for work, as usual," I said. "You know I work for whoever pays the most. I also was paid by Señor Obrillo in London to deliver a message that may interest you."

I knew that he had never heard of Obrillo and Obrillo had certainly never heard of a country town police commissioner like him.

"Ah, yes," he said. "Obrillo is a friend of mine. What message does he have for me?"

"It is a verbal message. I also have written messages but they are to be delivered farther south. Señor Obrillo wants it known in Spain that Señor Montaya, the Spanish purchasing agent in London, is diverting ships that are supposed to be carrying cargo to Franco in North Africa. These ships are now loading at Bremerhaven in Germany. Instead of delivering their cargo in Morocco, they will unload in Bilbao and turn their goods over to the Spanish government. Evidently this Montaya is working against Franco. If you act quickly, you may be able to get someone to stop the ships from leaving Bremerhaven."

I was playing a hunch that Regardo was a Franco man. He was the type. And Franco did control most of the military and police officials in Spain. I saw that my hunch was right. He was intensely interested.

"How do I know you are telling the truth, Capitán?"

"I have given you Obrillo's card. Do you think I would take the risk of returning to Spain and especially to Corcubion so soon after I escaped from your jail if I merely wanted to play jokes? I was well paid to come here and tell you this. My men are with me. They're outside."

"Your men? Then you have your boat again?"

"Yes. I told you I was looking for work."

"Bring your men inside. We will have wine together."

"How do I know you won't try to capture us again?" I asked.

"Oh, Capitán," he said, "we are now friends."

The men came into the house and Regardo told the taxi driver to go around to the servants' quarters for something to eat. We drank wine for two hours and talked about the coming revolution. He praised Franco and he was certain that the Republicans would be defeated quickly. He told us that the revolt would break out in July in Madrid, Barcelona, Seville, and La Coruña and that the police in these towns were completely Fascist.

That night the crew returned to the boat but Regardo invited me to spend the night at his home and I accepted his invitation. At breakfast the next morning he told me that he had talked with someone on the telephone in Madrid. The person in Madrid was very grateful for the news of Montaya's duplicity and the ships at Bremerhaven would be stopped from sailing. The story I had given Regardo about Montaya was, of course, just exactly the opposite of the truth. He was not keeping ships from Franco and sending them to the Spanish government. It was really the other way around. Regardo's telephone call to Madrid had caused trouble all around but he thought it had made him a hero in the eyes of the Franco people and he was in good spirits about it.

"So your friend in Madrid knows Obrillo?" I asked.

"Oh yes. And he also knows Montaya. You've been a great help to me, Capitán. Isn't there something I can give you? Have you enough stores and fuel for your journey south? Have you enough money?"

I needed neither stores nor fuel but I decided to take them. I couldn't refrain from taking something from Regardo, after all. He had five hundred gallons of fuel and two weeks' stores loaded on the boat. I told him I did not have enough money to pay for them. He asked me to sign for them and give him the name of the firm in England that owned the boat. I signed the name "George Black" and wrote down the name of a shipping firm that had not been in existence for twenty-two years.

"Are your men short of money?" Regardo said. "Let me give them one hundred pesetas each and add it onto the bill that I will send to your owners. The owners must have a lot of money. Let your men have some fun and let them pay for it."

So I signed for another receipt. Regardo asked me to spend another night at his home and I said I would. But that evening at seven o'clock we cast off and headed our boat down the coast. While I was standing at the wheel Ginger came rushing to me.

"For God's sake, come below," he yelled. "Fletcher and Harris are killing each other!"

I ran down to the cabin and found the two of them struggling on the floor. Their faces were bloody. When I separated them Harris was calling Fletcher every obscene name that had ever been imagined. Fletcher said nothing.

"Throw the bastard ashore, skipper," Harris said.

"What did he do?" I asked.

"He mailed a letter," Harris said. "He mailed a letter to England in Corcubion this morning. I saw him writing it and I saw him go ashore to mail it. The bloody yellow son of a bitch is no good."

I had issued a strict order against sending mail home while we were on the voyage. A postmark giving away our location could be fatal to us. No one was supposed to know what part of the world we were in at any time.

"I didn't mail a letter," Fletcher said. "I went ashore to get cigarettes and matches. I didn't mail any letters."

"Where's the letter you were writing this morning?" Harris shouted. "Where in the bloody hell is it?"

"Shut up, both of you," I said. "And wipe the blood off your faces or I'll throw you both ashore."

"He's giving us away, skipper," Harris said. "He's letting everybody in blasted England know where we are."

"Shut up, Harris," I said.

Fletcher told me he had merely been writing a list of things he wanted to buy ashore. I believed him. I could not imagine that any one of us would be fool enough to mail a letter and give away our location. When Harris and Fletcher were calmed down I got the men to raise the mast and sails and we headed toward the coast of Portugal as a schooner named *Leda*. My brother Jimmie had been a sign painter and decorator. His talent for making new names in various types of lettering came in handy.

The boys were anxious to go ashore at Lisbon for a bit of recreation, as we called it. When we landed I remembered that Regardo had talked to me about the Spanish consul at Lisbon. He advised me to have nothing to do with him if I stopped there. "He is an enemy of Franco and he will be the first to go when we come into power," Regardo said. The consul at Lisbon had been recruiting British, Irish, and Scotchmen for the Loyalist International Brigade which was then forming. "If you see him, he will urge you to join the government forces," Regardo had told me. "But have nothing to do with him. Franco will pay you better." Regardo hated the consul so much that I automatically put the consul down in my book as somebody who sounded like a good man. I decided to see him and let him know what Regardo had been saying about him.

When I had recovered from the hangover that followed our first night in Lisbon, I set out for the Spanish Consulate. I explained to the secretary that I was an English sea captain and that I had some private business to discuss with the consul. After a short wait I was shown into the consul's office. He was a courteous and intelligent man in his sixties who struck me as a real Spanish patriot. At first he thought I wanted to sign up to fight Franco and he told me of the plans to build up the Loyalist navy. But I explained that I had business in the south to attend to and that I had merely dropped in on him to tell him what I had heard in Corcubion. He was not surprised by what I told him.

"I deem it an honor to be an enemy of Franco, just as I deem it an honor to be an enemy of Hitler and Mussolini," he said. "Did you say you were going south? Are you familiar with the handling of explosives?"

I nodded.

"Would you be interested in making some money and, at the same time, striking a blow against Franco?"

I said that the prospect was not repulsive to me. I liked money and I disliked Franco.

The consul took a map from his desk and spread it out before me. It showed the northwestern corner of Africa: French and Spanish Morocco, Spanish Sahara, French West Africa, and Senegal.

"The Germans," he said," are building a railroad here."

He put his pencil at Casablanca and moved it south along the Atlantic coast and then brought it inland, skirting through the desert around the territory of Spanish Sahara, and kept moving it south to Senegal. The pencil stopped at Dakar.

"The Germans are building it?" I said. "But that is all French territory."

"Actually it is being built by a French company but it is being done with German money. Why are the Germans paying for a railroad in French Africa? And why at this particular time? Because Franco is gathering his forces down in Spanish Sahara and when the time comes for him to invade Spain he will be able to use this railroad to move men and supplies north to Spanish Morocco. The French have made a deal with Franco and Hitler. The Germans build the railroad and after it serves its purpose the French will have a railroad that connects Dakar with their railroads in French Morocco and Algeria. It will also connect the west coast of Africa with Mussolini's Libya. It is a rotten and dangerous deal."

"Does the League of Nations know of it?" I asked.

"The League of Nations?" he said. "Ah, that League of Nations!"

The railroad had been started from Dakar and from Casablanca. The northern end had gone as far south as the river that runs from Marrakech to the ocean.

"The bridge across that river has just been built," the consul said. "If it was blown up the railroad would be delayed for several months and that might be enough to make it useless for Franco. The bridge is only a short distance inland from the ocean. You could anchor your boat offshore at night and go in and plant the explosives and get away before the bridge goes up. I have explosives that can be set like an alarm clock."

I thought about it. Hall had told me to delay my arrival at Gibraltar. According to Regardo, the beginning of the Spanish war was three months away and Agent 11 would have no need for me until then. In the meantime I had to do something to keep from being bored to death. Besides, I liked to blow things up. I must have thought about it for all of twenty seconds before I told the consul that I would do the job for him.

I was not satisfied with the consul's map. The charts I had on the boat were more detailed. I returned the next day, accompanied by Harris, and went over the location again with the consul on my charts. Then we went down into the basement with him and he gave me two charges of explosives. Each one weighed about ten pounds and they looked like storage batteries from an automobile. He showed us how they operated. They were to be wound up like a clock with a square key and there was an indicator that could be set to explode the charge at anywhere from one to ten hours after it was wound and released.

Then the consul handed me one thousand Spanish pesetas in silver and shook hands with us and wished us good luck. I could have dropped the explosives overboard as soon as we left Lisbon and kept the money. But the consul and I both knew that I had no intention of putting the explosives anywhere except under that railroad bridge.

We went out to sea and made a wide circle around the mouth of the Mediterranean. Three days after we left Lisbon we passed Safi and the river where the railroad ended. We anchored about three and a half miles south of the river and about a half mile off the shallow and sandy beach. At dusk Harris and Fletcher and Ginger and I rowed ashore in the dinghy, leaving Jimmie to sweat it out on the *Girl Pat*. Fletcher and Ginger stayed on the beach with the dinghy to wait while Harris and I, dressed Arab style in blankets to protect ourselves against the desert sand, went inland carrying the two charges of explosives.

We found a road about a quarter of a mile from the beach that ran north in the direction we were heading but we decided to stay off it for fear that we might run into somebody. We continued into the desert for almost a mile before we turned north. It was hard going over the desert sand dunes and after an hour we came into a bad sandstorm. We stretched out on our stomachs with the blankets wrapped around our faces and heads but we almost smothered. The sand got into our eyes and noses and into our throats.

Finally we reached the bank of the river and followed it back toward the sea. Then in the darkness we came upon the unfinished end of the railroad. The bridge across the river was completed, as the consul had said, and the tracks from Casablanca extended across it to the south side of the river. There were two rows of white stakes going off to the south into the desert, indicating where the rails would be laid next. The engineers had built a siding on the south bank of the river and on the siding, in front of where Harris and I were standing, there were five boxcars and a flatcar that was loaded with building materials. The place was littered with cement mixers, railroad ties, and piles of tools and apparently it had been a busy scene during the day. But now, at eight o'clock at night, we could not see a soul in sight. The working crew probably spent its nights at Marrakech or Safi and rode out to the railroad in trucks every morning. If there was an Arab watchman he must have been asleep in a tool shed.

Harris and I left the explosives at the end of the siding and advanced cautiously toward the bridge to look the situation over. We walked along the boxcars on the siding, Harris on one side of them and I on the other. Between the boxcars we paused and looked to make sure that the other fellow was still walking. We walked across the bridge and looked around on the other side of the river. No one was there either.

Then we examined the construction of the bridge. It was a single span resting on two supports. Each support was steel and concrete imbedded in the bank of the river and around it was a semicircular wall of concrete to protect the support against a rising flow of water that might eat away the riverbank. Harris and I decided to put one charge of explosive under the bridge on the north bank of the river, between the support there and the protecting wall of concrete. That would take care of the bridge. We planned to put the other charge under the railroad siding on the south bank of the river. The blast would eat away the bank and topple the whole siding and the cars on it into the stream.

We went back across the bridge and took one charge and planted it in a hole beside the support, winding it and setting the indicator so that it would explode in four hours or around midnight. It was ticking loudly when we left it. We set the other charge at the siding for the same time.

Then we hurried away from the railroad. Instead of going back through the desert as we had come, we struck out down the river to the ocean and turned south at the beach. We made good time, walking fast and occasionally trotting along the hard sand at the water's edge, and it was much shorter in distance that way. In an hour we sighted the dinghy on the beach with Fletcher and Ginger sitting beside it. They were glad to see us. We lost no time pushing it through the lazy surf and rowing out to the boat. Jimmie was astounded when we told him we had done the job without seeing anybody. He was always pessimistic and he had been picturing the four of us dead and wondering how he would be able to get the *Girl Pat* back to England alone.

We weighed anchor and turned north. I was afraid to go too close to shore, as much as I wanted to hear the explosion. So we missed the pleasure of listening to the railroad and the bridge go to kingdom come. The next morning we went by Casablanca. I was bursting with curiosity about the explosion by this time and I wanted to go into Casablanca and see if there was any news of it there. Harris felt the same way but Jimmie was against it.

"Don't be a bloody fool, Dod," he said. "That's French territory and the French are still after you. Let's get away from here."

"You're too cautious, Jim," Harris said. "The skip and I performed a work of art last night and we want to know if it was a real smashing success."

We argued about it for a few hours and by that time we were past Casablanca and nearing Rabat. We compromised. I would stay on the boat so that I might not be recognized by the harbor police. Jimmie and Harris went into Rabat in the dinghy to see what they could find out about the explosion.

In less than a half hour we saw the two of them rowing back madly to the boat.

Harris stood up in the dinghy as they neared us and waved his arms.

"Weigh the anchor and start the engine," he yelled. "We've got to move out!"

When they clambered over the side we didn't even take the time to haul the dinghy aboard. We tied it behind us and turned the *Girl Pat* around and headed at top speed for the sea.

"What happened?" I said. "Are they after us for blowing the railroad bridge?"

"The railroad bridge!" Jimmie panted. "Who the hell cares about the railroad bridge? Look at this!"

He spread open a French newspaper and pointed to a big headline on its first page. The headline was in French and I did not understand all of it but some of the words in it hit me between the eyes. It mentioned "Orsborne" and *"Girl Pat"* and "Capitaine Solitaire."

We could not make out every word of the story underneath the headline but we made enough out of it to bring sweat to my forehead.

It said that Dod Orsborne and the crew of the fishing boat, *Girl Pat,* which had been reported missing off Dover in the storm of April 2, had been seen in Corcubion, Spain, where they had stolen money, stores, and fuel from the local authorities. The story sounded as though we had forced Regardo to turn over his money and the stores at the point of a gun. Furthermore, the story continued, the authorities at

Corcubion had positively identified Orsborne as Le Capitaine Solitaire, a British pirate who had recently killed two Italian soldiers in the Mediterranean. The story added that Orsborne was wanted also by the French government in connection with the disappearance of four hundred rifles from the French garrison at Algiers.

"We're sunk now," Jimmie said. "We're wanted for piracy and murder. How are we going to get out of this one?"

I tried to figure it out. We were reported missing in the storm after we left Dover. That ended the *Girl Pat* as far as the British knew. And as far as the rest of the world was concerned. How did they ever manage to connect the missing *Girl Pat* with the boat that turned up in Corcubion? How did they know that Le Capitaine Solitaire was Dod Orsborne, the supposedly missing skipper of the supposedly missing *Girl Pat?* We had not used the boat's real name in Corcubion and I had not revealed my name to Regardo or to anyone else in Spain. Nor had we used our own names in Lisbon, the only other port we had visited since we were reported missing in the storm off Dover.

"How did they know that the English boat at Corcubion was the *Girl Pat?*" I said.

Harris looked at Fletcher.

"I got my own ideas about how they knew," Harris said.

"Why, you bastard," Fletcher said. "I told you I didn't——"

"Shut up, Harris," I said. "And you shut up, Fletcher. God knows we have enough trouble as it is without fighting among ourselves too."

One thing was certain. We could not go to Gibraltar now. My name and the name of the boat were known to the Italians and the Spanish and the French and we were useless for Intelligence work. I wondered what Hall would say when he saw this in the newspapers.

I tried to think. We had to get back to England. But it was too dangerous to leave this African coast and head north past Gibraltar and Portugal and Spain at this moment. The part of the Atlantic that I would have to go through would be full of Italian and French ships. Even the British naval vessels might be looking for me. They didn't know I was a British naval agent. To them I was a runaway British fisherman with a charge of murder and robbery against me. I decided that it would be best to put in at some uninhabited island and hide there for a few days. I headed the boat for the Salvage Islands.

"That was where Captain Kidd used to hide," I said to Ginger.

"As long as everybody thinks we're pirates we might as well act like pirates."

The next morning at three o'clock a steamship passed within a mile of us. We doused our lights and shut off the engines and she went by without noticing us. She was headed toward the Canary Islands and there was a big sign on her sides, lit up by electric lights, that read, *"Daily Mail."* I did not realize it at the time but the ship was looking for us. Our story was big news in England and the British newspapers were trying to find me.

We found the Salvage Islands the next morning and anchored in an inlet surrounded by reefs with just enough water to float the boat. We slept around the clock and stayed there for three days, amusing ourselves by fishing for dogfish. Then we ventured out to sea again and went past the Canaries without being recognized. I decided to go south along the African coast to Freetown, a port in the British possession of Sierra Leone near Liberia, and to send a radio message from there to Donald Gillies in London. Donald was in close touch with Hall and the Admiralty and he was in a position to get advice from them about what my next step should be. And a radio message to him would not excite suspicion because the authorities in Freetown would assume that he was the owner of my ship. I hoped that the story we had read in the French newspaper from Morocco had not yet penetrated that far south in Africa.

We coasted along beside the Sahara Desert, changing the name of the boat again and repainting the black hull white. Outside of the Spanish port of Villa Cisneros I noticed a group of six or eight coastal steamers anchored a mile offshore. Small boats were going back and forth between these ships and the town. I wondered what was going on and of course I had to stick my neck out and take a close look. It was early morning and there was only a mild wind coming head on from the south so I did not have the sails up. I edged in toward the anchored ships and passed between two of them and then I saw two small motor launches coming directly at me. I veered away from them but they veered too and rushed toward us. I saw that they were both loaded with black soldiers who carried rifles. One launch rammed the side of our boat and the soldiers jumped up to come aboard us.

"What do you want?" I yelled.

"Amigos, señor!" they called to me. *"Amigos!"*

There was a box of emergency signal rockets beside me. I reached for one, lit the fuse, and tossed it into the launch. They thought it was a grenade or a bomb. As it burst, two of the frightened soldiers jumped overboard. The other launch turned and ran madly for the shore. I swung the head of our boat around and roared out to sea with the throttle wide open. The launch that had been alongside us stopped to fish the two soldiers out of the water.

"You and your God damned blasted curiosity," Jimmie said. "Now you've got us into a real pickle."

He was right. I should have kept away from the ships. And by refusing to be stopped and running away, I had practically told them who we were. I remembered that Villa Cisneros was a Spanish Foreign Legion headquarters. A wireless message would be sent out from there announcing that we had been sighted in that vicinity.

We were really in a bad spot.

CHAPTER 10

*P*ROBABLY THE MOST FASCINATING MYSTERY OF THE SEA
in modern times is the story of the *Mary Celeste*. She was an American
sailing brigantine that left New York on November 7, 1872, to cross
the Atlantic. The captain, a man named Briggs, was accompanied by
his wife, Sarah Elizabeth, and his two-year-old daughter Sophia. Mrs.
Briggs had been in ill-health since the birth of Sophia and the captain
felt that the rest and a change of scenery would be beneficial for her.

On the fourth of December the *Mary Celeste* was sighted by the sailing ship *Dei Gratia* about seven hundred miles west of Gibraltar. Some
of her sails were up. The cargo was intact and untouched. The table
in the captain's cabin was neatly set for a meal for three persons.
Clothing belonging to a woman and a small child were also found in
the cabin. The belongings of the crew were below in the crew's quarters. But the ship's papers were missing and the ship's only lifeboat
was missing and there was not a living soul aboard the ship.

The *Dei Gratia* mate sailed the *Mary Celeste* to Gibraltar where an
inquiry was held. There was no sign of violence or bloodshed aboard
the brig. Captain Briggs had a good reputation among seamen and
there was no reason to believe that there had been dissension in the
crew. There was no evidence that the *Mary Celeste* had been attacked
by pirates or that her crew and the captain and his family had been
washed overboard in a storm. Everything aboard was too neat and
carefully arranged for that. The last entry on the log slate was written
on November 25, ten days before the ship was found. The entry was
in the captain's handwriting and it said, "Sailing N.N.E. Sky overcast."
The absence of the ship's papers and the absence of the only lifeboat

pointed to one thing. Apparently the ship had been deserted by all hands. But why would a captain with a wife and a small child deliberately leave a ship in mid-ocean when the ship was not in trouble?

The captain and crew of the *Dei Gratia* were awarded seventeen hundred pounds sterling for salvaging the *Mary Celeste*. The case was never solved. No trace of the people was ever found.

I have read several accounts of the mystery of the *Mary Celeste* and several unsatisfactory theories about what happened to her. But on May 11, 1936, a few weeks after I ran away from Villa Cisneros, the *Girl Pat* encountered an amazing natural phenomenon which, I think, may explain why Captain Briggs left his ship.

When we left Villa Cisneros we went south along the African coast and past the end of Spanish territory. The first town we saw in French West Africa was Port Etienne, a fishing village at the head of an inlet where the ocean cuts for three miles into the red desert sand. I decided to stop at Port Etienne to see if there was any possibility of sending a radio or cable message to London from there.

"This is more damn foolishness," Jimmie said. "Every time you stick your nose into one of these French or Spanish towns we get into trouble. Why don't you keep going to Freetown? We can send a message from there."

"Maybe he's right, skip," Harris said.

I said, "Hold your water. Freetown is eight hundred miles down the coast. This is a fishing town and we're a fishing boat. Maybe we won't attract attention. If we can get a message off from here we'll be eight hundred miles ahead of the game."

I was right. Nobody in Port Etienne had ever heard of us and the two Frenchmen who managed the fishing industry there told us that the commander of the French Foreign Legion fort two miles south in the desert would be glad to telephone a message for us to Dakar. From there it could be radioed to London.

The commander of the Foreign Legion fort was a sick man. We found him lying on a wooden bed in a dirty white uniform, his thin and pale face soaked with perspiration. He spoke English perfectly and he was delighted to see somebody from Europe. His troops were all African Negroes. He had been stationed there for three years.

"Three years without another white man to talk to," he said. "It is a long time."

A supply ship from France was supposed to stop there every six weeks. The next ship was to bring an officer to relieve him but it was already four months overdue.

"I pray to God I will still be alive when it comes," he said. "I have been sick with this fever a long time and I don't want to die here. I want to see Paris again."

He made the arrangements for me to send a message to Dakar and to have it relayed from there to London. He also asked me to have the reply addressed to him. "You can wait here until it comes," he explained. "And that may give me the pleasure of your company for four or five days."

I worded the message to Donald: "Forward instructions. Destination at present Freetown. Registered ship number four five. Reply care of commandant military fort Port Etienne French West Africa."

I signed no name to the message. The numerals four and five, my laundry mark code number, would tell them who sent it.

Three days later the reply came from Donald: "Call on passage south for renewal of linen at De Gregorio Supply Company Dakar."

We lost no time heading for Dakar. The shore waters between Port Etienne and Dakar are largely unsurveyed and there are several "position doubtful" shoals and banks indicated on the charts. The only safe way is to go straight west about one hundred and twenty miles out to sea before turning south. I started to do this when I left Port Etienne but I saw a number of vessels that were barely visible on the horizon to the northeast. I had to choose between continuing west and meeting those ships or turning south by east and going into the uncharted water. I picked the uncharted water.

The day after we left Port Etienne the *Girl Pat* was making close to fourteen knots an hour with the engine going and the sails up. The wind was keeping the canvas full on the port tack. As often happens south of 40 latitude, the darkness came that night with no twilight immediately after the sun went down. I altered the course two points west to south by west. About ten o'clock that night I was standing on the afterdeck and I noticed the ship listing slightly to the windward. Ginger was at the wheel and I shouted to him, "How's her head?"

"Dead on south by west, skipper."

I looked for the sounding lead and found it. As I was starting to throw it overboard I noticed that the ship was not moving.

When I took the sounding I found that we were in only eight feet of water. The ship's draft was ten feet.

I yelled at Ginger to stop the engine and I went to the cabin hatch and called to the others, "All hands on deck. We're ashore."

They came up running. Jimmie and Fletcher were frightened and wanted us to take to the lifeboat. It took a lot of shouting to convince them that it would be best to stay aboard until we found out what had happened. There seemed to be no immediate danger. Although the water was leaving her sides fast, the ship remained on even keel. In thirty minutes the *Girl Pat* was high and dry. And even then she remained on even keel, as straight and as steady as if she was in dry dock.

It was uncanny. There is not much rise and fall of tide as you go toward the equator and in that area the ebb of the tide was never more than four and a half feet. It was as if some giant hand had grasped the bottom of the ship and lifted her firmly, but very carefully, out of the water. She felt as if she had been placed tenderly on a cushion.

"Let me go over the side, skip," Harris said. "I'll walk around her and have a look to see what's happened."

"Better not try it," I said. "We might be on quicksand."

Nothing could be done until daylight so we made coffee. I noticed that in the excitement none of us had thought about stowing the sails.

When daylight came we found that the ship was sitting in the middle of an island of sand, about a mile in circumference and three feet above sea level. We threw some things over the side and the sand appeared to be firm. Then Harris climbed over the side with a rope tied under his armpits so that we could pull him back if he began to sink. He walked away from the ship in the four directions of the compass and reported that the island was solid to the very edge of the water. The rest of us went over the side and walked about.

Every ten minutes one of them asked me what we were going to do. I did not know what to tell them. I told them to wait until the next day and then we would work out some sort of a plan. In the morning of the next day we saw another island to the north that had arisen from the sea during the night. It appeared to be smaller than ours but slightly higher. Early in the afternoon I saw surf breaking to the west of us. I watched through the binoculars and saw the surface of the water there become calm and then the gradual appearance of a third island above the water. Before dark the island to the north sank into the ocean. Its disappearance gave me hope. I called the men together and discussed the situation with them.

The nearest land on the African coast was at least eighty miles to the east. If we rowed there in the dinghy we would have to go ashore and walk on the desert either one hundred and twenty miles north to Port Etienne or two hundred and eighty miles south to St. Louis and undoubtedly we would die from thirst. Or we might be captured and killed by the cruel tribesmen in that part of French West Africa.

"If we stay here, on the other hand, there is a good chance that this island will sink," I said. "It may sink in a few days or in a few weeks, the way that island to the north of us sank this afternoon. I say let's stay here until our food runs out. Then if we're still stranded let's row ashore and take our chances in the desert."

The others agreed to that. That night we stayed up on the deck and tried to sleep. At nine o'clock I managed to doze off. When I awoke I felt the boat rocking from side to side. I thought I was dreaming. I looked at my watch and saw that it was three o'clock in the morning. Then I became convinced that I was really awake and the boat was really swaying. I yelled to the boys to get the sounding lead. They were awake and already taking soundings with great excitement.

Harris called to me and said that there was eight feet of water amidships. In twenty minutes we had fourteen feet of water below us and I started the engine. We began to move very cautiously because I was afraid of the other islands I had seen to the north and to the west. We kept on taking soundings. At times the water was thirty-six feet deep and at other times we scraped over the bottom. An hour and a half after we started to move we ran aground again in eight feet of water.

When daylight broke we saw that we were stuck on the northeast shore of another island. On the far side of the island we saw the rusted bow of a steamship sticking ten or fifteen feet out of the sand. I was sure we had moved four or five miles from our previous resting place.

We found that there was deeper water directly ahead of our bow. We put the anchor in the dinghy and rowed out to the end of its line and dropped it. By winching a few feet at a time on the anchor line and churning the engine through the sand at full speed, we managed to get the boat afloat again at noon.

But our engine pumps were full of sand. We worked on them for a few hours and put the engine into commission again and set the sails and trusted to luck. We drifted to the north and northwest for thirty minutes. Then we found to our immense relief that our sounding line, one hundred and twenty fathoms in length, was unable to touch the bottom. We were back in the deep Atlantic.

The engine gave out again and we drifted for twenty-two hours while we worked on it. Finally it started to work. Our stores were low so I decided to return to Port Etienne before going on to Dakar.

At Port Etienne I visited the commander of the French Foreign Legion fort again and told him of our strange experience. He said that the rising and falling sand islands were well known in that part of Africa. The natives call them the Phantom Islands. The natives and fishermen from St. Louis have found a deep-water passage between the islands and the mainland and use it for fishing. The commander said that French scientists attribute the islands to a great river which, they maintain, runs under the Sahara Desert and empties somewhere under the Atlantic about sixty or a hundred miles from the coast. The scientists believe that sand gathers in the outlet of this river and at certain intervals the sand clogs up the outlet completely. Then the dammed river increases its pressure and finally succeeds in belching the tremendous barrier of sand out to sea. This sudden upheaval of sand forms an island which later settles and sinks below the surface.

The commander asked me if we saw any remains of a French battleship that was lost in the Phantom Islands in 1919. A rising bank of sand lifted her out of the water and broke her back. The crew rowed ashore but only a few of them reached the fort at Port Etienne. The rest perished in the desert. I told him about the steamship bow we had seen sticking out of the sand. It did not look like a battleship, though.

I think it is possible that the *Mary Celeste* was lifted from the water by one of the Phantom Islands.

To be sure, the position of the *Mary Celeste* indicated in the last entry on her log slate (Latitude 37° 01′ North, Longitude 25° 01′ West) and the position where, according to the *Dei Gratia's* mate, she was found (Latitude 38° 20′ North, Longitude 17° 15′ West) are both more than six hundred miles north of where the *Girl Pat* ran aground (Latitude 20° 20′ North, Longitude 17° 50′ West). But the Phantom Islands undoubtedly extend farther north than the *Girl Pat's* position. And it is not only possible but also probable that the *Mary Celeste* could have sailed farther south than her supposed course.

It must be remembered that in 1872 most sailing-ship officers estimated their positions by dead reckoning, not by instrument. Modern steamships, which hold to a course more accurately than a sailing ship, are often twenty miles off their mark on a run of eighty miles between two ports in the British Isles when the navigation is done by dead reckoning. If a steamship can err twenty miles in an eighty-mile trip, it would be easy for a sailing ship to err six hundred miles in a three-thousand-mile crossing of the Atlantic—and they frequently did.

Furthermore, weather records on file at the Azores for November 1872 show that a bad storm with cold fronts and northerly winds was prevailing at the last known location of the *Mary Celeste* before her disaster occurred. When she was found, two of her sails had been blown away and another was lying loose on top of her forward house. This means that she had experienced a severe blow. With northerly winds pushing her square-rigged foresail, the *Mary Celeste* could have been swept much farther south than her captain realized. In the ten days that elapsed between the time of the last entry on her log slate and the time she was found alone and deserted, the brigantine could have covered an incredible amount of mileage. Those ships could do two hundred miles a day without a great deal of strain.

Presuming that the *Mary Celeste* was south of her course to begin with—and the best trade winds at that time of year are farther south —and presuming that the northerly gale of the storm drove her even more to the south, it is possible to picture Captain Briggs's ship running aground on a Phantom Island.

The *Mary Celeste*, weighing only two hundred and eighty-two tons, could have been lifted high and dry with an even keel and with no damage as the *Girl Pat* was. Only the lifeboat and the ship's papers were missing. The law of the sea says that the papers remain on the ship if it sinks but a ship is not considered sunk until her masthead is under water. The fact that the captain took the papers with him into the lifeboat indicates that the ship was above water when he left it. Undoubtedly the first instinct of the captain and crew of the *Mary Celeste* was to take to the lifeboat and head for the shore, as my men wanted to do when the *Girl Pat* went aground. Perhaps the lifeboat never reached the coast. Or if it did reach the coast the captain and his wife and child and the crew died in the desert.

And undoubtedly the *Mary Celeste*, left alone on the island, floated

136

north by itself when the sand beneath it submerged, as the *Girl Pat* would have done if we had left it.

The commander of the Foreign Legion fort sent a message for me to the De Gregorio Supply Company, informing them that the British sailing schooner *Morning Star* would be stopping in Dakar within a few days for linen and supplies. We arrived there on the morning of June 26 and anchored beside some ships in the middle of the harbor. I went ashore in the dinghy and located the supply company without any trouble. The manager was a cheerful Italian with a black beard. After we identified each other he asked me to have coffee with him. Compared to the black tar that Ginger had been brewing on the *Girl Pat,* it tasted wonderful. I told him what had happened since I left Spain.

"It will be safe for you to stay here until tomorrow," he said. "I'm sure nobody here has heard about you. Tomorrow I'll get you enough fuel and stores to make a non-stop run back to England. You must go out into the Atlantic and then north, keeping far away from the coast. I'll also give you a new set of ship's papers."

We made arrangements to store the boat in the morning and to load it with a thousand gallons of fuel at the Shell Mex Oil Company pier in the afternoon of the following day. The agent booked a room for the night for me at the Hôtel de Commerce under the name of Captain Nicholson. He went back out to the boat with me. I told the boys that three of them could go ashore that night but one would have to remain aboard and keep watch. They tossed a coin for it and Fletcher lost.

I also told them that the voyage and our troubles were over and that we were returning to England the next day.

"Blast it," Harris said, "I was just beginning to enjoy myself."

I told Fletcher that if anything came up during the night he could reach me at the Hôtel de Commerce.

"I have a room there under the name of Captain Nicholson," I said. "Sorry you can't go ashore and do the town tonight with the rest of the lads, Fletcher. But I'll let you have all day tomorrow off while their backs are being broken putting stores aboard the ship."

"Righto, skip," Fletcher said. "Have a good time."

He did not seem to be disappointed.

That night at eight o'clock the agent met Jimmie, Harris, Ginger, and me at the hotel for dinner and drinks. The place was crowded with girls and with seamen of all colors and nationalities and there was a jazz band that played loudly and continuously. As the night went on it became hotter, noisier, and more crowded and by midnight it was jammed. About one o'clock the three boys were on the dance floor and the agent and I were sitting alone at the table. Three young French naval officers came in and started to sit down at the empty places. The agent explained to them that the seats were taken and they apologized and looked around for another table. There was no other table empty.

"Oh hell," I said. "Sit down here and have a drink with us. Those boys have been sitting all night. They'll be dancing for a bit, anyway."

The French officers who sat down next to me spoke English. We talked for a while about this and that and then he said to me:

"Did you hear the wireless tonight? There was a broadcast about this fellow Orsborne, the Capitaine Solitaire."

The agent put down the drink that he was raising to his mouth.

"I didn't hear it," I said. "Orsborne? Is he English?"

"Yes. A *flibustier.*"

"A what?" I asked.

"An English pirate. He steals. He kills. Then he vanishes."

The agent spoke to the officer in French. And the officer spoke to him in French. The other two Frenchmen put in a word now and then. The agent turned to me and translated it into English.

"They say that they have received information that Orsborne is here in Dakar," the agent said. "They were told that he has a room in this hotel. They went to the room a few minutes ago but he was not there. However, they have stationed four French marines in the room and when Orsborne returns to it tonight he will be captured."

I laughed and the French officers laughed heartily.

"That Orsborne chap will be surprised when those marines grab him," I said. "I would like to see his face when he walks into that room. It ought to be funny."

The French officers agreed that it would be very funny indeed.

"And now let us have another drink," I said.

"By all means," said the officer who was sitting next to me. "And this time we shall pay for it."

"No," I said. "It goes on my bill. I insist."

After a few minutes the agent excused himself to go to the men's room and nodded at me to follow him. The agent was a nervous wreck.

"Captain, you must go," he said when we were alone. "You must leave immediately. If they ever find you out I will be ruined."

"How can I go?" I said. "I have no food and I have no fuel. Hide us someplace until we get stocked up tomorrow. Then I'll go to England."

The agent was almost in tears.

"Please, Captain. You must go now. Not tomorrow. Now. If they find out I've helped you they'll shoot me."

"But where can I go with no fuel?"

"Anywhere. The Cape Verde Islands. Use your sails. But please go now."

"All right," I said. "I'll tip off the lads first and then I'll leave myself. You sit with those Frenchmen and keep buying them drinks."

We went back to the table and sat down. I remarked that it was high time I did something about finding myself a woman for the night.

"By all means," said the officer who was sitting next to me. "If you don't hurry it will no longer be night. It will be morning."

The others laughed as though it was a big joke. Evidently the officer next to me had a reputation as a humorist.

I stood up and winked at them and wandered across the crowded dance floor. I bumped into Harris, who was waltzing with a dark-skinned girl, and told him to meet me at the bar. I found Ginger in a corner with another girl who resented my interruption and dragged him away. Jimmie was having a drink with another seaman. I motioned to him to join the three of us.

"Something's happened and we have to get out of here tonight," I said quickly when I had got them all together. "You three go to the boat now and I'll follow you in a few minutes."

"We stay here with you, skip," Harris said. "If there's going to be a fight I don't want to miss it."

"There's going to be no fight and you'll do as I say," I told them. "Go now to the ship. If everything's all right put on the bridge light. If the bridge light isn't on I won't come aboard."

"How about the dinghy?" Jimmie said. "If we use the dinghy to go out to the boat, how will you get aboard?"

"Never mind that. I'll find a way to get out there. Just go."

They drifted across the dance floor and eased out the door. I saw a girl at the bar and brought her back to the table with me. All the fairly good-looking girls had already been spoken for and this one was homely and as thin as a matchstick. She sat down and had a drink with us.

"You like them thin?" the humorous French officer said.

"The nearer the bone, the sweeter the meat," I said.

The agent had to translate that one and the French officers almost killed themselves laughing.

"Drink up," I said to the girl. "We must go have a look at the moon."

The French officers thought that was funny too. The girl and I went out a side door onto a veranda. I pulled thirty francs out of my pocket and handed them to her. I explained that the money was hers but I could not go upstairs with her because I had to go. She did not understand much English and she did not get the idea. She looked at the money and looked at me and shook her head.

"No," she said. "You come with me."

"No. The money is yours. I cannot come with you. Good-by."

I jumped over the rail of the veranda and walked to the street. The girl ran after me.

"You cannot come with me," she said. "I go with you. No?"

I didn't want to argue on the street in front of the hotel. We walked a few blocks toward the waterfront. Then I stopped her and turned her around so that she was facing back toward the hotel and I slapped her on the backside.

"Go," I said, pointing back to the hotel. Before she could argue I ran for the docks.

I looked everywhere for a rowboat. Several of them were tied to the docks but none of them had oars. I left the docks and walked along the beach, hoping to find one there. I heard an English voice in the darkness. "Sambo," it said, "stay there until we come back." About twenty yards ahead of me I saw the outlines of three men who were climbing out of a rowboat at the water's edge. There was a British trading ship anchored in the harbor and these must have been three of her sailors. I stood still until they disappeared in the direction of town. Then I drew my automatic and tiptoed toward the boat. Two natives were dragging it up on the beach. I put my hand on the shoulder of one of them. He jumped with surprise.

"*Vapori*," I said, pointing toward my anchored boat in the middle of the harbor.

He shook his head.

"No *vapori*," he said, pointing in the direction that the British sailors had gone. "We wait *Angleterres*."

"*Vapori*," I said. Then he saw the gun and nudged his companion. They pushed the boat back into the water and got into it while I climbed into the stern. I held the gun on them while they rowed. When we eased up against the *Girl Pat*, I made them hand me the oars. I threw the oars overboard. One of them started to jump into the water to swim after them. I waved the gun at him and he sat down. I climbed aboard the *Girl Pat* and tied the rowboat with the two natives in it to her stern. I looked down at them and pointed the gun at them.

"Stay here," I said. They made no move to leave.

The light on the bridge was on and I assumed that everything aboard was all right. But I found Harris, Ginger, and Jimmie sitting in the cabin and saying nothing. They looked as though something bad had happened.

"What are you sitting here for?" I yelled at them. "For Christ's sake, let's get this boat going."

"We can't go," Jimmie said. "Fletcher's gone."

"To hell with Fletcher," I said. "We can't wait for him to come back. We'll have to go without him."

"He's not coming back. His gear is gone too. And so is the compass and all the charts. He's fixed us good. And how can we go without a compass?"

It took me a moment to realize what they were saying. The compass was gone. Fletcher had run away from the ship and he had taken the compass with him.

"That dirty bastard," I said.

"I tried to tell you that back in Spain," Harris said. "But nobody listens to me."

"He must have sold us out to the French," Ginger said.

I had been wondering how the French had known that I was registered at the hotel under another name. Nobody knew I had a room there except the agent and the men in my crew. Ginger had given me the answer. Fletcher had come ashore and turned himself over to the French. He told them that I would be staying that night at the Hôtel de Commerce under the name of Nicholson. The French had boarded the boat and had removed the compass and charts to keep us from sailing it out of the harbor.

"Compass or no compass, we've got to move out of here," I said.

We turned on the power and began to move out of the harbor. When we were well away from it I walked back to the stern and turned my hand flashlight on the two natives who were dragging behind us in their rowboat. They looked frightened. I threw a handful of silver into their boat and cut it loose. When they saw the silver they began to salaam me.

We left the steaming lights on until we were clear of the harbor. Then we doused the lights and headed west northwest, which I remembered as the direction to the Cape Verde Islands from Dakar. We used the Southern Cross star, abreast on the port side, as our bearing.

When daylight came I called the boys together.

"We can do one of two things," I said. "We have enough fuel to reach the Cape Verde Islands. They are Portuguese and the Portuguese seem to be the only people in the world who aren't chasing us. We have money and we can buy stores and fuel and some kind of a compass and charts there. The other thing is to go back to Africa and sink the ship and split the money between us and then take off, every man for himself. If we head for the Cape Verde Islands we'll have to go without food for two days. What'll it be?"

"Cape Verde Islands," Harris said. He turned to the other two and said, "Right?"

They both nodded.

"Fine," I said. "We still have a little coffee left. Ginger, make us all a cup of it. And, Harris, there's a small-scale chart of the Atlantic in that chest in the cabin. Bring it to me up on the bridge."

Harris came to the bridge livid with rage.

"Even that small chart is gone, skip," he said. "There isn't a map or a chart on the bloody boat. Even your rulers and dividers are gone. Fletcher cleaned us out proper."

"Wait till I lay my hands on him," I said.

"I knew he was yellow the first day after we left Dover," Harris said. "Remember that bad storm when we were crossing the Bay of Biscay? I didn't say anything to you about it but twice I had to take his spell at the wheel because he got the wind up. He kept saying we were going to founder and he was afraid to go on deck."

I found a piece of paper and a pencil and drew a rough map from memory of the west coast of Africa and the Cape Verde Islands.

"Don't worry," I said to the boys. "If we stick on this west northwest course we'll see ships going to and from the islands in two days. Then we'll be able to follow them into port. Let's take turns standing two hours each at the wheel."

At four-thirty that afternoon Jimmie came below and woke me from a nap. There was a plane circling overhead. When I came up on deck it dived on us and passed our starboard so low that we could see the pilot. He waved to us and we waved back to him. It was a French plane. It turned east and headed toward Dakar. I did not like it but there wasn't anything that could be gained by worrying about it.

The sky was clear and full of stars that night and we had no trouble keeping on our course. In the morning dark clouds gathered behind us on the starboard quarter and northeast winds came from that direction. I put up the sails because the wind was just right for traveling west northwest. We painted out the name, *Morning Star,* but we did not bother to paint on a new name. It was really useless to try to camouflage ourselves any longer because Fletcher had undoubtedly told the French about our masts and sails and our bogus smoke funnel.

At eleven o'clock that morning another plane circled over us and headed east like the one the day before. The clouds in the northeast grew darker and closer and we saw lightning there. The swells on the sea became bigger and rougher and topped with whitecaps. We were in for a tropical storm. Harris shouted at me:

"There's ships in that storm astern, skip!"

We all looked but we saw nothing. Then after a few minutes we were able to make out in the darkness behind us the outline of three gunboats. I knew what they were. They were French naval vessels that I had seen at Dakar.

I ran to the wheel and swung the *Girl Pat* to the southwest so that the swells from the approaching storm would hit her dead astern and push her away faster. We heard a sound like thunder. There was a splash on top of the water ahead of us. The gunboats were firing at us.

"Please, God," I prayed, "bring that storm on us fast. And make it a heavy one."

There was another shell landing closer. I waited until I heard the sound of the guns again. Then I twisted the wheel and threw her off to the port side. I waited and saw two more splashes ahead of me and twisted the wheel, zigzagging back to the starboard. Then the storm hit us.

The *Girl Pat* went down until I thought she was heading for the bottom and then she arose slowly to the top of the waves, shaking and shuddering while the water swished off her decks. Down she went again and then up again with another shudder. The wind screamed and howled. Ginger staggered up to me and grabbed my arm and pointed at the sails. They were beginning to go but there was no time to run them down. The wind screamed again and the sails tore loose and hung for a moment like a flag whipping in a stiff breeze. Then they ripped and vanished into the storm, leaving only a few small ribbons that flapped and danced madly on the quivering masts.

There was a cracking noise and the boat leaned sideways and trembled all over. A shell from the gunboats had hit her on the starboard side. Harris lurched toward me and shouted into my ear to make himself heard above the scream of the wind:

"We're hit amidships! Above the water line! Two timbers driven into the engine room!"

There was no more firing and I turned and saw the reason why. The storm had blotted the gunboats from our sight. Then the rain came. It rained as it can rain only in the tropics. We could see nothing around us except a thick curtain of it driving downward like hail. The waves arose above our heads and then went down until we seemed to be floating in air. I hoped that the storm would keep up until darkness came.

Jimmie and Harris came up from below and told me that they had stuffed the shell hole in the side with sacks and had nailed timbers across it. Every time the boat rolled to the starboard she was taking water but not badly.

"Good," I said. "Call Ginger. I want to talk to the three of you."

They stood beside me, exhausted from fighting the storm and weakened from not having eaten since we had left Dakar. I stood at the wheel, holding the boat on the southwesterly course with the waves behind her, and talked to them with my eyes on the rising and falling bow ahead of me.

"If this rain stops we're done," I said. "Those gunboats will blow us out of the water. If I turn back and surrender they'll put us in jail. It's a safe bet Fletcher's blabbed about that railroad bridge in Morocco."

I glanced at them. They looked beaten and discouraged. I took one hand from the wheel and reached into my pocket for the key to the medicine chest. I handed it to Ginger.

"Go to the medicine chest," I said. "There's a bottle of brandy in it. Bring it up here."

I said nothing until Ginger returned with the bottle. Then I started talking again.

"Our only chance is to stay on this southerly course until it gets dark. The gunboats won't follow us that way if they can't see us. They'll figure that we are running west to the Cape Verde Islands and they'll head that way, thinking that we're in front of them."

I gave that a little time to sink in.

"So we can escape from the gunboats by going south. But if we go south, God only knows what will happen to us. It will take us away from the Cape Verde Islands and tomorrow morning we'll be lost and off our course with damn little fuel and no food and no compass and no sails. If we run south tonight we'll be adrift tomorrow with no idea of how to get to the nearest land. And the nearest land will be a hell of a long way off. Ginger, open that brandy bottle."

He opened it and we passed it around. Each of us took a good-sized drink. We felt it fast on our empty stomachs.

"What'll it be?" I asked. "Do I run south and get away from the gunboats and lose the Cape Verde Islands and let us take a chance on starving to death? Or shall we surrender?"

They were silent for a few minutes. Harris was the first to speak.

"To hell with them," he said. "Keep going. Let me have the wheel for a spell, skipper."

Jimmie said, "I don't want to rot in a stinking prison. If we're going to die we may as well die here."

I looked at Ginger. He seemed even younger than his seventeen years. His skinny face was flushed by the brandy. He smiled at me.

"What about you, son?" I said.

"I'm aboard," he said. "I'll do as you say, skip."

"All right," I said. "We go southwest."

Toward dusk the rain turned into a drizzle and after dark the sky cleared. We saw no ships that night. Apparently we had lost the gunboats. Ginger found a lot of bilge water in the engine room so we manned the deck pumps and took turns pumping the rest of the night. At daybreak I went into the engine room and discovered, to my horror, that the main feed line of the oil tank had broken loose at the base during the storm. All night long we had been pumping fuel oil into the sea.

It was a fine situation. I took a sounding in the tank and found that we had less than thirty gallons of fuel left. The compass was gone and all the charts were gone and the sails were gone. There was no food and now there was no fuel.

And we didn't know where we were.

CHAPTER 11

*T*HE DAY THAT FOLLOWED WAS HOT AND STILL. WE drifted on the lazy swells and lay on the deck with the sun beating down on us and felt the hunger pains that tore at our stomachs. Jimmie went below and came up with his mandolin and tried to sing a song. Nobody encouraged him. He put the mandolin aside and lay down and closed his eyes. No one said a word for the next few hours. Harris was stretched out on his stomach with his head on his arms. I sat with my back against a hatch staring out to sea and Ginger was sprawled on the deck, leaning on one elbow. It was no longer necessary for one of us to stay at the wheel. We were not going anyplace.

Ginger pointed to the deck near the bridge. A flying fish was lying there, stunned and fallen after hitting against the superstructure.

"Can we eat it, skip?"

Harris sat up and looked at the fish.

"Why not?" he said. "I've eaten worse things than that."

I said to Ginger, "Come on and I'll help you cook it."

We cut up the fish into small pieces and put every bit of it, fins and bones and head, into a pot of boiling water. Ginger happened to look into the bin where we had kept our vegetables and in one corner of it there were seven small potatoes and a few moldy peas. We counted the peas. There were twenty-three of them. We wiped the mold carefully from each pea and put them and the potatoes into the pot with the flying fish. Harris appeared and proudly exhibited two more flying fish that he had picked up on the deck. We cut them up and put them into the pot too.

While the stew was cooking we made a thorough search of every locker to see if we could find anything else edible. All we could muster up, besides the coffee that we already knew about, was salt and pepper and a tin of curry.

We cooked the stew until every bit of the fish was dissolved into liquid. We dished out one plateful for each man and saved the rest to drink that night. It tasted wonderful and made us lose the weak feeling for a few hours.

I decided to look through the pockets of my extra clothing to see if I might find something that could be eaten. In the breast pocket of a monkey jacket that I had not worn since before I had gone to the Mediterranean, I felt something heavy. I pulled it out. It was a schoolboy's atlas.

I wondered how it had got there. Then I remembered. My last voyage before Inspector Leyland introduced me to Hall was a shake-down first voyage of a new ship called *Lea Tiger*. There were only a few of us aboard and there was no cargo; it was an informal and brief trip around the North Sea to observe how the ship took to the water. So my mate, Benny Woods, had brought along his little boy and a few of the boy's schoolmates. I had got to be great friends with these youngsters, especially one of them who called me "Kipper" because he had difficulty pronouncing "Skipper." This lad was following the course of the cruise on his atlas and I used to spend a lot of time looking at his maps with him. He left the atlas behind in my cabin one day and I put it into my pocket, meaning to give it to him. That had been more than a year and a half ago. I had not worn that jacket since then.

I looked at the atlas. It was the kind that used to sell at the Woolworth stores for a sixpence. It was small, about seven by ten inches, and the maps lacked detail. But at least the maps in it had meridians marked on them. That was something. Meridians could give you an approximate idea of distance.

I sat down with the atlas and began to study it carefully.

Our position was then somewhere south of the Cape Verde Islands and north of the equator, about five hundred miles southwest of Dakar. Supposing for the moment that I had sails, I began to consider the possibilities.

I could try to head north for the Cape Verde Islands. That would be a long-shot gamble. I could miss them easily. It is practically impossible to aim at such a small spot on the ocean as those islands unless you know where you were starting from. I didn't know where I was starting from.

If I did attempt to hit the Cape Verde Islands, I would have to sail north for a week before I could tell whether or not I had missed them. Then I would have to search westward for them for another week and eastward, against the trade winds, for a third week. That would be three weeks' sailing without food and with about one chance in fifty of sighting land. The Cape Verde Islands were out. I crossed them off my list.

The west coast of Africa was about five hundred miles to the northeast. The wind would be against me and it would take me three weeks. And when I landed we would be captured and imprisoned. That was out too.

There was only one thing to do. That was to try for South America or the West Indies.

It seemed silly to attempt a crossing of the Atlantic from a position so close to Africa but I realized that actually it would not be so silly. That is one of the narrowest parts of the Atlantic. We were about twenty-two hundred miles from British Guiana and less than three thousand miles from Trinidad and Barbados. And, most important of all, if we sailed westward we would have the trade winds at our back. If we had luck we might be able to make the crossing in two weeks. Furthermore, I had friends in the West Indies.

I sat in the cabin and thought about it for a while. While I was thinking I noticed the covering on one of the cushions. It was canvas. There were several cushions in the cabin. The covering on the mattresses was canvas too.

I went up on deck and looked at the remains of our sails. The edges of the mainsail were still attached to the mast. That would give me something to start with. I called to the boys.

"Do you want to sit here and die? Or do you want to do a little work that might get us out of this fix?"

We started collecting canvas. We took off the hatch covers and tarpaulins and ripped apart the cushion covers and mattress covers. I began to sew them together and then sewed them onto the remains of the mainsail. I was not too happy when I found that I was the only one aboard who could sew a herringbone stitch. An ordinary stitch is no good for a sail because if one stitch pulls loose the whole seam is likely to go with it. I sewed all that night by the light of a lantern and by morning we had a green, black, and white mainsail. We ran it up on the mast and the northeast trade winds filled it out. When I saw the boat beginning to move west my heart began to beat with excitement.

My hands were a mess from sewing and I was sleepy but there were still some coverings that we had not used and I began to work right away on a jib and a mizzen. We hoisted them that afternoon. I slept for four hours while the boys began to rip apart the seams of all our clothing, even the shirts that we had been wearing. I sewed all that night and all the next day. We ran out of thread but the boys made more thread by unraveling fishing lines and ropes. We tore apart a fishing net for twine to tie the sails down. On the sixth day after we had left Dakar the *Girl Pat* was carrying as much sail as she could hold—two jibs, two topgallants, a large mainsail and mizzen, and even a small staysail.

We watched these sails like a jealous wife watches her husband. We knew they could never be replaced; they had consumed every inch of canvas and silk on the boat. We inspected them every hour and the slightest hole or the smallest loose stitch was repaired immediately. If we saw a few clouds that even remotely suggested an approaching squall the sails were lowered and secured.

The northeast winds were steady and constant. We could navigate in the daytime merely by watching the wind on the sails and at night by the stars. I measured out a mile of fishing twine by marks on the rail of the boat that were ten yards apart. I tied a piece of wood to the end of the twine and let the twine run out after throwing the piece of wood overboard astern. This is the old-fashioned method of estimating the speed of a boat. It took about eight minutes for the mile of twine to run out. Figuring very roughly, this enabled me to estimate a speed of seven miles an hour or approximately one hundred and seventy miles a day. Some days it was less and some days more, depending on the wind.

My little Woolworth atlas did not have a map that showed the whole Atlantic between Africa and South America. I had to figure part of the route on one page that showed Africa and then turn back several pages to another map to find the last half of the route. I found that sixty miles on these two maps was about the size of the end of a wooden safety match. Each day I marked my progress in the atlas by dabbing the end of a match in soot from the galley stove and then pressing it upon the map. If I covered one hundred and eighty miles, I would increase the length of the black line on the map by three more match-end prints, each one, of course, touching the preceding one.

Considering the rate of speed that the sails had given us, I figured that we might be able to reach British Guiana on the South American coast in sixteen or seventeen days. But even this news did not bring much cheer to the men. They felt hopeless and discouraged. Hunger is very demoralizing.

On the fifth day we cooked two more flying fish. After that we had nothing except the coffee. On the eighth day we drank the last of the coffee.

"My belly feels as though my blasted throat had been cut," Jimmie said.

That sort of prolonged hunger makes it difficult for you to stand on your feet. As long as you lie flat or crawl about on your hands and knees, the weakness is bearable and not too disturbing. But when you attempt to stand up your head aches and your stomach becomes nauseated and your knees feel as though they were not there. We were always drowsy and we slept a lot. After we had slept and rested the hunger pangs would start anew. But if you stood up the hunger went away. The act of standing made you so sick that it was impossible to be hungry.

There was one pack of playing cards aboard the boat but when the men tried to pass the time by playing a game of cards there was usually an argument between them. They were always irritable and they had no patience. They were always snapping at each other and at me. Jimmie was the worst one. He was naturally inclined to be pessimistic and gloomy. And because he was my brother he felt freer to complain and to criticize me.

"Do you know where the hell you're taking us to?" he would say. "You ought to have your head examined. Imagine trying to sail this blasted scow to South America. You might as well try to go to Alaska."

"With these trade winds behind us, we can't miss," I'd say, trying to sound encouraging to Ginger and Harris.

"Trade winds?" Jimmie would say. "These aren't the trade winds. We haven't seen a ship since we got hit by those gunboats."

That was Jimmie. He would never say "since we got away from those gunboats." It was always "since we got hit by those gunboats."

By the tenth day the taste in our mouths was unbearable. The emptiness of our stomachs and our intestines caused gas to accumulate in them. We belched and hiccuped often and when we belched the smell that came from our mouths was foul. To take the taste away, we mixed curry powder with our water.

Luckily the water supply held out well. We replenished it with rain water during the first week of the voyage but it did not rain at all on the eighth, ninth, or tenth days and it began to run low. On the afternoon of the eleventh day, however, there was a downpour that lasted for more than an hour. We put every pot and pan under the sails and caught as much water as we could. While the pans were filling, we stretched out on the deck and let the rain soak into our bodies. It felt wonderful. We wore only shorts because the rest of our clothing had gone into the sails and our skin was burned brown and dry by the relentless sun.

Our only reading matter was one Western story magazine from America. We read each story in it so many times that we could recite the dialogue and the passages of description word for word. We also memorized the advertisements about getting instruction through the mail that would enable you to become a fingerprint expert or a guinea pig breeder.

"How would *you* like to earn big money and travel as a railway mail clerk for Uncle Sam?" Harris would proclaim.

After the rain on the eleventh day I remembered that there was a package of linseed meal in the medicine chest. It had been included with the medicine in case we needed to make a poultice. It could be cooked and it would be quite nourishing. I was overjoyed by the idea and I wondered why I had not thought of it before. I decided to go below and prepare it myself on the stove to surprise the men.

"Would you lads care for a nice, hot, tasty dish of porridge?" I asked them.

Jimmie turned to the other two. "He's gone balmy," he said.

"If you're going to start cooking, skip," Harris said, "don't bother with porridge. It's too troublesome. Just make us something simple like ham and eggs or mutton chops with brussels sprouts and hashed brown potatoes and a dish of sliced onions on the side."

I went below, picturing their astonishment when I showed them a pot of steaming gruel that I would make from the linseed meal.

My fingers were trembling with anticipation when I opened the medicine chest. The linseed meal was still there. But apparently the medicine chest had fallen and overturned during the storm and several bottles of poisonous antiseptics in it had been smashed. The antiseptic fluids had dripped into the linseed meal and the meal was swollen and discolored and saturated by them.

I sat there and looked at it, with my heart broken.

Then I removed the linseed meal from the chest and took it up on deck where the men would not see me and threw it overboard. I was afraid to leave it in the chest. One of the men might find it and eat it without realizing that it was full of poison.

On the twelfth day I announced that we would begin to take a daily sounding. I explained to the men about the continental shelf that juts out about one hundred miles from the South American coast. The line of our sounding lead was one hundred and twenty fathoms in length. When it began to touch the bottom of the ocean we would know that we were within one hundred miles of land.

I did not expect to touch the bottom on the twelfth day or for several days thereafter but I felt that taking soundings would be good for the morale of the men. It would give them the feeling that perhaps land was not too far away. They needed encouragement badly at that point. In our weakened condition taking soundings was terribly hard work. The sounding lead weighed fourteen pounds. Pulling fourteen pounds up out of one hundred and twenty fathoms of water is tough enough when you are eating three meals a day. To us it seemed almost impossible. But it gave us something to look forward to each day.

By that time we had given up walking. When we wanted to move from one place to another on the deck we crawled on our hands and knees. We rarely went below deck. We did not even stand up when we steered the ship. We crawled to the wheel and lay beside it with one hand on a lower spoke, guiding the course by watching the sails above us in the day or the stars at night. Lying beside the wheel, we could not see the water in front of the boat but we had no need to see it. There was no danger of bumping into anything.

On the morning of the thirteenth day Ginger became delirious.

He sat on the deck forward and kept pointing out to sea. His eyes were glassy and his voice was a croak.

"Land, skipper, two points on the starboard bow," he repeated over and over again. "I see land there. It's an island with four palm trees on its right-hand corner. Look at it, skipper. Two points on the starboard bow."

I tried to pacify him. "I see it, Ginger. I see it. We'll soon be there, son."

"Four palm trees. See them, skipper?"

Jimmie sat up and growled, "Isn't it bad enough on this damn boat without listening to him too?"

Harris told Jimmie to shut up.

"Two points on the starboard bow," Ginger said. "Do you see the four palm trees?"

He went on like that all day and all night except for a few hours here and there when he dozed into a restless sleep. I thought he would drive Jimmie insane. We wanted to shut him up but we didn't have the heart to hit him. Or the strength. There was a fair breeze that night but the sun arose like a red ball the next morning and the wind died down. By nine o'clock the sun was burning hot and there was not a ripple on the sea. I worried about the water, which was getting low. Ginger started talking about his island again and I thought about getting him to move into the shade on the bridge but I decided that it was cooler on the deck even though he was in the sun there. My head was aching worse than ever and my eyes were sore.

Then we saw the ship.

Harris saw it first. He was at the wheel and he shouted to me that there was smoke on the horizon. "It's a ship!" he yelled. "It's a ship!" Jimmie and I looked and saw the tiny speck to the northwest and watched it grow larger. Jimmie grabbed my arm. There were tears in his eyes.

"Great God!" he said. "Suppose he doesn't see us?"

I said, "We'll start a fire. He'll see the smoke."

We went below and gathered up the stuffing that we had taken out of the mattresses and cushions when we made the sails. We piled it on the deck and lit it. We watched the ship again for a while and then we saw that it was unmistakably headed for us. As it drew closer we recognized its American flag and saw the crew gathered along the rail, looking at our little craft. We ran down our sails and drifted. I expected the ship to put down a lifeboat but it edged near to us, examining us carefully. I will never forget her name. It was the *Lorraine Cross,* registered at New Orleans. I saw an officer on the deck who seemed to be the captain and I shouted at him.

"Can you give us some food? We've had no food in fourteen days."

The captain was in no hurry to answer me. He waited until his ship was on top of us. Then he cupped his hands at his mouth and called down to me.

"Who are you? Where are you from?"

"We're a British fishing boat! Can you give us food?"

He looked us over for a moment and turned and talked to some men from his crew who were standing near him.

"Don't kid us!" he yelled. "You're not British. Why isn't there any name on your boat? You are escaped convicts from Devil's Island."

I was in no mood to hold a conversation. All he had to do was to drop us a little food.

"We're British, I tell you! We were lost in a storm off Africa. Just give us enough food to get us to Georgetown. We'll pay you for it."

He shook his head.

"I can't feed escaped convicts. Give up that boat and come aboard my ship and we'll feed you. Come aboard."

I could not believe my ears.

"I can't give up my boat," I yelled. "Just drop us a little food. We'll pay for it."

He shook his head again. I was not going to give myself up after all that we had gone through. In asking him to drop me some food I was making a fair and reasonable request and he was violating the common courtesy of the sea when he refused me. He had no right to attempt to force me into giving up my ship. A feeling of wild rage swept over me. I shook my fist at him.

"To hell with you!" I shouted. "Take your food and stick it!"

The captain stood there and laughed at me. He walked away from the rail. The ship eased away from us and turned and started to steam off to the east. As I sat on the deck, feeling disheartened, sick, and completely furious, the whole thing seemed like a bad dream. I watched the stern of the ship growing smaller as it went farther into the dis-

155

tance and I wondered if its captain's words were something that I had imagined. I did not understand how any living person could have been so heartless and cruel.

"That miserable son of a bitch," Harris said. "I wish I had my hands on his throat. My God, I'm hungrier than ever now. I could taste that food."

"Why did you let him go away?" Jimmie yelled at me. "Why did you tell him you didn't want his food?"

"Oh, shut up," I said.

"Too damn proud to take the man's food," Jimmie said. "Can you beat that one, Harris? He was too proud to take the man's food."

"Shut up," I said.

"Here we are starving and he tells the man to take his food and stick it. My own brother won't take the man's food. My own brother. A great God damn family I come from."

"By God, that was the last straw for me," Harris said. "I'm so hungry now I could eat anything."

I noticed Harris staring in a crazed way at something on the deck. He was looking at the Western story magazine. It was lying on the deck, tattered and torn, with its pages swollen by rain and bleached by the sun. Before I could say anything to him or stop him, Harris had it in his hands. He began to tear out the pages and stuff them into his mouth.

I crawled toward him. I wanted to punch him but I was too weak to do it. I threw myself on top of him and held his arms and brought my knee up hard against his chin. He went limp. I crooked my finger and put it inside his mouth and scraped out the paper that was in there. I knew I did not get it all. It had taken me a long time to get to him and I had seen him chew and swallow a lot of it.

When he came to, Harris lay on the deck the rest of the day cursing the sun, the sea, and the captain of the ship that had passed us by. Ginger still mumbled about the island with the four palm trees. "To hell with everything," Jimmie said. "I'm going to lie here and I'm not going to get up until somebody picks me up dead." I crawled to the bridge and fixed some hatch covers in a position that enabled me to see the water around me as I steered. If the captain suspected us of being escaped convicts from Devil's Island, our position must be near the South American mainland, I reasoned. Besides, the sight of that ship indicated that we must be close to the South American coastal shipping lanes. I felt that we might sight another ship soon.

That night was a bad one. I was sick and thirsty but I was afraid to drink because the water supply was nearly gone. There was a strong breeze and I became nearly exhausted trying to hold the boat on her course. Along about midnight I realized that I had not heard a sound from Ginger, Jimmie, or Harris. I had a moment of fright, wondering if they were still alive. I called to Ginger.

"Yes, skip?"

"Do you still see that island?"

"Yes, skip. It's nearer now and I can see it better now. There are four palm trees at the water's edge on the right-hand corner of the island. And three palm trees, big ones, up on the top of it."

Jimmie's voice came out of the darkness, telling Ginger to close his bloody mouth.

The sun rose the next morning in a clear sky and I searched the ocean eagerly but I saw neither a ship nor land. I went to the galley and drained the last of the water into a bottle and crawled up on deck to the men. Jimmie was asleep and so was Harris. I put the bottle to Jimmie's mouth. He shook his head and turned away. "Leave me be," he said. "I'm dreaming." I poured some water into Harris' mouth and he sat up, swearing. Ginger drank and asked for a little more. I drank some and then gave the bottle to him to finish. I went back to the bridge. It seemed to me to be the end. As long as you have water you can live. And as long as there's life there's hope. But when the water is gone there is nothing left.

I sat for three or four hours and stared at the blue water. I was about to lie back and close my eyes when I saw two birds sitting on the rail at the starboard side. I wondered if I might be able to catch one of them and eat it. The birds must have read my mind. They flew away to the west and then as I watched them disappear I realized that they were land birds. I sat up and yelled at the boys.

"Cheer up!"

"Why?" Jimmie muttered.

"I just saw birds."

"Well, what of it?"

"They're land birds. We must be near land."

I crawled from the bridge and found the sounding lead and line.

I crawled to the rail and dropped the lead overboard and let the line run out through my fingers. Then it stopped. I felt it touching the bottom. I looked at the line. The bottom was less than one hundred fathoms. I dropped the line overboard. To hell with hauling it up, I thought. We've hauled it up for the last time. We are within one hundred miles of South America. Let it stay on the bottom.

I told the boys about the sounding but they seemed to be too weak to care.

Just before sundown I thought I saw an island through the binoculars at the very tip of the horizon. But I couldn't be sure because there was a slight haze that obscured it. Later that night after it was completely dark I saw a tiny light flash in that same direction. Again during the night I saw the light flash from time to time, sometimes strong and sometimes weaker. I kept heading toward it and I thought that daylight would never come. Finally at daybreak I saw the outline of the island clearly. Looking through the binoculars at it, I was thunderstruck. The island was exactly the same as the one that Ginger had described in his delirium two days before. There were four palm trees at the right of it and three large palm trees on top of it. And it was two points off our starboard bow.

At six o'clock that morning I pulled the clutch that held the anchor. The cable flew out and the anchor splashed into the water and the *Girl Pat* swung around with her head to the wind and her sails flapping in the breeze.

A longboat rowed by twelve men came out to meet us. I saw that the oarsmen were stripped to the waist and in chains. Two other men in white uniforms sat in the stern. They circled and hailed us. I tried to shout at them but my voice was only a hoarse whisper. I waved to them to come alongside.

The two men in uniform climbed aboard.

"*Anglos*," I said. "No food. No water." I rubbed my stomach.

One of the officers said, "English explorers?"

I nodded and asked the name of the place. They said that it was the French penal colony at Devil's Island.

The oarsmen were convicts. The officers released two of them from their chains and they lowered each one of us into their boat. They took us to the home of the governor of the colony on the island of Royale where they fed us spoonfuls of food and champagne as we lay on the floor with pillows under our heads.

CHAPTER 12

$\mathcal{D}$EVIL'S ISLAND WAS NOT THE TERRIBLE PLACE THAT the Sunday supplements of the newspapers make it out to be. Actually there are three islands: Joseph, Royale, and Devil's Island itself, the one with the palm trees that Ginger had seen in his delirium. We stayed on Royale with the governor for nine days. I found that the convicts enjoyed considerable freedom. They lived in their own huts and worked on the roads or in the fields and were paid thirty francs a month, which they spent on red wine, chocolate, cigarettes, and small luxuries. Joseph was managed the same way. There was only one prisoner on Devil's Island. He was serving three months of un-guarded solitary confinement there for some crime that he had com-mitted against the other prisoners on one of the two main islands. His food was sent to him every morning in a basket attached to a pulley and a line.

Harris took longer than the rest of us to recover. He was taken to the hospital, where the paper of the Western story magazine was re-moved from his stomach. Ginger, Jimmie, and I got to be friendly with the colony officials. I told them I had been on an expedition in Brazil and Dutch Guiana and that we had got lost at sea and had drifted for fifteen days without food. This was not really an untruth. I had been on an expedition in Brazil and Dutch Guiana many years before with Major Ryan. And we had drifted for fifteen days without food.

The day that we were taken ashore the governor sent a cable for me to Donald Gillies in London. It said, "Reached French penal set-tlement island Royale alive and well."

Donald's reply arrived nine days later. It said, "Congratulations. Proceed carefully to Trinidad. Will contact you."

By the time we received Donald's message we were physically fit and ready to move again. Unfortunately there was no fuel oil to be had at the penal colony but for six hundred and fifty francs I was able to buy enough food and stores to last us for a month. I could not replace the compass or the missing charts but I did not need them to navigate from Devil's Island to Trinidad. I planned to cross the fourteen miles from the penal colony to the South American mainland and to follow the coast northward to the West Indies. I could have navigated in the West Indies with my eyes shut.

We weighed anchor and left the islands at dusk. The next afternoon when I was passing up the coast I saw a steamer from the south bearing down on me. We were close to some swamplands and we saw the mouth of a river and swung into it to avoid the ship. The breeze carried us around a bend in the river that hid us from the sea but as we rounded the bend we saw an airplane flying along the coast and we wondered if it had spotted us.

About three miles up the river we saw a wide creek on the starboard side. We crept into it and dropped anchor. Some natives came out of the bushes on the bank of the creek and stared at us. We waved to them and they smiled at us and went back into the bushes. In a few minutes about twenty of them in two canoes paddled down the creek and came alongside the *Girl Pat*. We talked with them in broken English and traded washers and small metal objects for some bows and arrows.

We stayed there for the night. After dark Harris came to me and said that there were a lot of logs floating in the water beside the boat. I went on the deck and saw dark shapes in the water. I lit a match and leaned over the side to get a better look at them. I found myself looking straight into the eyes of a tremendous alligator.

In the morning we sailed back to the mouth of the river and looked out to see if the coast was clear of ships. While we were making up our minds about whether to start another run northward toward Trinidad a small plane flew overhead and circled us. It looked like the same plane we had seen the day before. Then it circled quite close and dropped a small parachute, which dropped into the water near us. We fished it out with a boat hook. Attached to the parachute was a tin can and inside the can, wrapped around a stone, was a note. It said:

"Are you Dod Orsborne? If so return up the river and mark your position. Friend."

At first I did not know whether to follow the directions in the note or not. But then I decided to do so. We went back to the creek where we had spent the night. I smashed a mirror in the cabin, climbed a palm tree on one side of the creek, and put the piece of glass on the top of it so that it would reflect the sun upward. Then I climbed another tree on the other side of the creek and put another piece of glass on top of it.

We spent the rest of the day at the creek. I showed the boys a trick for hunting alligators that I had learned in India. We caught some small fish. There was a hundredweight of carbide in the cabin that we used in the lamps. I stuffed a lump of carbide into one of the fishes and threw the fish into the water. An alligator came to the surface and swallowed the fish and submerged. In a few moments the white, swollen belly of the alligator appeared on the water with the astonished alligator on his back trying frantically but futilely to keep it below the surface. We took the native bows and arrows and drove them into the helpless creature. The carbide had formed gas in the alligator's stomach and it had lifted him like a balloon to the surface against his will.

About four-thirty that afternoon the same plane circled overhead and spotted the reflection on the mirror glass. It swooped low and dropped something in the trees beside the creek. One of the natives brought it to me. It was a bundle of newspapers, some British, some American, and some from British and French Guiana. Every one of them had a story about the *Girl Pat*.

The stories were amazing.

One British paper showed a picture of two men carrying a stretcher across a lonely beach. Under the picture the caption said, "The End of an Epic Voyage. Dod Orsborne and his crew, last sighted by an American vessel off the South American coast, have been washed ashore in the Bahamas, apparently drowned in a storm."

Another story told of our escape from Dakar. It said that the *Girl Pat* had gone down in a storm near the Cape Verde Islands. There was a report from London that a member of Parliament had demanded that the British government do something to capture this pirate who was jeopardizing our relations with the Spanish, Italian, and French governments.

The stories differed here and there but the main gist of them was that I was merely a British fisherman who had run away with my owner's boat in search of excitement and adventure. I had got money and stores and fuel through fraud in Spain (some papers, being romantic, hinted that I had forced the Spaniards to restock the boat while I stood over them with a pistol in each hand) and then I had gone on some sort of crazy voyage around the world. There was no mention of Fletcher deserting the ship. But they must have known something about him because one story said that the *Girl Pat* had run away from Dakar with no compass or navigation charts. There was no mention of the blowing up of the railway bridge in Morocco. That was a load off my mind. Fletcher must have said something about the bridge but perhaps they did not believe him. He knew nothing of the details of the explosion, anyway. Nor was there any suggestion of the fact that I had been in contact with agents of the Admiralty. I was merely a prodigal fisherman who had got into a lot of amusing trouble. The newspapers said nothing about the kidnaping of the Italian guards or the stealing of the French rifles on my previous trip to the Mediterranean. Thanks to Regardo, I was sure that the Spanish, Italian, and French governments knew that Orsborne and Le Capitaine Solitaire were one and the same man. But the British public did not seem to know Le Capitaine Solitaire. Perhaps the Admiralty had hushed up that angle of my story or perhaps the British newspapers were not sure enough of the facts to be able to publish them.

The pilot of the plane, or whoever had sent him, had written a message across the headlines of each newspaper. It said, "Remain there until I come."

While we remained until he came we discussed our predicament.

"We've become bloody celebrities," Harris said. "When I go back to Yorkshire blokes will be asking me for my autograph."

I said, "We've made a balls of it. I'll catch hell from the Admiralty for all this newspaper publicity. I've done just what Hall and Donald told me not to do."

"What about the chap who dropped the papers from the plane?" Jimmie asked. "What if he turns out to be a reporter? What'll we tell him?"

162

"We'll make up a story right now," I said. "If we're discovered at any time before we get back to England each one of us will stick to that story. Understand?"

They said they understood.

"Here's the story. No matter how many questions they ask you, tell them no more than this. We are fishermen from Grimsby. We got blown across the Bay of Biscay in a storm and then we decided that we were bored with fishing and we decided to take a trip and see something of the world. Remember that. The trip was just a lark and nothing more."

"A hell of a lark," Harris said. "A great way to spend a holiday, starving to death in the Atlantic."

"You can tell them what happened at Corcubion but don't go into details. Forget about Lisbon and the blowing of the railway bridge. If they ask you about Fletcher, tell them he got scared and deserted the ship at Dakar. Somebody stole the compass and the charts at Dakar. We don't know who. Don't say anything about the agent in Dakar and don't say anything about the wires I sent to London. And don't say anything about me being in the Mediterranean before we took this voyage. For God's sake, remember that. Have you got it now?"

They said they had it. That night we went ashore on the bank of the creek and the natives brought us some bush rum. Jimmie played his warped mandolin and Harris got tight on the rum and danced with the natives. I reread the newspapers. When I read again the story about our being washed ashore dead at the Bahamas and looked up and saw Harris dancing with the natives, I couldn't help but laugh.

The next morning a motor launch came into the river. In it were four Negroes and a white man. The white man was Herbert Chandler, representative of a bank in Georgetown, British Guiana. His London office had asked him to contact me. He did not say who in London had asked his office to contact me and I did not ask. I knew it must have been Donald or the Admiralty. He was the one who had dropped the newspapers from the plane.

Chandler told me that he had been asked to instruct me to get to Trinidad as soon as possible. There was money awaiting me in a bank there. When I reached Trinidad, I was to sink the *Girl Pat* and destroy everything aboard her. Then we were to use the money that we would get from the bank to make our way back to England.

"As you can see from the newspapers, everybody thinks you're dead," Chandler said. "Let them continue to think so."

I thanked him for his help and shook hands with him and he left us. We pulled out of the river the next morning and headed north, hugging the coast. Late that afternoon the same plane circled over us and dropped a message:

"Are you Dod Orsborne? If so, wave both arms."

I assumed it was Chandler again so I waved both arms. The plane flew away and came back in an hour and dropped a second message which we fished out of the water.

"Drop anchor and wait," it said.

We dropped the anchor. I remarked to the lads that perhaps Chandler had received a second message from London, canceling the plan to sink the boat in Trinidad.

We were then only three miles off Georgetown. Darkness came and I wondered how long Chandler expected us to remain in such a conspicuous spot before we were seen and investigated. About eight o'clock a motor launch could be heard approaching us.

"Who's that?" I yelled. "What do you want?"

An English voice answered me.

"Al White, *Daily Express* reporter. I want to come aboard and get your story. I dropped those messages this afternoon."

I thought about it for a moment.

"Does anyone else know I am here?" I called.

"No," he said.

"All right," I said. "Go back and get me one drum of Diesel fuel oil. Then I'll let you come aboard and give you the story."

"Okay," White called. "Thanks. I'll be back in an hour."

I figured that if White brought me the oil I could get to Trinidad very quickly. I wouldn't tell him where I was going. But I would tell him everything else. By the time the story appeared I would have drawn the money from the bank in Trinidad and nobody would be able to find us. In a little more than an hour we heard White's boat approaching us again. We turned a flashlight on him. With him in the motor launch were a number of armed Negroes. We saw no drum of fuel.

"I'm coming aboard," White announced. "I've come to capture you!"

He was not satisfied with an exclusive story. He wanted to capture me, no less. He was probably picturing in his mind the sensational headlines about the dashing *Daily Express* reporter who brought the dangerous pirate back alive. The double-cross made me furious. The Negroes started to climb aboard the *Girl Pat*. We grabbed everything within reach, belaying pins, pots, pans, and rope. When hands appeared on the rails we smashed them on the knuckles and they dropped back into their boat, yelping and crying.

"Turn the machine guns on them," I shouted.

That was enough to make White and his expedition back away fast. We weighed anchor and ran up the sails but there was not a breath of wind. As we drifted that night we could hear White's launch circling at a safe distance. When daylight came it was lying a half mile away.

Then we saw a larger boat approaching us. This one had a few white officers, wearing revolvers, and about sixty native troops. It drew alongside and one of the officers ordered me to surrender.

"Go to hell," I said.

It seemed like something in the moving pictures but just at that moment a breeze sprang up and started to carry me out to sea. They tried to ram into me but I managed to avoid their boat by pulling the wheel over hard. We had astern some fishing nets, fitted with cork to keep them afloat. While the boat was turning about to follow us we threw these nets out behind us on a line. They caught in the propeller of the boat that was pursuing us and wound around it like thread on a spool and slowed it down. I ran to the cabin and the bridge and collected all our firearms and our logbooks and threw them overboard. The breeze died again and the boat moved alongside us and I waved politely to the officer who had ordered us to surrender.

"Having trouble with your propeller?" I asked.

He was peeved. "We are staying beside you until you surrender," he said.

"I don't quite understand what you mean," I said. "Aren't you from Georgetown?"

"Yes," the officer said.

"But I am on my way to Georgetown," I said.

"Then let's go in together," the officer said.

"That's agreeable to me," I said. "But I want no one to board this ship."

We lashed the *Girl Pat* to the official boat, which was called the

Pomerroon, and entered the harbor of Georgetown. When we reached the quay at east twenty white men came aboard, all of them looking important and giving orders. Georgetown had not changed a bit since my last visit to it. I expected somebody to ask me how I had escaped from Devil's Island. Georgetown was still a three-ring circus.

One of the officials informed me that he was the chief of police. He asked me to turn over my firearms.

"Firearms?"

"Machine guns and rifles and pistols," he said.

"I never carry such things."

"Do you deny that you are Dod Orsborne and that this is the boat that the whole world is looking for?"

"I deny nothing. But why are they looking for me?"

"You have no compass on this boat. Where is it?"

"I ate it," I said. "I was awfully hungry."

They took us ashore. We had been eating regularly since we had landed on Royale and we looked and felt quite healthy. As we walked ashore somebody ran up to me and handed me a banana. Absentmindedly I unpeeled it and started to eat it. A camera light flashed. Later we saw the picture. The caption said, "Four Starving Pirates Eat Bananas after Dramatic Capture at Sea by British Guiana Ship *Pomerroon.*"

The distance from the dock to the police station was about three hundred yards. Lined up along this route were approximately one hundred mounted policemen and two hundred policemen on foot to keep the four desperadoes from committing violence.

At the prison we were given cots in one room. We hoped to get some rest because we had not slept all night. But the police chief appeared with a half-dozen other dignitaries and began to ask questions. We did not talk until the police chief produced a bottle of rum.

"Where did you get the ship?"

"We stole it."

"Where were you going?"

"On a vacation."

"Why?"

"We were tired of catching fish."

"There were five men on the boat when you left Dover. Where is the fifth one?"

166

Harris, who had been paying no attention, sat up on his cot.

"That bastard?" he said. "We ate him. Just before we ate the compass."

"Were you planning to sell the ship?"

"No, we intended to sink it."

"Who told you to sink it?"

"The owner."

"Who is the owner?"

"How should we know?"

The local newspaper the next day hinted at cannibalism.

The questions and answers went on and on. Finally they allowed us to sleep and after I had slept for a few hours somebody woke me and asked me to sign a typewritten record of my testimony. "Don't bother me," I said. He persisted and I leaned over and signed it.

The next morning the whole situation changed. I learned that London had ordered Jimmie and me to be brought back to England to stand trial for conspiracy and fraud. Harris and Ginger were to be released. The conspiracy charge involved the boat. When it was reported missing the insurance company had tried to pay for it but the Mustag Shipping Company, nominal owners of the *Girl Pat,* had tried to avoid receiving the insurance money, knowing that it was probably safe and somewhere near Gibraltar. The Mustag Company could not very well explain this to the insurance company, however. Then when it was revealed that the boat was not sunk the insurance company pressed the shipping company into bringing charges against me for stealing it. There was nothing else that the shipping company could do. In order to have a conspiracy you must have more than one defendant. Jimmie's name was not on our original crew list; I had brought him aboard unofficially as an added starter. So they decided to make Jimmie the other half of the conspiracy.

The fraud charge was brought by the company in Corcubion that had been holding the empty sack since I signed a false name to the receipt for the fuel, stores, and money.

London had also ordered the officials in Georgetown to release Jimmie and me from prison and to treat us well until we boarded the next ship for England.

The chief of police became very polite and gracious.

When Jimmie and I checked out of his jail and checked into the hotel he provided us with clean clothing and a bodyguard of two detectives to fight off annoying journalists. He told us that there was money awaiting us at the bank.

The clerk at the bank asked me to identify the person who had cabled the money.

"I don't know," I said. "The cable was probably signed D.D."

"You must give the full name. What is the name of this D.D. person?"

"You can keep the money if that's your attitude," I said, walking away. The initials, of course, were the ones that Donald used in signing messages. I called back to the clerk, "If you must know, it probably means the Duke of Dunfermline."

The clerk called me back and begged me with apologies to accept the money.

That afternoon the local newspaper said, "Was Duke Concerned with Mystery Ship and Her Skipper?"

The next day there was some sort of a ceremony that I still don't understand. But I found myself attending it and saluting passing troops from a grandstand.

Leaving the parade ground, a newspaperman attempted to take our picture. Jimmie nudged me.

"Isn't that our friend Al White of the *Express?*" he said.

It was.

Jimmie reached for the camera, opened it and took out the film, and threw it away. He dropped it on the ground and walked away. I punched White on the nose.

"Have you been capturing any pirates lately?" I asked as he sat on the ground and felt for broken bones.

That night Harris and Ginger flew to New York on a Pan American clipper plane to get a liner to England and Jimmie and I went back to prison. We were being sued by Al White for assault and for damages to his camera.

We stayed in prison for twelve days, receiving messages and cables from all over the world. A brewer in England wanted us to endorse his beer and somebody else wanted us to be the judges of a bathing beauty contest. Several newspaper syndicates wanted our exclusive story. When one of them offered five thousand pounds I decided to take it. I dictated to a stenographer in the jail for two hours and sent off the result to them. The story appeared later in serial form in the Sunday papers and I enjoyed reading it. Most of it was completely new to me. It included things about hunting for gold in Devil's Island and romantic tales about the Grimsby fishing boats.

We went back to London on a Harrison liner and, although we paid for a first-class passage, the captain kept us confined to the ship's hospital for the whole voyage. He was afraid to give us the freedom of the ship. He thought we might rob the passengers.

At Gravesend several Scotland Yard detectives came aboard and the captain led them to us proudly, as if he expected to be complimented for bringing such desperate criminals safely back to England. He seemed a little bit surprised when the inspector in charge of the detectives extended his hand to me and said, "Well, Dod, how in hell are you? It's good to see you."

It was Leyland, my old friend.

"There's a big crowd of people waiting to get a look at you up the river where the ship is supposed to dock," Leyland said. "We've come to smuggle you and Jimmie off here."

The captain said something about giving the detectives some men to assist them with the dangerous task of bringing us ashore. Leyland glanced at the captain with astonishment.

"Why?" he said. "Dod is a friend of ours. Nobody has to guard him. Come along, Dod."

The captain could not make head or tail of it.

Leyland took us to Old Bailey in the subway tube. We waited there for two hours to see about bail. Donald and Lucille came to see me.

"Now what have you gone and done?" Lucille said. "When are you ever going to stop all this nonsense and stay home with me and enjoy life?"

Donald drew me aside.

"You'll have to stand some sort of a rap for this, Dod," he said. "But it won't be bad. Remember now—not a word about Hall. And don't attempt to go and see him or to get in touch with him."

After the Scotland Yard men vouched for my character and assured the judge that I was not the desperate character that the newspapers had made me out to be, I was allowed to go out on bail. The bail of two thousand pounds was put up by Sir Hugh MacIntosh, a gentleman well known in British sporting circles. I had never met him.

I found to my surprise that everybody in England was still talking about the *Girl Pat*. They were even making jokes about me and the boat on the music-hall stages. The *Queen Mary* was then being built and one comedian was saying that they had better tie her down securely fore and aft or Dod Orsborne would make off with her before the launching. Mae West was then appearing in London and she had a gag in her act about us.

"Who is this Girl Pat who was found with four exhausted men?" she would say. "I would certainly like to have a private talk with her."

The trial began a month later and lasted a week. I had engaged one of the best counsels in London to be my representative and we worked carefully on a defense that he considered airtight. The day before the trial was scheduled to open my lawyer was stricken with a sudden heart attack and died. The lawyer who replaced him was not prepared to handle the case.

I opened my mouth only once during the trial. That was when the prosecutor charged that the Mustag Shipping Company, registered owners of the *Girl Pat,* had ordered me to sink the boat. I stood up and said that it was a lie. The prosecution promptly produced the signed statement of the silly story we had told in Georgetown and asked, "Is that not your signature?" I had to admit that it was.

Fletcher appeared at the trial as a witness for the prosecution. He told the whole story of what had happened at Corcubion. He said that he had written a letter from there to his girl in England expressing fears about the sort of company he was traveling in because the visit to Regardo's house made him nervous.

As Harris had suspected, that letter was the thing that connected us with the incident at Corcubion. The girl reported to the British authorities that the *Girl Pat* was not missing in the storm as it had been reported previously. She showed the letter as proof that it had been in Spain after the storm. That letter gave us away. If Fletcher had not mailed it we might have never got into trouble.

Fletcher also testified that he had deserted the boat in Dakar and that the French there had paid him twenty-three pounds in English money to return to the boat with two of their men and to remove from it the compass and navigation charts.

He did not mention the blowing up of the railroad bridge in

Morocco, however. And my experiences in the Mediterranean were not brought out in the trial.

To all outward appearances, I was guilty of stealing the *Girl Pat* from her owners and running away with her. The owners tried to avoid making this charge. If I had only used my head and landed at Georgetown with some evidence to show that I had been fishing in the Atlantic and looking for new fishing grounds near South America, I might have beaten this accusation. But all the evidence was against me. I had said too often that I had run away for a vacation to avoid fishing. In court that looked bad.

The forging of a false name and a non-existent company to the receipt for the stores, fuel, and oil in Spain was very bad of course. On that count they had me cold.

So the jury found me and Jimmie, as co-conspirator, guilty. The judge sentenced me to twelve months of hard labor at Wormwood Scrubbs prison and gave Jimmie six months.

CHAPTER 13

I COULD WRITE A WHOLE BOOK ABOUT MY IMPRISONMENT at Wormwood Scrubbs. Maybe I will if I ever finish this one. After Jimmie and I were convicted the newspapers began to speculate about how long I would remain in prison. The newspapers were apparently beginning to believe their own stories about me and pictured me as a sort of Scottish combination of the elder Douglas Fairbanks and Superman. They confidently predicted that Jimmie and I would break out of prison in a few days. When we didn't they must have been disillusioned.

As a result of the newspaper stories the Home Office, the branch of the government that is responsible for the prisons, ordered Jimmie and me to be separated. Jimmie was transferred to Brixton, where he promptly got himself a soft job and was released for good behavior before his six months were up. The governor of Wormwood Scrubbs summoned me to his office and had a fatherly talk with me.

"I do hope you are not planning to attempt an escape or any such nonsense as that, Orsborne."

"Indeed not," I assured him.

"Of course we feel here, as you do, that the sentence was unfair."

"I don't feel it was unfair. I was lucky that I didn't get fifty years. Besides, I need some peace and quiet for a change."

As a matter of fact my friends at Scotland Yard had told me that the six months' sentence was a Godsend because the prison walls would protect me from the Spanish and Italian agents who might still be on my trail.

"You're the first prisoner who ever came here feeling that way," the governor said. "I don't think you'll be too badly off."

After a week of hard labor I was put in with the privileged prisoners in D Block, where there was a radio and a recreation room with newspapers, and I was put in charge of the work in a ship where they made brushes. There is no smoking allowed in the English prisons but I soon found out that you could get cigarettes if you were willing to pay extra for them. In fact you could get anything if you were willing to pay for it. Two of my closest friends at Wormwood Scrubbs were a pair of celebrated stock swindlers. The night before they were released they threw a party in D Block which featured all the whisky the guests could drink.

The only thing about being in prison that really annoyed us were the people who came to lecture to us about the evils of sin and the attractions of the straight and narrow path. We called them Bible Punchers. One of the Bible Punchers who appeared regularly at Wormwood Scrubbs while I was there was a member of Parliament who was particularly sanctimonious. He was always pointing out that he was sacrificing his valuable time to come to the prison and inspire us. I took great satisfaction in discovering a few years later that he himself had been sentenced to eighteen months at Wormwood Scrubbs for selling commissions in the British Army.

While I was supervising the workers in the brush shop I made an eight-inch model of a sailing ship and engraved on the side of it the date and the words, "Made in Wormwood Scrubbs Prison by Dod Orsborne." The prison officials admired it.

"What a pity you can't take it with you when you leave," they remarked. "You are not allowed to take anything whatsoever out of here, you know."

Two days later the ship model was delivered at Donald Gillies' office in London. And none of the prison officials had anything to do with smuggling it outside. The job was handled by one of the Bible Punchers, who was quite willing to undertake it for a reasonable financial consideration.

After six months in Wormwood Scrubbs I was released quietly under the condition that I would stay out of the public eye for a while and not let the newspapers know that I was free. I left the prison lying flat on the floor of a sedan. In prison I had grown again the beard that I had shaved on Devil's Island and no one recognized me except Lucille. She and I went north for a holiday.

One day we were having tea in a shop at Edinburgh and heard two girls at the adjoining table discussing the exploits of Dod Orsborne, which were then running in serial form in the Sunday newspapers. I could not resist interrupting them.

"You shouldn't believe that stuff," I said.

"Why not?" one of the girls said. "It's all true!"

"Get away with you. It's all rubbish made up by the newspapers."

The two girls stood up and glared at me. "If you're so smart," the other one exclaimed, "why don't you try pinching a boat and crossing the Atlantic yourself!"

Three months later we were stopping at a hotel in Lincoln and after dinner one evening I walked into the lounge bar and found a crowd of people gathered around three young men. The young men were regaling everybody with stories of their adventures aboard the *Girl Pat*. Everybody was buying them drinks. I sat for a while and listened to them. They were quite entertaining.

Finally I tapped one of the lads on the shoulder and said to him, "What sort of a chap is this Dod Orsborne?"

"Oh, very regular. Just like one of us seamen."

"Stop it," I said. "You've never seen Dod Orsborne."

Somebody shoved me and several people became indignant.

"Who asked you to put your nose in here?" a woman cried.

"Imagine this for nerve!" somebody else said. "Want to punch this bloke on the nose, boys? We'll help you!"

"Look at who's saying they don't know Dod Orsborne! What does he know about Dod Orsborne!"

I backed away from them and said, "I ought to know Dod Orsborne. I was one of his crew myself."

This brought only hoots of laughter and boohs. I had to get away from the lounge bar in a hurry.

The real members of the crew of the *Girl Pat* did keep in touch with me for a while after I left prison but I soon lost track of them. I gave Jimmie, Ginger, and Harris each one thousand pounds of the five thousand pounds I received from the newspaper syndicate for the use of my name on the largely fictitious account of our travels. Ginger went right back to sea. Harris drank up his share of the money in his home town. Jimmie spent his share quickly and then went to the Mediterranean, where he had an exciting time running refugees from Spain to Algeria. Later he went to Canada and he was reported missing in

Singapore when it was invaded by the Japs in 1941. Our family never heard from him again.

Fletcher had a bad time after he testified against us at trial. He was so unpopular from then on that he took his life in his hands whenever he put his head inside a waterfront pub anywhere in England or Scotland. A friend of mine in Hull whose name also happened to be Fletcher was badly beaten one night by some seamen who thought he was the Fletcher who deserted the *Girl Pat*. Finally, after being turned down everywhere that he sought a job, Fletcher gave up and went to Australia, where he was not known.

A few months after I was released from prison I visited Hall and told him the whole story of the *Girl Pat's* voyage. It was quite a session. Hall was furious with me. He cursed me for stopping again in Corcubion to get revenge from Regardo. When I told him about blowing up the railroad in Morocco he almost went out of his mind. Looking back on it then, I can't say that I blamed him for being disgusted with me. As a valuable member of the Admiralty's Intelligence network I was pretty much of a bust. We parted friends, though. Hall told me that he would send for me the next time he needed me. I knew he would not be sending for me for a very long time, if ever.

Some of the newspaper people recognized me when I went back to London and my picture was again plastered in the papers with stories announcing my release from prison. I received offers to appear on the stage and on the screen, and quickly turned them down. I received another offer, however, that I quickly accepted. It was to command a ship that was to go on an expedition to the Amazon River.

I spent several months planning the voyage and fitting out the ship in the river Humber. She was a fine ship, named *Hermosa* after the schooner that I had sailed as a free trader in the West Indies. But by the time she was ready to go to South America it was 1938 and the possibilities of war were strong in Europe. The backers of the expedition were warned against attempting such a voyage at that time and I was instructed to sell the vessel. The day after I placed her in the hands of the brokers I received a wire from London.

To my utter astonishment, it was from Hall. He wanted to see me. The following day I found myself sitting in a room with several Naval Intelligence officers and two civilians, discussing Oswald Mosley's British Fascist Union.

175

The proposal that was made to me was neither particularly dangerous nor melodramatic. A lot of people in England, who did not know me personally, assumed at that time that I felt disgruntled and peeved at the government for putting me in prison. The Admiralty Intelligence men figured that I would be welcomed with open arms by the British Fascists if I applied for membership. They wanted me to mix in with these Hitlerites, merely for the purpose of getting acquainted with the members and listening to their conversation.

One of the civilians in the room was already an established member of the Fascist Union in good standing. The next day he took me to four Fascists at the Union headquarters and introduced me as "Skipper Dod Orsborne, who should be a handy chap to have around." They were evidently convinced that I was sore at England and favorably inclined toward Hitler. They gave me a membership card, made a few disparaging comments about the Jews in England, and assured me that Mosley had half a million loyal followers in London alone. I went to a few of Mosley's lectures. Then I met a Captain Montgomery who was one of Mosley's bodyguards and closest advisers. Montgomery wore a golden swastika on the underside of his lapel, which meant that he rated highly in the esteem of Hitler.

If Hitler rated Montgomery highly, it was no wonder that Hitler lost the war.

Montgomery sent me to Grimsby and Hull for the purpose of getting skippers to join the Fascists. I couldn't imagine British sea captains joining anything but of course I assured him that I would do my best. He did not want seamen or bosuns or mates. Just skippers, if you please. I checked into the Yarborough Hotel at Grimsby with an armful of Fascist Union application blanks. After six weeks I sent Montgomery thirty signatures. They were all friends of mine who signed the applications as a joke and not one of them was a skipper. I explained to Montgomery that the British skippers were too hardheaded and stupid to see the benefits of Fascism.

Then he got me involved with a motor fishing boat that he had bought. He planned to fit it with a radio transmitter and to broadcast from it at sea a few true facts about the Jews in England. He figured that a broadcast from a moving fishing boat would be difficult to trace. And of course he wanted me to be the skipper of the boat.

I told him that the voyage on the *Girl Pat* had ruined my stomach and that I could not set foot on any kind of a boat these days without becoming seasick.

Of course I told the Admiralty what Montgomery was up to and they saw to it that the transmitting equipment he ordered was never delivered. I persuaded him to take the boat out for a trial run without the radio to see how she acted in the waters of the North Sea. I recommended a friend of mine as a skipper and instructed him to run her into trouble in the Shetland Islands. He did. That was the end of Montgomery's broadcasting scheme.

While I was working for Montgomery in Grimsby, I received a letter from another Fascist I had met in London, a fellow named Lee who had said he was a newspaperman. In his letter Lee said he had something of importance to discuss with me and asked me to meet him at 117 Kilburn Road in London as soon as possible.

I felt that Montgomery needed watching at the time so I sent the address to the Admiralty and suggested that they check on Lee. They told me that the address was apparently a phony and asked me to drop Montgomery temporarily and come into London and look into the matter myself. I showed Lee's letter to Montgomery then and Montgomery said, "A very nice fellow. By all means go to London and see what's on his mind."

When I went to 117 Kilburn Road, I ran into something that was like a sequence in an Alfred Hitchcock movie.

There was no house or office at 117 Kilburn Road. It was a big restaurant. One of those average-price places with no tablecloths and paper napkins. I figured at first that Lee had made a mistake when he wrote the address. But I went into the restaurant and ordered coffee. I asked the waitress if she knew of a Mr. Lee who lived near by. I explained that he had given me 117 Kilburn Road as his address and perhaps he had the number wrong.

"I never heard of him," the waitress said.

But I noticed that she went straight to the hostess and told her the story and both the waitress and the hostess turned and looked at me carefully while they were talking. I stood up from the table and walked toward them and asked the hostess if she knew Mr. Lee. She shook her head.

"I thought perhaps that he used this place to get his morning coffee," I said. I took out the letter from him and showed it to her. The letter made all the difference in the world.

"Oh," she said, "I think I know the person you mean. When you finish your coffee I'll have one of the girls show you where you want to go."

I returned to my table and drank the coffee. Then a waitress took me back through the kitchen and out a rear door and down a narrow alleyway to another street. Then we turned into another alleyway that led to the back door of a house that had several huts and sheds in its yard. The waitress knocked several time on the door before it was opened by a woman of about sixty who spoke English with a thick German accent. She asked me to come inside and the waitress went back to the restaurant.

The woman took me upstairs to a room where the shades were drawn and the electric light was on, even though it was broad daylight outside. She brought me a cup of tea and sat down and talked about Lee, whom she referred to as Albert. I gathered that he was her son. She explained that he was in Berlin on a holiday but that he would return to London within a week.

"He had hoped that you might be able to go to Germany with him," she said. "A friend of his is in town, though, and he wants to meet you. He will be here in a few minutes."

And in a few minutes the friend walked into the room. I wondered where he had come from. I was sure that he had not been in the house when I arrived. And still I had not heard any doors downstairs opening or closing. He introduced himself as Mr. Ryan and shook hands and began to talk with me as though we were old friends. He seemed to be English or Irish.

"Albert told me he wanted to take you to Berlin with him," he said. "You'd like Berlin. I've been there several times."

The next thing I knew Ryan was showing me a new type of camera that he had acquired and before I could open my mouth to object he had snapped a picture of me and Lee's mother.

When Ryan and I left the house I still had no idea of what I had been sent for. We went to a hotel and had a few drinks. Ryan insisted upon paying for them.

"I'll let you know when Albert returns to London," he said.

"Same address?" I asked, wondering if I would have to go through the kitchen of the restaurant again.

"Same address."

I wondered how many people knew of that address. I could not make head or tail of the whole thing.

I told the Admiralty what had happened and went back to Grimsby. Ryan must have got in touch with Lee very quickly because four days later I received a letter from Lee. It had been written in Germany but there was a London telephone number on the envelope. The letter perplexed me. It said:

> Berlin—Neukoelin
> Hermanstrasse 51,11
> Germany
> 21st March 1939

Dear Skipper:

Yesterday I had a letter from my mother, enclosing your photo and telling me that you had called on us. I am sorry not to have been there. She further added that you would drop me a line so I am dropping you a quick note first. From the above address you can see where I am. I arrived a week ago last Sunday but do not know yet when I shall be home again. I do not suppose, however, that I shall be much longer than a fortnight.

Well, old Sea Bear, how are things going with you? What are you doing? I should like very much to see you again as soon as I am back where we can renew old college acquaintance. It seems years since I was there but it is really just over a month ago.

Now that I am in Berlin, life takes on a rosy look again and things look good. Have you made your trip to Germany yet as you intended? Boy, what fun we could have here. I do not know whether you will get this in time but I shall be pleased to hear from you.

Will close now with my kindest regards and best wishes until I see you again.

> *Sincerely yours,*
> *R. O. Lee*

I did not get the chummy, old-friends and Sea Bear stuff. I had met the man only once briefly in a pub with a lot of other people and here he was talking to me like a brother. Furthermore I wondered where he had got the idea that I was planning a trip to Germany.

Early in May I had to accompany Montgomery to London in search of his missing radio transmitter. At the earliest opportunity after we reached the city I went into a telephone booth and called the number that had been written on the envelope of Lee's letter.

A girl answered and said that there was nobody there by the name of Lee.

I looked up the number in the phone directory and found that it was not listed. I called the number again and got the same girl. I explained that a gentleman named Lee had asked me to call him at that number.

"Wait one moment," she said.

A man's voice came on the phone.

"Whom did you want?"

"Mr. Lee. He's a friend of mine."

"What's your name?"

"Orsborne." I spelled it out slowly.

"Who told you to ring this number?"

"It was in a letter that I received from Berlin."

"Oh! Won't you wait a moment, please?"

The next voice was apparently Lee's.

"Hello! Is that you, skipper?"

"Albert? I've had a hell of a job getting you."

"I'll explain that later," he said. "Can you meet me for lunch in a half hour at the Three Nuns?"

I said I would be there and I found Lee waiting for me. I asked why he wanted to see me and he said he would explain after lunch. I asked why I had trouble reaching him on the telephone and he said that he worked under another name. He was no longer in the newspaper business. He was with a new wireless and telephone company on Euston Road. He gave me the firm's card.

"I'm taking the afternoon off," he said. "I want you to come home with me and talk to a couple of chaps."

We went to the restaurant on Kilburn Road and walked through the kitchen and out the rear door and through the alleyways to his mother's house. I asked if he always went to his house through the restaurant kitchen.

180

"Yes," he said. "My mother owns most of these stores and it is wise to make an appearance in them regularly. Makes it look as though you are taking an interest."

At Lee's house we found Ryan and a man named Smythers who was really a German. He seemed to be the leader of the group. We talked for a while about various things. Then Smythers asked me if I could smuggle a girl from Germany into England without the British government discovering it.

"I want to marry this girl. The British government won't allow her to land because she is a German Jewess. Do you think you could get her in if you had a ship?"

I could imagine his wanting to marry a German Jewess. Or any kind of a Jewess.

"It would be easy," I said. "But I couldn't do it myself because my stomach can't stand the sea since the *Girl Pat* voyage."

"I could arrange for you to take a ship out of Hamburg as its skipper. The money would be good."

"I really couldn't. I'd like to but I can't."

Smythers brought out a map of Scotland and spread it on the table.

"Could you show me a few places where we might be able to land someone without being seen? A place where there are very few inhabitants."

I pointed out several such places. In a few moments they were praising the Nazis and Hitler and damning the Jews. They lifted their lapels and showed me proudly the gold swastikas that they wore underneath.

"They could use you in Germany," Smythers said. "You should let us send you there. Think it over."

I said I would think it over and I left them. I knew that I would be followed from the house. I took a cab to Charing Cross Road and the tube from there to Lucille's house. At two o'clock the next morning I had quite a time persuading Lucille to get out of bed and drive me to Donald's apartment in Chelsea. At last she gave in.

"When you get one of these queer notions there is no peace until you carry it out," she growled.

I woke up Donald and gave him a full account of what I had seen and heard that day. I gave him descriptions of Lee, Ryan, and Smythers and the address of the radio firm on Euston Road. I told him of the plot to smuggle a girl from Germany into Britain and wrote down the names of the places in Scotland that I had suggested as landing points. I knew that I could not go near the Admiralty or phone there. Donald agreed to hand over all the information and to have the three Nazis watched and to advise the Admiralty of the places in Scotland that I had suggested to them.

I stayed in London another week and heard nothing from Lee or Smythers. Then I returned to Grimsby. That was in May. During the summer I stayed with Montgomery for a while and did a few other odd jobs. On September 5, two days after war was declared, I was at Lucille's in London. A captain in the War Office named Simpson called me and thanked me for my help in reporting Lee, Ryan and Smythers. The government had captured thirty-seven Nazi fifth columnists at the restaurant on Kilburn Road and at the radio firm on Euston Road.

"Did you say the War Office?" I asked. "I turned my report in to the Admiralty."

"Yes, but the case was turned over to us," Simpson said. "There is one other thing, Orsborne. This fellow Montgomery. He seems to have vanished completely. Can you remember anything about him that might assist us in tracking him down?"

I described Montgomery's chic wife and then I remembered his two red cocker spaniels. I had heard him speak of the dogs often and it seemed as though he loved them more than anything in the world. I told Simpson to look for the two red cocker spaniels. I was sure that Montgomery would never part with them.

The declaration of war put a damper on another adventurous project that I had planned for more than a year. Since the voyage of the *Girl Pat,* I had had a lot of discussions with various people about the problems of navigating without instruments. The average fisherman hardly ever uses a compass and would look askance at the direction-finding devices that are installed in the modern luxury liners. Land can be seen from eighteen miles at sea but it is not unusual for a fisherman to find his way straight to his dock from fifty miles at sea without the aid of instruments, even in a thick fog. When you have lived on the water a long time you can find your way about on it just as you are able to find your way about on the streets of a city where you have lived a long time. You can tell where you are by the color and the tides and the currents in the water and by the winds and the stars.

While I was in prison at Wormwood Scrubbs, I thought about making a voyage alone in a sailing boat without navigating instruments. I wanted to prove that man's knowledge alone is a capable and efficient direction finder. The best way to prove my contention would be to make such a trip from Southampton to New York over the route of the *Queen Mary* and the then uncompleted *Queen Elizabeth*. I resolved to do it.

I designed a boat for the voyage while I was in Wormwood Scrubbs. After I was released I began to have her built. Naval architects said it was the most perfectly constructed boat of that type that they had ever seen. I spent all my money on her. I decided to sail her from Southampton on the same day that the *Queen Elizabeth* left there on her maiden voyage to New York. So I named my boat the *Little Elizabeth*.

It took nine months to build her in a yard on the Thames. Lloyd's of London registered her as the smallest seagoing vessel in the world. She was twenty-four feet over all and three tons. She was carvel built with a hollow steel keel that was divided into thirty compartments for the storage of fresh drinking water. As I emptied the two gallons of fresh water from each compartment the compartment automatically filled with salt water to maintain the balance of the keel. The truck of the mast was glass with a blinker light at the top of it that could be used to signal in Morse to passing ships. I had three sets of sails: one flax, one hemp, and one silk to suit varying wind conditions. Relying entirely on sails and using no charts or navigation instruments, I planned to reach New York from Southampton in sixty days. She responded perfectly to all tests after she was built. I even had her pushed under water on her side by a heavy crane. When she was released she bobbed upright immediately like a cork.

But the arrival of the war called off the maiden voyage of the *Queen Elizabeth* and the maiden voyage of the *Little Elizabeth* too. I put her up in a yard at Brentford on the Thames. In 1940 the yard was hit by a German land mine during an air raid and the *Little Elizabeth* was completely destroyed. I have been able to forgive the Germans for some things but not that one.

When England declared war I expected to receive a naval commission. I was still working at that time for the Intelligence people. I might have got a commission then if I had not lost my temper one day.

When I lost my temper I told off a group of high-ranking Intelligence officers in rather colorful and shocking language.

I was working on the problem of camouflaging motor torpedo boats so that they would look like fishing vessels. I had also been told to mix in with fishing-boat skippers from the Continent who came to the British ports and to report any information that I might be able to pick up from them.

Back in 1928 I had befriended a Swede named Emmel who needed a job. I had found him a place as an interpreter in a Grimsby firm that dealt with foreign fishermen. Two weeks after war was declared I met Emmel again on the Grimsby fish docks. I told him in confidence what I was doing. He was always closemouthed and I knew that he was in a position to help the Admiralty.

"I'm working now with six skippers," he said. "Three Danes, two Norwegians, and a Dutchman. They just came in from Europe yesterday."

"Bring them to the Exchange Club tonight," I said. "We'll have some drinks with them."

After a few drinks that night two of the Danes told me something that seemed to me to be very important news for the Admiralty. The other skippers corroborated it emphatically.

They said many Danish fishing boats were bringing German agents into British ports and carrying espionage reports from England to German agents in Denmark. The Danish skippers at the table, all of them violent anti-Nazis who were disgusted with what their countrymen were doing, also told me that German submarines were being refueled and restocked in Danish ports and that Danish fishing boats had actually laid German mines off the British coast. They said that Denmark's sympathies in the war were about sixty per sent pro-German.

I hurried back to London and reported my findings to a group of Intelligence officers at their headquarters. They were skeptical.

"Where did you get your information?"

I said, "From Danish skippers who have no intention of returning to Denmark."

"Are you trying to make us believe that Denmark, a neutral country, is waging war against us?"

"I am telling you that the Danes are violating their neutrality. I

184

think you ought to restrict the movements of Danish vessels on our coast or at least watch them closely."

One of the officers in the room guffawed. The others smiled indulgently. That was when I lost my temper.

"Take your damn Intelligence job," I said. Then I told them what they could do with it. "I'm going into some branch of the service where I can fire a weapon."

With that I turned and walked out of the room. The officers were horrified.

Donald was also horrified when I told him about it. "You can't talk to the Navy like you talk to the merchant marine," he said. "You shouldn't have done that, Dod. It may hurt your chances of getting a commission."

In the mood I was in, I did not much care if I ever received a commission.

A few days later I had a drink at the Southern Cross Bar in Whitehall with Captain Simpson of the War Office, the fellow who had been looking for Montgomery. He told me that they had found a man with two red cocker spaniels holding down an important and confidential defense position as an engineer at the naval dockyards in Harwich. It was Montgomery. After we had another drink to celebrate his capture Simpson asked me if I knew any parachutists. Incredible as it seems now, the British Army in 1939 had no paratroops. It was trying frantically to organize such a force. Simpson told me that he was seeking experienced parachutists only. The Army had to do some experimental work in the field before it would be ready to accept untrained volunteers.

It sounded intriguing to me. The next week I visited a friend of mine at a moving picture studio in Denham and had him write a letter which said that I was a movie stunt man who had made several parachute jumps. I had never jumped in my life actually. I went to the War Office and offered my services. The letter made quite an impression. I filled out the necessary papers and, on November 3, I was ordered to report to Norton Camp near Watford. There I became one of a group of twenty-five parachutist specialists, attached to the Army as civilians at the pay of a pound a day, plus twelve shillings for each jump.

We didn't do much until January, when I made my first jump.

Eight of us went up in a Flamingo plane and from the moment that I strapped the parachute to my back I began to visualize myself splattered all over some lonely field. We were supposed to jump from two thousand feet. In those days there was no line attached to the plane that automatically opened the chute after you jumped. You were supposed to leap out of the plane with your finger in the ring attached to the rip cord and count from seven to eleven before opening the chute. I was supposed to be the second man to jump. If I had been the last one I don't think I would have left the plane. I jumped with my eyes closed and my arms flew out and the rip cord was pulled before I had a chance to count. The jerk of the parachute across my chest opened my eyes and I found myself drifting gently above a church spire and across some open fields that looked like a checkerboard. I felt peaceful and secure until I looked down and saw the ground rushing up toward me at a tremendous rate of speed. I started to move my legs in the running motion that we had been told to use when landing and I hit the earth hard and ran for about thirty yards before I fell. To my surprise I found that no bones were broken. Two men came running toward me and asked if I was all right.

In a weak voice I said, "I think so."

After that we jumped as often as three times in a day and I got so that I could even make a good landing from five hundred feet if the winds were favorable. We were attached to the Hertfordshire Regiment. England then feared the arrival of German parachutists and the whole country was warned to be on the lookout for enemy agents who might drop from the sky. In April there was a maneuver exercise in which the local Home Guard and a regiment of regular soldiers were to guard ten square miles of Hertford County. Just before dawn twenty of us parachutists were to drop into the area. We were told to do anything that a German would do to avoid capture. If we were not captured by the Home Guard or the soldiers in four hours we were to return to our camp and give an account of our movements.

When I jumped that morning I landed in a clump of bushes near a golf course. I hid my parachute in the bushes and waited until daybreak. It was clear and sunny and it didn't seem as though we would be able to move far without being spotted and captured. I was on high ground and near me I noticed a number of private automobiles parked near a road that ran downhill to a railroad bridge. The government had recently issued an order that all cars standing idle in such places would be confiscated. It was feared that German agents could use such vacant and unguarded automobiles to make a getaway in if they slipped into England.

I crept toward the parked cars and found one Austin with its window open three or four inches from the top. I took off my tunic and worked my arm into the opening and opened the window the rest of the way. I climbed inside the car and let off the hand brake. Nobody was anywhere in sight. I found a metal marking rod near by on the golf course and used it as a crowbar, working the car forward, a little at a time, until I had it out on the road at the top of the slope. I gave the car a slight push and jumped into it as it began to roll down the hill. It gathered speed as it rolled along.

Two Home Guards and a regular soldier were standing at the railroad bridge. When I went by them I waved and put my head out of the car and said, "What do you think of this for a lovely spring day?"

"Oh, it is lovely, sir," one of the Home Guards said.

I coasted beyond them for about five hundred yards before the car came to a stop on the level ground. I got out of the car and left it on the road, walking through a small wood to a hayfield. I lay down in the hayfield and went to sleep. When I awoke it was ten-thirty. The four hours had elapsed so I set out for my camp. I went back to the road. The car was still standing where I had left it. I walked along the road and came to a little inn called the Black Swan. I went inside and asked an old lady, who was the proprietress, if she had anything to eat.

"Nothing but bacon and eggs, I'm sorry to say. And if that's good enough for you, you'll have to take the bacon down from the rafters yourself. I cannot lift it and my man is gone away today to visit our son."

Nothing but bacon and eggs? I was amazed to see the bacon hanging on its hook. Bacon and eggs were already something that the British people remembered vaguely and lovingly but had not eaten since the start of the war. I helped myself to a few thick slices and some eggs. After this delicious breakfast I had two bottles of beer and ambled slowly back to camp.

When I arrived in camp that afternoon I heard that one of the Home Guard captains had lost his car. I assumed that it was the one that I had borrowed. I tried to contact him but he had left for London.

I reported the incident to the police and two days later, at the insistence of the irate captain, I was summoned to court and booked and fined two pounds.

I went to my commanding officer and explained the circumstances to him.

"After all," I said, "I was supposed to act as an enemy parachutist would have acted. And an enemy parachutist would have taken that car."

The commanding officer asked me for a detailed account of my movements. When I mentioned the Black Swan and its bacon and eggs, the commanding officer's face lit up with interest. The upshot of the whole thing was that the captain was reprimanded and stripped of one of his pips. He was foolish to have made a fuss about the car. It only called attention to the fact that he had disobeyed a regulation by leaving it there unattended.

Later I went back to the Black Swan but there was not a bit of the bacon left. The old lady told me that business had been very heavy. The commanding officer and his friends had practically lived there for a whole week.

And then I was promoted to the rank of acting captain and made an instructor. I don't think the promotion was due to my ability as a parachutist. I'm quite sure that it was given to me in recognition of my discovery of the bacon and eggs.

On May 11 a staff officer came into our mess after supper and told us that the Germans were overrunning Holland and Belgium.

"We are doing our best to stop their advance to the coast. Do any of you know anything about demolitions?"

I raised my hand and said I knew about nitroglycerine, dynamite, and bombs. The officer asked where I had got my experience.

"Well, that is rather a long story," I said.

"Good. I won't ask you to tell it now. Any of the rest of you care to have a go at it?"

There were eleven of us in the mess and everybody said, "Yes."

We went to a hangar where the officer uncovered a great supply of various types of explosives. He lectured to us about demolition work for an hour. Another officer came in and asked us if we were familiar with Holland and Belgium. I said I was well acquainted with the coast. He announced that he was sending up two planes in a half hour with four parachutists in each plane. We would be briefed before the take-off.

We sat around the hangar, smoking and listening to an air raid on London, and got our first taste of the horrible ordeal of waiting that all of us in every army and navy became so accustomed to later in the war. The half hour came and went, of course, and nothing happened. At midnight an officer came into the hangar and told us to go to bed.

At two-thirty in the morning two days later I was awakened and told to report at headquarters. We had been drinking heavily up until midnight and my head felt awful. I pulled myself partially together with a cup of tea and the next thing I knew we were being briefed for a jump on Holland.

The briefing officer said that four of us would be dropped west of the town of Aardenburg, near the Belgian border. We were to blow up a railway bridge there and then we were to move west to a canal and to destroy the locks of the canal if they were not already destroyed by another group of British parachutists. Then we were to get back to the coast as best we could. There were still British forces on the coast to receive us.

We took turns memorizing the map of the bridge and the canal. Each of us carried ten pounds of explosives. When our plane took off at quarter of four that morning it was dark and raining. It did not take long for us to get over the position. The navigator of the plane came to me because I was to be the first to jump.

"It's a bit cloudy," he said. "We'll circle and then go down a bit before you go out."

I went to the open door. I was anxious to get it over with so I yelled to the navigator, "Never mind going down. Tell him to ease it a little and we'll be off."

He gave me the signal and I jumped.

I was not particularly frightened. The briefing officer had said that this area was not yet occupied by the Germans and the task of blowing up the bridge did not seem too difficult. I could see nothing but blackness below me and I landed in the branches of a tree. I shook and pulled at the tangled cords of the parachute and then I dropped from the tree and fell on something that turned out to be the hind end of a terror-stricken cow.

The cow kicked viciously at my legs and then ran away. I lay on the ground until I got my wind back but when I stood up I found that I could not walk. I crawled to the trunk of the tree and leaned against it and discovered that I was covered with fresh, hot cow dung. One of my legs was painfully swollen. The other one was broken at the ankle.

When daylight came I looked around and saw that I was in a pasture surrounded by a stone dike. I knew that there was a road about three hundred yards from me on the other side of the dike so I dragged myself to it. I managed to crawl up to the top of the dike. And I saw a column of troops approaching along the road on motorcycles. At first I thought they were British troops but then I recognized their helmets as German.

I was helpless. I couldn't run away. I decided to surrender.

When I waved to them they smiled at me and gave me the Nazi salute. I tried to call to them, "I am English." But the roar of their motorcycles drowned out the sound of my voice. They disappeared down the road without stopping.

I dropped back from the dike into the field. About an hour later the old farmer found me. He came into the field with a youth to bring the cows out for milking. I pointed at my battered legs and said, "I am *Anglais*."

He understood me. He pointed at the dike and said, "Boche."

The old man took out a knife and cut open the legs of my pants. He looked at my legs, which were black and puffy. He said something in Dutch to the boy and the boy went away. The old man sat down beside me in the field and lit his pipe. I explained to him about the explosives in the haversack that I had left at the tree and told him to get rid of them. The boy came back pushing a wheelbarrow and they put me in it and took me to a small cottage beside the road, where the old man's wife helped them to get me inside and put me to bed. The wife gave me hot milk and the old man wrapped my legs in cold towels.

I stayed there for three days. The road was full of German Army traffic and troops for the first two days. Often the German soldiers would stop in the cottage dooryard and ask the old man's wife for permission to get water for their canteens at her pump. Once a group of them saw me in bed through the window and waved and smiled at me politely. The old man spoke some English because he had visited England as a seaman when he was young. He explained that he could not get a doctor for me because the Germans had forbidden the people in the countryside to use the roads. "But don't worry," he said. "Stay here until you are well. This war will not last long. The Germans tell us that they are merely protecting us against the French."

The old man put a splint of kindling wood on my broken ankle and the second day I was there I was able to stand on the other foot. After the second night the traffic on the road eased off and the old man heard that Rotterdam had been bombed by the Germans. That worried him because his daughter, the mother of the boy in the cottage, lived there. Then he heard that the King of Belgium had abdicated and that the whole British Army on the Continent had been wiped out. I thought it was merely German propaganda.

But I was nervous and I begged him to take me to the coast. At first he was reluctant but finally he agreed to take me to Heist, a small Belgian fishing village where he had relatives. We made the trip with me covered with hay in a cart that was pulled by a pony and four dogs. It took us all day. The old man carried a jug of cider on the axle of the cart and gave me a drink from it now and then. When we arrived in Heist about six-thirty in the evening we found a few German soldiers standing about on the streets of the town, chatting with the people. I went into a house near the water with the old man and sat down on a bench inside beside three men who looked like native fishermen. They spoke to me in English. One was a British Army lieutenant whose regiment had been either killed or captured in Belgium. He had escaped the Germans by coming down a canal on a barge. The other two men, a hotel manager and a travel agent, were Englishmen who were fleeing from Antwerp.

I was in luck. The hotel manager had hired a fishing boat to take them and some other English refugees to England that night and there was enough room aboard for me. The other men would be able to walk aboard, posing as Belgian fishermen, but because I had to be carried I would have to wait until after dark. At nine o'clock the three of them left for the boat, carrying fishing nets on their shoulders. The old man shook hands with me. I apologized for not being able to pay him for his kindness.

"No need to pay," he said. "After the war come back and visit us."

I was left alone in the house, a weird and lonely place lighted only by a single candle. I kept hearing noises outside and wondered if the

Germans had found out about the boat and were coming to capture me. Then, as midnight came and went, I wondered if the fisherman who owned the boat had decided to leave me behind because my presence would be too cumbersome. But at one-thirty the owner of the boat came into the house with a husky Dutch seaman who motioned to me to climb on his back. The beach was only across the road from the house. The seaman carried me piggy-back fashion to a dinghy and they rowed me out to the boat.

That trip to England was a terrible ordeal but all of us were too thankful to be on it to complain about it. Besides us four men, there were the two wives of the Englishmen from Antwerp and their seven children and another woman. The sea was rough and the fishing smack stank of rotten fish and fuel oil and everybody was sick. We landed at Margate. I left the boat on a stretcher and was taken in an ambulance to the hospital, where the police questioned me. I had no identification papers and they suspected that I was a German agent. I persuaded them to call Donald Gillies in London. Before he arrived my legs were X-rayed. The right leg had a compound fracture and torn muscles and the left one had a sprained ankle and torn muscles.

Donald told me about the fall of France and the evacuation of Dunkirk. Only then did I realize how lucky I was to get out of Europe alive.

CHAPTER *14*

THREE DAYS LATER I WAS TRANSFERRED FROM THE HOS-
pital at Margate to the Northwood Hospital, thirty miles from London, and I left there on crutches at the end of June. I was notified
that my injury disqualified me from further paratroop duty but I was
offered an infantry commission in the Hertfordshires. I turned it down
with the explanation that I was a sailor and not a soldier.

The doctors told me to wear boots instead of low shoes for a year
and to take it easy until my legs regained their strength. I went to
Grimsby to take some additional courses at the Nautical College but
I began to get restless so I applied to the Admiralty for a Royal Navy
Volunteer Reserve commission. Then I began to get a run-around.
Apparently my blowup over the Danish fishing boats was not forgot-
ten in certain offices at the Admiralty.

I was interviewed by an officer who looked at my record and said I
was just the type of man that the Navy needed. I took a physical examination and passed it. But ten days later I was notified that my
services were not required. I went back to the officer who had interviewed me and talked about it.

"It's beyond me, Orsborne," he said. "They are crying for men with
practical sea experience and yet they turn you down and accept others
who don't know the difference between fresh water and salt water.
Why don't you try the RAF? They've been advertising for men with
navigation experience who know combustion engines."

So I tried the RAF. At first I was enthusiastically received. They
wanted crews for crash boats. I passed another physical examination

and reported to the commanding officer of the RAF depot at Lincoln for duty.

"I don't know where to put you," he said. "We are merely looking for crew members for this boat squadron now. Your experience seems to call for a commission."

"I don't care about rank, sir. If I can get into the Air Force, I hope to be able to rise according to my ability."

"Of course, but we already know your ability. You'd better wait until I talk with London about you. You really should be the officer in charge of one of these speedboats."

Four days later I received a letter from the RAF which said that there were no vacancies.

I gave up and started to study Diesel engineering at Grimsby. In the next month, the memorable August of 1940, the invasion scare reached its peak in England. Tank traps were laid on the beaches. The shores were mined. The German air raids increased with ferocity. The rest of the world will never really understand how close to defeat England was then. The Germans were assembling invasion craft in the Channel and we had nothing to stop them. On August 28 every able-bodied man in Grimsby and Hull was asked to come forward and volunteer for emergency sea duty. Regardless of rating and rank, we were asked to go out prepared to fight. We signed emergency orders, agreeing to go anywhere in any capacity for one voyage.

I was assigned as first mate to a trawler which had as its skipper a man of sixty named John Newton. We were given one machine gun and one rifle for each man and we patrolled the North Sea coast, sometimes carrying aboard a platoon of seasick soldiers and sometimes keeping watch by ourselves. I will always remember the official order we received from the Admiralty. I have a copy of it beside me now:

FIGHTING INSTRUCTIONS FOR AUXILIARY PATROL

Your first duty is to sight and report immediately any suspicious vessel or enemy.

Use the radio telephone if you can. But on a dark night you may not have time to report by this means before you are attacked.

Therefore do not hesitate to make a firework signal or to fire a gun while you are calling up.

Have everything loaded.

Be ready always to get your report through somehow.

Remember other forces depend on you to do so.

Unless you have special warning of the approach of our own ships, assume that any vessel seen approaching from seaward is hostile and treat her accordingly. *Shoot before she does.*

Do not assume that the enemy will have been reported by some other vessel which may appear to be nearer to him than you are.

Continue to make reports about the enemy, giving especially his strength, type, course, speed and position.

If you see gunfire and alarm signals, steam towards the engagement. You will be told if you are required to remain in your own sector.

If you merely intercept an enemy report on the radio telephone, remain in your own sector and look out for invaders.

Your second duty is to cause the utmost damage and confusion to the enemy with every weapon you have and by all means in your power.

If you can make the enemy stop before he reaches the shore, you are doing your job. Leave him then and go for another one.

Don't waste time trying to sink a disabled ship. *Let her sink and do not waste time trying to save prisoners.*

Follow the enemy. Show where he is by gunfire.

Do not hesitate to fire upon him from any direction, even in the direction toward shore, if necessary.

REMEMBER, *where he can go, you can go.*

NEVER LET GO.

Where there were not enough rifles to go around, the Admiralty issued cutlasses. I remember one of the seamen looking at his cutlass and saying, "We're only blooming pirates, wearing civvies and patrolling with guns and knives. Jerry won't have have no mercy on us sort."

We stayed at it, day and night, until September 13. By then the invasion scare had lessened because on the tenth of September the RAF caught the main force of German invasion barges off the French coast and sprayed them with liquid fire and set them aflame. Then our fast speedboats went in and machine-gunned and torpedoed them. The charred bodies of German soldiers floated in the English Channel and the North Sea for days afterward.

When I left the trawler I went to London and that was when I started working as a courier for Donald Gillies. It was often an exciting job. I carried important messages to and from the War Office and the Admiralty and the Prime Minister's office on a motorcycle. One night when I was speeding through the blacked-out city a German bomb fell behind me and lifted me into the air and dropped me ten yards from the cycle. Neither the cycle nor I was scratched. I picked it up and continued on my way. Another night I drove the cycle into a bomb crater that was full of water from a damaged main. The cycle was wrecked. I delivered my papers at five the next morning after hitchhiking and walking for ten miles.

I met a lot of important people and heard a lot of interesting behind-the-scenes stories. One of the stories concerned a man I would like to know someday. I never saw him but I heard about him from time to time and Donald and I followed his career carefully during the rest of the war.

Before the fall of France this man—he was British—managed a small and disreputable night club on one of the Channel islands. The island was evacuated when the Germans took over the Continent and the people were given their choice of remaining and taking their chances under the Germans or returning to England. A lot of them went. Some of them stayed and one of them was our night club manager. When the Germans arrived they asked him why he had not accepted the chance to go to England.

"I don't want to have anything to do with England," he explained. "I'm wanted there for forging checks. If I return they'll put me into jail."

He was a shady character but a shrewd one. The Germans were rather impressed by him. They asked him if he wanted to work as a German agent.

"I'll work for you if you pay me well," he said. "All I'm interested in is money. The easier it comes the better I like it."

He was sent to Germany and trained in the espionage and sabotage schools. His first assignment was in Lisbon. A British merchant ship was refueling there before going out to meet a convoy. He was to get aboard her and to plant a time bomb in her hold that would explode after she went to sea.

He got aboard the merchant ship and he planted the bomb. But he did not release the firing mechanism. Then he went to the bridge and asked to see the commanding officer. He told the astonished commanding officer that the bomb was in the hold but that it would not explode.

"Now here's what I want you to do," he said. "Don't join the convoy. Go straight to Liverpool from here and tell the Admiralty what has happened and get them to announce in the newspapers that this ship was destroyed at sea by the Germans. In that way the ship will be saved and still my reputation with the Germans will remain good."

It took quite a bit of convincing. The British officer did not believe his story at first. But finally he did as the night club manager directed him to do. The merchant ship hid in Liverpool and a week later it was announced as missing. The man went back to Germany, where he was complimented and praised by his superior officers.

His next assignment was in England. He was to be dropped by parachute and to plant an explosive at a plane assembly plant in the Midlands. He landed safely but he went to the War Office and told them what he was supposed to be doing. A number of empty sheds were quickly thrown up beside the assembly plant and they were destroyed by the British so that the scene would look like destruction to the pilots of German observation planes. It was announced in the newspapers that the plant had been badly damaged in an air raid. Again the Germans were highly pleased with the night club manager's work.

He went back to Germany and a year later he returned to England. This time he brought a short-wave transmitting set. He was ordered to send out range corrections and damage reports to the buzz-bomb operators who were scheduled to begin firing their missiles at London the following month.

Again he went to the War Office and described the buzz bombs and what they would do to England. The officials in the War Office refused to believe him. The buzz bombs sounded preposterous.

But when those guided rockets began to land in London the War Office looked up the night club manager in a hurry and apologized profusely for not having listened to his warning. They set him up in an apartment outside of London with his transmitting set. He sent incorrect range adjustments to Germany and France. His radio messages were the main reason why the buzz bombs did not do the great damage in London that they might have done. It was impossible, of course, for him to guide the rockets away from London entirely. The

Germans would have discovered his treachery then and his directions would have been ignored. But he did manage to keep the bombs away from strategic targets.

After the war I made it a point to look up an Intelligence officer I knew who had worked closely with the night club manager. I asked him what had finally happened to the man.

"He stayed in England after the buzz bombs stopped," the officer said. "He was pardoned for his previous sins and rewarded handsomely by the government for his great services. He was allowed to start life anew with a clean slate. But now he's in jail."

"What for?" I asked.

"As soon as the war ended he started to forge checks again."

I worked for Donald Gillies all that winter and still I heard nothing from the Admiralty about my commission. I thought about going to see the Intelligence people and apologizing to them for losing my temper but my pride was too strong to allow me to do that. Still I was restless and I tried to think of some way of getting into combat. I did not want to sit out the war on a motorcycle in London.

On the morning of April 1, 1941, I had breakfast with Donald. I remarked to him as we lit cigarettes over the coffee that five years ago that day I had sailed from Dover in the *Girl Pat*.

"I always do something foolish on April Fools' Day," I said. "I have a feeling that I'm going to do something foolish today too."

Donald looked at me warily. "Now what?" he asked.

"I am going to enlist in the Navy as an ordinary seaman."

Donald shook his head. "Don't be ridiculous, Dod," he said. "I've told you that the people at the Admiralty are merely letting you cool your heels to take you down a peg. If you go to them and admit that you were wrong in telling them what to do with that Intelligence job they'll think more of you. And then they'll give you a commission."

"No," I said. "I'm going to a recruiting office and sign up as an ordinary seaman. I've made up my mind. Will you give me a release that will show that I am no longer needed by your firm?"

Donald saw that it was useless to attempt to reason with me.

"All right," he said. "I'll give you the release. Deliver this last dispatch for me. Then you can turn in the cycle at the garage and you'll be through work."

I delivered the dispatch and turned in the motorcycle and went to a naval recruiting station on Edgeware Road. The clerk who filled out my application blank was not very bright.

"What is your present occupation?" he asked.

"Courier."

"What's that?"

"I'm a dispatch rider."

"You mean you're in the Army?"

"No. I carry messages from place to place for a private concern."

"Oh, I see. You are a message boy."

He wrote down "message boy" and that occupation is still on my Navy papers. The next day I reported for duty as an ordinary seaman at the H.M.S. *Europa*, a naval depot which served as a training station for six thousand new recruits. I spent a few days drawing my uniforms and equipment and learning how to drill. On the fourth day we were taught how to tie knots. I tied all the Navy knots and then showed the instructor a few knots that he had never seen before. He looked at me suspiciously.

"You've been at sea before," he said.

I admitted that I had been at sea a few times.

"You shouldn't be in this class," he said. "I'll see the commander and have you put in with the able-bodied seamen."

When I joined the able-bodied seamen I attended a class on the Lewis gun. The instructor asked for a volunteer to attempt to strip the gun. I stripped it and put it together again in two minutes. The next day I was a gunnery instructor with the rating of leading seaman.

I attended a class in navigation that was conducted by a lieutenant who had obviously never been to sea. I asked him a few questions about difficult navigation problems that he was unable to answer. It was an unfair thing to do but I could not resist it; I was still mad at the Navy and I had to take it out on somebody. He asked me to box the compass. I boxed it backward and forward and then recited for him the cobbler's compass, an old sailing-ship trick of naming the points on a compass as if they were parts of a shoe. He had never heard it before.

"You must have been at sea quite a lot," he said.

"Yes, sir. I've been a quartermaster and a bosun for years."

"Then you don't belong in this class."

The following day I was promoted to petty officer. There were only thirty-seven men in this class. The officer in charge of it asked if any of us were familiar with the various types of ship design and construction. I said I was. He asked me to conduct a blackboard lecture. Two days later, and only fifteen days after I had reported for duty as an ordinary seaman, I was made a chief petty officer.

My first assignment as a chief was to march the petty officers from the barracks to a dock where a Royal Navy Volunteer Reserve lieutenant would meet us and accompany us aboard a mine sweeper. The lieutenant was to conduct a sight-seeing tour.

The mine sweeper was lying at anchor in the harbor and we rowed out to it in two small boats. When we came alongside the ship the lieutenant said to me in a very knowing manner, "Chief, see to it that the painters of the boats are loose enough for the rise and fall of the tide."

I glanced at him to see if he was joking. He wasn't.

"You'd better see to that yourself, sir," I said.

"Are you being insolent?"

"No, sir, but I've been at sea long enough to know that you don't have to worry about the rise and fall of the tide when you tie a small boat to an anchored ship. The anchored ship also rises and falls with the tide. You don't need to loosen the rope that is tied to it."

We went aboard the mine sweeper. Her captain came forward to meet us. He yelled, "Hello, Dod, you old bastard!" I shook hands with him warmly while he ignored the lieutenant. He had been a second mate under me in the old rum-running days.

"What are you doing in that chief's uniform?" he asked. "Come along and have a drink and bring your young lieutenant friend with you."

We went to his cabin and broke open a bottle. Before I could tip off the captain to keep his mouth shut he was asking me about the *Girl Pat*. The lieutenant, who confessed that he had been a banker up until a few months ago, became fascinated with our conversation. I made the lieutenant promise that he would say nothing about my past at the barracks.

But in a few days all the older merchant marine men on the waterfront were making jokes about the fact that Dod Orsborne was a chief petty officer at the H.M.S. *Europa* training station. The next time we had a parade the commanding officer of the station, a crusty old commodore, stopped in front of me while he was reviewing the men. He peered at me intently. I stood stiffly at attention without moving my eyes.

"What's your name?" he growled.

"Orsborne, sir."

"Are you Orsborne of the *Girl Pat?*"

"Yes, sir."

"Come to my office after Divisions."

I knew that the jig was up. When I went to the commodore's office he stood up and glared at me. He was a short man with a face that was normally fat and very red and as he glared at me it grew purple with rage. He banged his fist on the desk and everything on it danced.

"Orsborne, what the bloody hell do you mean by coming into this barracks and making fools of my officers? You, a master mariner, wearing a seaman's uniform and asking questions that you damn well know these landlubbing lieutenants cannot answer! I've never been so insulted! I'll make you pay for this little joke, Orsborne! I've already phoned the Admiralty about you and, by God, if I can do it I'll have you thrown out of the Navy! Get out of here! Get out!"

The next day I was ordered to draw an officer's uniform allowance and to report to Whitehall for a commission as a lieutenant skipper in the Royal Naval Reserves. On the twenty-sixth of April, less than a month after I had enlisted, I was assigned to command the H.M.S. *Corsaire,* a corvette in the Northern Patrol based at Londonderry in Northern Ireland. It is customary in the Royal Navy for an enlisted man to appear before his commanding officer for a blessing before he leaves to get a commission. The commodore, however, never sent for me.

CHAPTER 15

*T*HERE WAS AT LEAST ONE HIGH-RANKING OFFICER IN the British Admiralty during the war who had a sense of humor. I did convoy duty on the North Atlantic for a few months in command of the *Corsaire* and then the name of the corvette, when linked with my past reputation, became a source of merriment at the officers' mess in Londonderry. I became known as Dod the Pirate. I wrote a letter to the Admiralty, pointing out respectfully that the *Corsaire* was a little too appropriate in view of some of the things that had been said about me. My request for another ship was granted and I was ordered to Belfast to pick up a new corvette that was being commissioned there. I was happy until I saw the name on the corvette.

It was the H.M.S. *Filibuster*. "Filibuster," of course, is a synonym for cutthroat privateer. I remembered that one of the French officers had used it to describe me that night in Dakar.

I stayed with the Northern Patrol until February 1942, when I was ordered to the H.M.S. *Pembroke* at Chatham Depot, where I had trained as an ordinary seaman during World War I. There I was transferred to Specialized Service, which made me eligible for duty with any branch of the armed forces, although I still retained my R.N.R. commission. I was told that I would be assigned to a flotilla of motor launches and motor gunboats that would be organized in three weeks. Lucille came down from London and spent the three weeks with me. We walked in the country lanes and woodlands and found it hard to believe that there was a war on.

After the flotilla was organized we began to study maps of the French coast until our eyes almost fell out. We were being prepared for the attack on the German submarine base at St. Nazaire. That battle will always remain in my mind as the worst experience I had in the war. Perhaps I feel that way about it because it was the first time I had seen large-scale bloodshed since Zeebrugge in the other war. Whatever the reason, I hate to remember St. Nazaire.

I cannot describe the combat at St. Nazaire and I doubt if anyone else will ever be able to describe it. There was too much happening at one time. Our flotilla of MLs and MGBs went into the estuary of the port at full speed, with the formation so close that we practically scraped each other's sides, and the RAF planes dived in over our heads so closely that we could see their tracer bullets. Our purpose was to land the troops who were crowded on our decks and then to go back in a second time and bring them out after they had completed their damage. The moment we went into the estuary the Germans opened up on us with everything they had and they had plenty. There was no element of surprise in the attack. The only surprise that the Germans must have felt was surprise that the British would have the courage and foolhardiness to attempt a raid on such a well-prepared and thoroughly alerted objective.

There was no cover of darkness. The gunfire was so heavy and constant that the whole place looked as if it was lit by the sun. Somehow we disembarked the troops with the shells dropping all around us and as we tried to maneuver and kill time until the troops did their work ashore the Germans murdered us. One boat after another broke into flames or exploded. The Germans remained completely in command of the situation ashore and our soldiers there were getting much the worst of it. But the hardheaded commander of our small-boat flotilla refused to believe that it was futile for us to attempt to return to the end of the estuary and re-embark the troops. Twice he ordered the flotilla's flagship to go in but the crossfire was so heavy from both sides of the estuary that only three members of his crew escaped injury. He finally had to give the order to withdraw. This meant that the soldiers on the shore had to fight until the end with no means of escape. But we had no other choice.

In fact it was bad enough trying to withdraw. To do it we had to run a gantlet down the estuary and then face more shore batteries at the mouth of the inlet. I saw one ML beside me limping down the estuary on one engine. She broke out in flames. The skipper, realizing that he could not escape, turned on a German gun position at the water's edge and went straight at it with every one of his guns blazing. Just before the ML ran ashore she exploded and went into the air in fragments.

When I think of St. Nazaire, I always think of Tapping.

Tapping was a tall blond leading seaman on my ML, a quiet and bright boy about nineteen. When we were edging out of the estuary our ship was sprayed by one burst of machine-gun bullets. I felt something sharp hit my hand. Tapping was standing beside me. He said, "You've been wounded, sir." I held up my hand and the little finger was dangling from it, held only by a strip of flesh.

Tapping took off the black silk muffler on his neck and gave it to me to wrap around the hand. Then he turned and walked to a hatch and climbed down a ladder about eight feet to the galley and poured a cup of coffee and put rum in it and carried the cup of coffee back up the ladder to the deck and handed it to me. Then he walked away and sat down on the deck, resting his back against a coil of rope.

A few minutes later one of the seamen said to me, "Sir, I don't think Tapping is well." We looked at him. He was dead.

He had five machine-gun bullets in his chest. The only time he could have been hit was the time I was hit on the finger. I tried to estimate the time he had spent in giving me the muffler and going below and getting the coffee and rum. It could not have been less than five minutes. I talked to a doctor about it later. "He was practically dead when he gave you the muffler," the doctor said. "But he didn't know it. He probably did not feel a thing."

When we returned to England I went to a hospital in Wales. Then, after three weeks' sick leave that I spent with Lucille, I reported for duty as a training officer with Special Service. I did not know what Special Service was then but I soon found out. It was the branch of the forces that later became known officially as Combined Operations and popularly as the Commandos.

As I've said before and as I'll no doubt say again, it is the little thing that changes the course of your life. There was once a man who stopped every evening for his beer in the Cheshire Cheese, the famous pub that is frequented by London newspapermen. This man said little and none of the Cheese's regular clientele knew anything about him until one day during the blitz when he finished his beer and asked to have a few words with an editor who was a friend of mine. The man explained to the editor that he had a great deal of money hidden in his home. He was afraid that his house might be bombed and he wondered how the money could be safeguarded. The editor explained to him some of the elementary facts about banking. The man was skeptical of banks. But the editor convinced him that a bank was the only place in London where a large sum of money would be secure during an air raid.

Sensing a story for his newspaper, the editor made all the arrangements for the man to deposit his savings in a bank. I forget the exact figures now but they were big. The man had more than twenty thousand pounds, or nearly one hundred thousand dollars, in a box under his bed. And his business and property holdings were worth eighty thousand pounds. He was a successful junk dealer.

The bank official who received him was naturally impressed by this wealth. When he asked the man to sign a deposit slip the man explained that he could neither read nor write. The bank official was even more impressed.

"Great heavens!" he exclaimed. "Imagine how much more money you would have made if you had been able to read and write."

"You're wrong," the man said. "If I had been able to read and write I would have been the attendant in the men's lavatory across the street from this bank."

It seems that in his youth the man was penniless and looking for work. He heard about a job in the men's lavatory and applied for it. But it was a civil job because the lavatory was a public one and in order to qualify for the position it was necessary to be able to read and write. So the man was turned down. He went into the junk business instead and made a fortune.

And it was a little thing that got me into the Commandos. I might have finished the war on a corvette or some other ship if I had not lost my temper and bawled out a superior officer.

It happened in Londonderry before I went to St. Nazaire. After Christmas we hunted German submarines near Iceland and lost two corvettes. When we returned to Ireland and turned into the Foyle River we came abreast of a line of destroyers that were also heading up the river. I could have fallen back and followed them but my first officer and I had been invited to a party that the American Navy people at Londonderry were giving that night and we were impatient to get to our dock. I stayed beside the destroyers and then I saw that the river was narrowing and I would have to cut across the bow of the second ship in the line. I judged the distance and dashed in front of the destroyer and made it safely. The commander of the destroyer was furious. He blew seven or eight quick blasts on his siren and shouted and cursed at me. I pretended I didn't hear him and kept going full speed up the river.

As soon as we tied up we washed and dressed for the party and as we were leaving the ship we were both ordered to report immediately to the destroyer's commander.

"Now we'll get it," the first officer said nervously.

I was very fond of the first officer. He was an R.N.V.R. lieutenant who was a teacher of mathematics at a university in civilian life. A corvette is a rough ship and he was always seasick but he refused to give it up for a desk job ashore, which he could have had. There are three kinds of officers in the British Navy and the caste line between them is strongly underscored. Everybody looks down on the R.N.V.R. officers because they are not professional sailors but only temporary volunteers. The R.N.R. officers, such as I am, are more respected because they are experienced and qualified merchant marine officers. The R.N. officers, of course, are the old school tie regular Navy men, like the Annapolis graduates in the United States Navy.

When we went to the destroyer the first officer was wearing his blue jacket with the wavy braid of the R.N.V.R. plainly visible. I was wearing a plain black raincoat that concealed the R.N.R. insignia on my sleeve. As we entered his cabin the commander glanced at the first officer's uniform.

"Oh," he said, turning up his nose in disgust, "R.N.V.R. men. I might have known."

Then he turned to me.

"You are the commander of that corvette? I am reporting you the first thing tomorrow morning to my Lords High Commissioners of the Admiralty for the bad seamanship that you showed in crossing my head. Were you not taught the Rules of the Road when you entered the service?"

I became angry at his manner and I did not like the remark that he had made about my first officer's R.N.V.R. rating.

"Go ahead and report me," I said. "I will also make a report. The Lords High Commissioners will be delighted to know that they have a maniac in command of one of their best destroyers."

I thought he would burst.

"How dare you?" he exploded. "How dare you speak to a superior officer like that?" He turned to my first officer. "You heard what he said, didn't you?"

"Yes, sir," the lieutenant said.

"Will you repeat that statement before some of my officers?" he said to me.

"Certainly," I said. "I'll be glad to."

My first officer looked at me with imploring eyes. The commander quickly summoned six officers into the cabin. I had been standing and the raincoat was cumbersome. I took it off. The commander noted with surprise the R.N.R. stripes on my jacket.

"Oh, I see you are R.N.R.," he said. "I'm surprised that a man from your branch would conduct himself like this. Now repeat before your officer and my officers what you just said to me."

"I will if you'll repeat the remark you passed when we entered here."

"That's not what I'm talking about."

"But I'm talking about it. I regard your remark about the R.N.V.R. as an insult to my lieutenant. He and the officers in his branch are making a greater sacrifice in serving here than you are or I am. The war and the Navy have interrupted their professions and they are giving us several valuable years of their lives. We should respect them. Furthermore, when I crossed your bow today you behaved as badly as I did."

"What do you mean?"

"I have a master mariner's certificate and I know the laws of the sea. The correct signals with a siren are either one, two, three, or four blasts, meaning port, starboard, astern a tug, and assistance. A master is supposed to remain cool, calm, and collected at all times. When a master of a ship gives seven blasts on his siren and shouts and curses, I don't consider him calm or cool or collected."

The commander became much more polite.

"Sit down, both of you," he said. "Now, after all, you will admit that cutting through between two destroyers like that was rather a dangerous thing to do."

"It was dangerous," I said, "and foolish. But we were in a hurry to get to a party."

"Why didn't you say so before? That's a valid reason for crossing anybody's head. Won't you have a drink?"

Out came the gin bottle. We did not get to the Americans' party that night. We had several drinks with the commander and by the time we left the destroyer he and I were fast friends. A few nights later in a hotel in Londonderry the commander and I had a drink with Lord Louis Mountbatten, who was then in command of that destroyer flotilla. Not many people know that Noel Coward's excellent moving picture, *In Which We Serve*, was based on the actual experiences of the *Kelly,* the destroyer that Mountbatten commanded early in the war. Mountbatten allowed the picture to be filmed on the condition that a large share of its proceeds be turned over to the families of the men who had died on the *Kelly.* I did not know it at the time but when I met Mountbatten in Londonderry he was already slated to succeed Sir Roger Keyes as head of Combined Operations. I also did not know until later that the commander of the destroyer whom I had called down for not being calm, cool, and collected recommended me to Mountbatten as the sort of officer who could be useful in the Commandos. That was why I was transferred to Mountbatten's command after I recovered from the wound I had suffered at St. Nazaire.

The war left me with a profound respect for British royalty. Marina, the Duchess of Kent, was stationed as a Wren at a naval base where I was attached at one time and I never met a finer woman. One night I was at a party that she attended with several Wren officers. One of the men in our group got sick and made a terrible mess of the room. Although there was no necessity for doing it, Marina got down on her hands and knees and scrubbed the floor with soap and hot water until it was clean. Mountbatten, the King's cousin, was an excellent commanding officer, a colorful and relaxed leader who inspired his men and brought out the best in them. I shall always remember the day he made his first appearance at our small Commando training camp on the Isle of Wight.

I had a group of two hundred men, most of them hard and tough bargemen and dock hands from the East End of London. Mountbatten was scheduled to inspect them at ten o'clock on this particular morning and they lined up in formation a few minutes before that time. It started to rain. We never wore raincoats in a formation and the men began to get wet to the skin. A half hour and then an hour went by and still there was no sign of Mountbatten. The men became restless and impatient and then really fed up with the whole thing. I began to hear muttering in the ranks about the blasted blue-blooded brass hat who was keeping them standing in the rain. By the time Mountbatten's car appeared at quarter to twelve the men were openly hostile.

He climbed out of the car and walked toward us. We noticed that he was wearing no protection against the weather. An officer ran up to him and held out a raincoat. Mountbatten waved him aside.

"These men have been waiting a long time in this rain," he said. "I guess I can afford to take a wetting too."

Instead of going through a formal inspection as any other officer would have done he told the men to break ranks and to gather closely around him in a circle.

"Stand easy and light up your cigarettes," he said. "Have a good look at me and I'll have a good look at you and we'll get to know each other."

Then he apologized for keeping them waiting and explained why he had been delayed. He told a funny story. It was the one that was new at the time about the girl who wrote to her sailor overseas, asking what the women there had that she didn't have. The men loved it. Then he talked to them about the Commandos. I remember how he closed his remarks.

"When the time comes I will be able to get you in there against the enemy. But I'll be damned if I'll be able to guarantee that I'll get you out."

The men hung on every word and when he left them there was not one of them who would not have been willing to follow him into hell if he asked them to do it.

"What a blinking gent!" one of the Cockneys exclaimed. "A regular toff if there ever was one!"

The Commandos were an unusual collection of fighting men. They came from the Army and the Navy and the Marines and straight from civilian life. They included such people as Evelyn Waugh, the effete author, and university professors and bartenders and longshoremen and movie actors and professional football players and farmers and steeplejacks and some others who, I'm sure, must have committed a little robbery in their prewar days. They were picked carefully for some special physical or mental talent and because the work required above everything else coolness and courage their family histories were carefully examined for signs of insanity or nervousness. The physical examination was rigorous.

The Commandos were trained for swift and silent missions that involved only a few men. They were taught to swim under water and to scale rocks and walls that seemed impossibly steep. They learned navigation and the use of small boats and the reading of maps and the firing and construction of all types of weapons. But above all they were taught to use a knife and to kill by the knife instead of a gun whenever it was possible. The Commando knife was only six inches long. The approved method of using it was to stick it only one and a half inches into the kidneys at the small of the back. That makes the victim die with no sound except a sharp intake of breath, no louder than a sigh.

A typical Commando mission was one that involved making a contact with the French or Belgian or Dutch underground partisans. Sometimes three or four of us would slip into France and spend a few days in occupied territory, instructing the underground men in sabotage or the use of British or American weapons or in the tapping of telephone wires. Or a few of us would cross the Channel to take a captured quisling from the underground and bring him back to England for questioning. Commandos parachuted into Germany to commit sabotage or to contact anti-Nazi groups and made their way safely across France and Spain to Gibraltar. It seemed as though the Commandos practically lived on the beaches of Normandy during the six months that preceded the invasion of France. They removed mines, made soundings to determine the depth of the water in various sectors of the beaches, and made reports on the enemy coastal defenses. A group of five or six men would land in a rubber boat and hide for three or four days under the cliffs, waiting for a carefully timed RAF raid that would divert the enemy's attention and make it possible for the Commandos to move inland. If they came to a steep cliff or a wall they would climb it with their toddle ropes. Each man carried around his waist a length of rope that had a small eye spliced in one end and a small wooden peg spliced in the other end. Six men attaching their ropes together could make a line long enough to enable them to go over a thirty-foot wall with ease. One or two of the men in the group would wear battle tunics with thick leather on the front. If they had to cross a barbed-wire entanglement these men would lie face down on the barbed wire and the others would walk across their backs. One of the buttons on each man's tunic was a luminous compass.

Because the Commando training schedule was designed to build up individual initiative and self-reliance, the system of discipline was much different from that of the Army or Navy, where the aim is to instill the idea of mass obedience to orders from above. The Commandos did not live in a barracks. When they were not busy with their training their time was their own. They lived in private homes and supplied their own meals. If a training exercise was to be held on the following day at a town forty miles away the officers would tell the men what time to be there. How to get there was up to them to figure out. When they were off duty they wore the uniforms of whatever branch of the service they belonged to before they were assigned to the Commandos. They discussed their work with no one.

My function in the Commandos was that of a training officer in navigation and small-boat work but, in order to correct and improve training methods, the training officers themselves went frequently to the big raids and invasions and on small missions like the placing of the flares around the factory at Blankenberghe. I had charge of training at the Isle of Wight until July 1942, and then I went as an observer to the Dieppe raid. After that I went to the Mediterranean for the raid on Tobruk, where I was stabbed in the neck by a German during the fighting in the rooms inside the enemy barracks. I went back to England for hospitalization and then I returned to the Isle of Wight for the winter. It was pleasant there. I lived in a pretty cottage near the camp and Lucille joined me for a while.

The following July I was with a Commando unit that landed in the invasion of Sicily. We went all the way back to England after it was finished but two weeks later we went back to Italy for the landing at Salerno, which was probably one of the most fouled-up operations of the war. Confusion reigned supreme at Salerno and the security was terrible. A German prisoner told us that they knew two weeks in advance exactly where we would land. The British and American troops in General Mark Clark's Fifth Army were all mixed up when they reached the shore. I was supposed to be the beachmaster in a sector between the British and Americans but it was practically impossible to direct landing craft. When we came out of the water we found the Germans entrenched a few yards directly in front of us. I ran toward them, reaching for my revolver, and discovered that I had lost the revolver in the water. A star shell went up, lighting the beach like daylight, and I found myself standing in front of a sandbagged machine-gun parapet with four Germans in it. I took off my steel helmet and threw it at them and fell to the ground, expecting to be sprayed by bullets. But a number of American Rangers rushed by me, dropping the Germans with tommy-gun fire.

After the capture of Naples, I went back to England and in January we began to prepare for the invasion of Normandy.

CHAPTER 16

FOR THE INVASION OF NORMANDY I WAS ASSIGNED AS
beachmaster to the 37th Marine Commando Group, a mixed force of
British Commandos and American Rangers that was to land as the
first wave at Arromanches. After I joined this unit at a depot near
Southampton it was restricted and we sat down to await D-Day. The
day before we left for France I was brooding over a beer in the house
that served as the officers' mess and another naval Commando officer I
knew walked into the room.

"Hello, George Jarvis," I said. "What are you doing here?"

"I was up in Scotland on another job," he said, "and they ordered
me down here. I'm to be the beachmaster for the 37th Marine Commando Group."

"No, you're not. Your orders must have been fouled up."

"Why?"

"Because," I said, "I am the beachmaster for the 37th Marine Commando Group."

He sat down and had a beer with me and while we were talking
another officer we both knew, a fellow named Edward Innis, sat down
at the table with us.

"I didn't know you were here, Innis," I said.

"I wasn't until an hour ago. I just arrived. I am supposed to be the
beachmaster for the 37th Marine Commando Group."

I looked at Jarvis and Jarvis looked at me. We decided that the
situation could bear some looking into and the three of us went to
see the executive officer of the group. At first he evaded our questions.
Then he broke down and told us the story.

"If you must know, there is no mistake in the orders," he said. "This group will have three beachmasters. Orsborne goes in first. If the beach is as hot as we expect it to be there's a good chance he may be knocked off within the first fifteen minutes. Then Jarvis will go in and replace Orsborne. There is also a good chance that Jarvis may get it within a half hour. If so, Innis will be available to replace Jarvis. Now go along out of here. I have work to do."

With that send-off, I naturally went ashore with trepidation on the morning of D-Day. I had written letters to Lucille and Donald, saying good-by to them. When I saw those letters later I could hardly believe that I had written them. As the endless flow of ships made its way across the Channel our small LCMs were herded between cruisers and destroyers. Through the darkness we saw the flicker of big-gun flashes and the orange and yellow lights from the shore where the air forces were dropping bombs. As we drew closer the din of the anti-aircraft batteries was deafening. We stopped about four miles off the beach. The big ships behind us opened up with broadsides that seemed as though they would never end. "Blimy, there'll be nothing left for us," a marine beside me said.

The sky became gray and we saw the outline of the beach in front of us where we were to land. It was known to us as Gold Sector. To the left were Juno and Sword and on the right was Omaha, where the Americans had it toughest of all, and Utah. Our sector was the place where the vital artificial port was to be built. Zero hour had been set for six-thirty. At five minutes past six we received the signal to go in. I turned to Major Martin, who was standing beside me, and said, "It's a bit early, isn't it?"

"Yes, but there's no mistake about the signal."

Our engines roared and we rushed to the beach. The tide was low and we saw steel tank traps sticking out of the water ahead of us. We threw grenades at them and waited until they exploded. Before we reached the shore we went aground on the sand and the men climbed over the side and ran for it. In every battle there is always somebody who says something utterly incongruous at a time like that. The marine in front of me looked at the pink sky behind the beach and said, "My, what a red sky. It will be a fine warm day." He did not realize that the sky was lit by the glare of burning buildings.

When I came out of the water I saw heads behind a concrete wall in front of me. I ran for the wall and jumped over it and found about ten Germans running before me down a narrow path through the sand dunes. I ran after them, firing a tommy gun. Strangely, I never thought of taking cover and all of us were acting the same way. I almost fired by mistake at a group of marines who ran past me shouting like madmen, "Kill the bastards!" There was bloody hand-to-hand fighting in the remains of some ruined houses behind the beach and in a wood that stood on a high ground.

Major Martin ran up and told me that he had located a German staff headquarters a quarter of a mile from the beach. While he was pointing out the direction to me he shook his head and dropped to the sand. I picked him up and saw a small black bullet hole in his forehead. I joined his lieutenant and about twenty men and went with them along a winding lane with a hawthorne hedge beside it until we reached a large, three-story farmhouse. There was an apple orchard behind. We surrounded the farmhouse and closed in on it, firing at the windows and the doors. I followed two marines through the front door and ran upstairs behind them. In the narrow hallway on the third floor I was hit on the shoulder by a rifle butt and the impact knocked my revolver out of my hand. I saw a German officer in front of me raising a pistol. As he fired I dodged into a room. A marine was in the room and when he saw the German officer coming through the doorway after me he drove the spike-shaped bayonet on the end of his tommy gun into the officer's chest. The officer stayed on his feet and the marine struggled with him and turned to me and shouted, "I can't get it out!" I pushed the marine aside and grasped the tommy gun and put my foot on the officer's stomach and pushed. The bayonet pulled out of his chest and he went backward and through a window and fell to the ground outside. The marine took the tommy gun from me and stepped to the window and fired down at him, finishing him off.

We searched the rest of the house and found nobody else alive in it. There were thirty-five dead Germans, ten of them staff officers. We had only two dead and three wounded. From the farmhouse we had a fine view of the beach, which was covered with troops and vehicles. When we went back to it we found that only 240 men were left out of our original landing party of 1040. That afternoon shells were still falling on us and mines were still exploding. The shore was jammed with disabled landing craft and damaged ships and we worked hard all that night and all the next day to clear the beach and to bring some sort of law and order to its confusion. We had to issue orders forbidding any ship that was disabled offshore to land on the beach. Space was at a premium and we had to make room for supply craft. This was a hard order to carry out at times. Once that night an LCT carrying six tanks and the tank crews came in signaling that it had been hit by a mine. We signaled the officer not to land but he ignored us and kept on coming and I had to walk out into the water and yell at him, "Go astern or we will blow you to hell."

The officer, a young and frightened man, begged me to let him beach the ship. "We're sinking and we've got injured men and tanks aboard," he yelled back at me. But we had to order him away.

Snipers gave us a lot of trouble during the next few days. After three of our men were killed near me on the beach we decided that there was a sniper in the small field of wheat behind us. We surrounded it and set it afire with gasoline. Two Germans came out of the wheat with their hands up. Farther inland there was a place on a road where passing troops were getting fired upon by a single sniper who was very accurate. We watched the area and noticed a pretty French girl, standing at a gate in front of an orchard and a barn and waving to our men as they moved along the road. Twice during the morning a soldier who stopped to talk with her was dropped by the sniper's bullet as he hurried to rejoin his ranks. The girl was working in collaboration with the sniper. He would get his aim as a soldier spoke with her. We surrounded the barn in the orchard and found the sniper, a German soldier, in the hayloft. We took him outside and debated about what to do with him. There was a Scottish sergeant standing near by, a big strapping man about six feet three, and the discussion evidently bored him. He picked up the sniper in his arms, walked to a well in the orchard, and dropped him into it. Then he took out a grenade and pulled the pin and dropped it into the well and strolled away. He did it all so casually that the rest of us were amazed. We stared at him and at each other and then it dawned on us that the grenade at the bottom of the well was about to explode. We ran like mad.

Finally the artifical harbor was built and the beach became a main thoroughfare for all the Allied forces and supplies that were pouring into Normandy. I stayed at Arromanches until the end of July, when I received three telegrams, one telling me that my mother had died and another that Donald was seriously ill. The third wire was from headquarters and it ordered me to return to London as soon as possible. Lucille met me at Waterloo Station when I arrived. I was still unshaven and dirty, in battle dress with a steel helmet on my head. Normandy seemed to me then like a bad dream.

I was given an indefinite leave and I stayed with Donald until he died. He was the closest friend I had in the world, the one I always went to when I needed advice or help, and his death hit me hard. I had a harder time trying to recover from it than I did recovering from any combat ordeal I went through in the war.

By the end of September I had still heard no word from the Admiralty summoning me back to duty and that was all right with me. I was no longer hungry for action. I felt that as far as the war was concerned I had had it. If I had received a discharge from active service then I should not have minded it in the least. I figured that I had stretched my luck out to the limit in not getting killed on D-Day in Normandy and I had no desire to see if it would stretch any further.

I presumed that the Navy had no further need of beachmasters because there were no more beaches in Europe to be invaded. But I wrote to the Admiralty and told them where they could find me if they needed me. "Perhaps they'll give me a desk job," I said to Lucille.

I received the following reply from Combined Operations Headquarters:

> *In the absence of the Commanding Officer, we acknowledge your letter of October 8th, informing us of your change in address.*
>
> *Your sailing instructions were dispatched to your former address by registered letter on October 7th. We shall be glad if you will inform us on receipt of this letter whether the letter of October 7th has reached you.*

Sailing orders? I went to the place where I had lived previously and found the registered letter awaiting me. It told me to be prepared to sail from Glasgow on October 27. I was to travel light and I would be told of my destination after the ship was at sea. I went to the headquarters and made a few discreet inquiries. I found out that my destination was Burma. The same Marine Commando unit that I had landed with in Normandy was now out there. I was to rejoin it, again as beachmaster.

When I arrived in Bombay I discovered, as might have been expected, that nobody in the Southeast Asia Theater of Operations had even heard of my unit. I spent a week there trying to locate them and another week trying to get travel orders to join them. One day I would be scheduled to go by air and the next day that would be changed and I would be informed that I was going by boat. But the delay did not annoy me. I was delighted to find myself in India again. It was still my favorite country. At last I left Bombay by train and went across India and on the twenty-seventh of January I caught up with the Marine Commando group at Chittagong near the border of Burma.

Our first operation there was a raid on Japanese outposts on the Irrawaddy River. We wiped them out. We did various jobs of sabotage and sneaked through the Jap lines to supply the Burmese tribesmen with arms and ammunition and gathered information in the jungles near the Gulf of Martaban that enabled the RAF to raid the enemy supply lines. Once we penetrated far up the Salween River and came upon a party of Japs and Burmese laborers, working in the jungle. We surprised them and overpowered them easily with knives and bayonets. After we questioned them we were about to withdraw in our collapsible boats when we saw a fleet of Jananese sampans coming across the river, straight at our position. They were evidently on their way to pick up the labor unit that we had attacked. The sampans were loaded with troops and supplies. We hid in the foliage and waited until they touched the bank and then we threw grenades into the sampans. The troops that were not killed were carried away by the swirling current of the river.

But on the other hand three boatloads of Commandos approached a Jap outpost on the Irrawaddy one night and heard somebody on the bank calling to them in Cockney English, "Come alongside here, chums." They came alongside. The Japs threw a searchlight on the boats and cleaned out two of them with machine-gun fire.

Rangoon was recaptured on May 3 but the Japs remained in force farther east. We staged a landing operation at a beach on the east bank of the Sittang River, about twenty miles inland from its mouth. The plan was to land and to advance into the jungle and to disrupt

Jap supply lines between the Sittang and Salween rivers. We expected no opposition on the riverbank but there was a possibility that we might run into small numbers of the enemy when we penetrated inland.

Our Intelligence reports were erroneous and misleading. Instead of finding no Japs when we landed, we walked into a big concentration of troops and artillery. There were only two hundred Commandos and we were slaughtered. The three mother ships were forced to draw away and leave us when the artillery began to shell them. The ships signaled to us to hold onto the beach because we were about to get air support. The air support arrived but instead of dropping their bombs on the Japs in the jungle the planes dropped them beside us on the beach. We fought for three hours but we had no means of getting ammunition or reinforcements and no avenue of withdrawal. We were badly beaten. As we used up the last of our bullets there was nothing to do but wait for the Japs to come out of the jungle and take us. They advanced toward us, holding their fire, and surrounded us and covered us with their weapons. We did not surrender. They motioned to us to come forward and herded us together and marched us inland on a jungle trail. As we walked I tore off the beachmaster's arm band on my sleeve and threw it away.

The Japs led us to a clearing where thousands of their men were encamped and lined us up in a column of twos and searched us. I was surprised to find that so many of us were still alive. There were fifty-four of the original two hundred left. The Japs took everything from us; they even stripped me of my watch and the last letter I had received from Lucille. They kept us standing for two hours in the sweltering sun. The private next to me muttered, "What will they do to us now, skipper?" I said I didn't know.

One of the guards came over to me and spoke in Japanese, digging his rifle into my chest.

"What do you want?" I said.

That made him dig the rifle into me again. Somebody down the line called to me, "Don't talk to him, skip." The Jap ran down the column, seeking the man who had spoken, and dug the rifle into him. Three Jap officers appeared on the scene and talked among themselves about us. Then we were marched to a freshly cut jungle road and we began a long and exhausting walk of about fifteen miles. A truck moved in front of us with a group of soldiers on it who covered us with a machine gun. There was another truck behind us with another machine gun that pointed at our backs.

It would have been less tiring if we had been allowed to walk at a faster pace. But the truck ahead of the column had a difficult time getting along on the jungle trail and we had to slow down accordingly. Sometimes we walked haltingly like a wedding procession and there were frequent halts and long periods of waiting and we were not allowed to sit. We stood, shifting our weight from one foot to the other, while the truck ahead labored to get out of a muddy rut in the road. It seemed as though the march would never end. My green denim tunic and pants stuck to me and the insects bit us and buzzed in clouds around our heads. Four times we heard the machine gun behind us chatter. We were afraid to look back but word passed down the column that if anybody fell by the wayside they would be machine-gunned by the truck in the rear as it passed them.

We stumbled and inched our way along the trail all night and about an hour after sunrise we stopped near a native village. We were herded together in a bunch, still standing on our feet. My tongue felt like a piece of leather and my throat was parched and hard. I had no fight left in me. I decided to sit down even if it meant getting shot. When I sat the guards paid no attention to me. Gradually the other men began to sit, too, and soon all of us were sitting.

The natives came close to us and looked at us as though we were curiosities. I heard one of them say, "Europeans." I looked at him and said, "Yes, English."

He smiled at me and said, "I English too. Me ten years in Rangoon. Work there as coolie."

I asked him for water and he went away and came back with a brass bowl that held about a quart of it. I drank half and gave the rest to the marine next to me. The Japs did not object so other natives brought water to the rest of the men. We drank a lot of it. It was brackish and sweet but it tasted to us like champagne.

Two Jap officers appeared in an armored car. One of them, a fat man with a sword decorated by jewels, seemed to be in command. He walked around us and looked us over and sneered, "English pigs." I could not help muttering, "Yellow bastard." He swung around sharply and barked, "Who said that?" Nobody answered. He shouted, "Stand up!"

We got to our feet and he ordered the officers and non-commissioned officers to step forward. There were nine of us in the group.

"So," he said. "You are the well-mannered and disciplined English."

We said nothing. Then I asked him if we could have some food.

"You will get food when you reach the rest of your kind," he said.

Then we were loaded like sardines into two trucks, standing upright and packed so tightly that we were unable to raise our arms. We rode in the truck for the rest of that day and toward evening we reached what turned out to be a transient prison camp. It was a collection of mud huts and tents, surrounded by a barricade. Our nine officers and non-coms were separated from the rest of the men and lined up outside one of the huts, to be taken inside one at a time for questioning.

When it was my turn to be questioned I was taken inside to face a stern, elderly high-ranking officer. The fat Jap was sitting beside him, acting as an interpreter. I saw that my discarded beachmaster's arm band was lying on the table in front of him.

"Where are you from?"

"England."

"What army?"

"British."

He shouted at me, "We know that. We are not fools. The ships that put you ashore, where did they come from?"

"Calcutta."

"Don't lie. We know you came from Chittagong."

"If you know, why do you ask?"

"Who is the beachmaster?"

Four other officers had been questioned before me and I wondered if one of them had revealed that I was the beachmaster. "I don't know," I said. "Perhaps he is dead. I haven't seen him since we landed."

"He is not dead. If he was dead he would be still wearing this arm band. He is either among you or he is hiding with some others in the jungle. We shall soon know."

He talked to the other officer in Japanese and then turned to me and said, "All right. About turn." As I turned to go he snapped, "Wait. Don't you salute your betters in the English Army?"

I looked at the two guards who were standing behind me with fixed bayonets and decided that discretion was the better part of valor. I gave the officer a halfhearted salute.

I went outside and waited until the rest of the officers and non-coms were questioned. Apparently none of them revealed that I was the beachmaster. We were marched to a compound about two hundred yards square. There we met other prisoners, most of them Indians and a few British officers who had been in command of Indian troops. One of the officers was a doctor. I had a slight wound in my right hand and as he dressed it he told me that we were the first prisoners who had been brought into the camp since he had arrived there in April. His troops then numbered 1300 and now, after three months of imprisonment, there were only 532 of them alive. The others had died of disease, in most cases dysentery. At first they had died at the rate of sixty a day but, the doctor said, things had improved recently. He had been able to beg a few medical supplies and the rice ration had been increased. The death rate had gone down to seven a day.

I walked around the compound. The only covering and shelter from the sun and the rain in the whole enclosure was a bamboo and palm-leaf hut in one corner of the fence where the doctor attended his patients. A *chong,* or small river, ran along one side of the compound, its bank just outside the fence. The chong was about one hundred yards wide and its current was swift and it was full of crocodiles that slithered up and down its muddy edges. In the doctor's hut there was a commode where the sufferers from dysentery were always sitting. The commode was over a deep and foul-smelling hole in the ground and at the bottom of the hole there was a big drainage pipe that carried the human filth under the ground beneath the fence and emptied it outside at the bank of the chong. The drainage pipe was big enough for a man's body to pass through it and I noticed that the fence beside the chong was unguarded at night, although a sentry was stationed there during the day. The Japs probably figured, quite correctly, that no prisoner would be able to stomach the thought of lowering himself into the indescribable filth of the dysentery hole. And if he did try to escape through the drainpipe the crocodiles in the chong would take care of him.

The only other sanitary arrangement in the compound was another hole in the ground in a corner of the enclosure. It was understood that the one in the doctor's hut was for the dysentery cases and the one in the corner was for everybody else. When it became apparent that the dysentery cases were about to die the doctor would carry them out of the hut and leave them on the ground by themselves until the end came. There was nothing he could do to help them. We lived as much like pigs as men could.

Rice was issued twice a day. One urn of it was shared by ten men who dipped their fingers into the mound of rice until it was gone. Water was issued twice a day, too, immediately after we ate the rice. It came from a well outside the barbed-wire fence. Each man had a pot that held about a pint of water. He would take it to the fence and hand it through the wire to a native who filled it and handed it back to him. The doctor was sure that the water was causing the dysentery but there was nothing else to drink except rain water and that was hard to get.

Once a day for the first three days we were in the compound the fat Jap visited us and asked for the beachmaster. It got so that the very sight of his flabby face filled me with an almost uncontrollable rage. Just before the time for the evening rice issue on the fourth day I was sitting with four other officers playing a game we had invented called "Bury the Peg." While the others turned their backs one of us would bury a small piece of bamboo in the sand. Then he would shout, "Buried," and the others would try to find the piece of bamboo. The finder would have the next turn at burying it. While we were playing the fat Jap entered the compound and walked toward us and ordered us to stand. He asked us if we were prepared yet to tell him which prisoner was the beachmaster. I was feeling hot and tired and my nerves were raw. Something came over me and made me lose all judgment and caution. I screamed at the Jap, "Why don't you find him yourself, you flat-faced bastard?"

The Jap smiled at me. "I will find him," he said. "There will be no rice issued tonight. And there will be no rice issued after tonight until you find him for me."

I rushed at him with my head down and rammed it into his stomach. I knocked him to the ground and I was about to grind my foot into his face when a guard came at me with a bayonet. He lunged at my chest. I put out my hand to defend myself and the palm of my hand met the bayonet. The bayonet went through my hand and my hand slid down the blade to the tip of the rifle. Another guard grabbed me around the neck from behind. As if in a dream, I heard the voices of the other Commando officers calling to me to calm down and to get a hold on myself. I became quiet then and helped the first guard remove his bayonet from my hand. I noticed then that about twenty Japanese soldiers were inside the compound, covering the other prisoners with fixed bayonets.

The fat Jap told the doctor to bandage my hand. "We'll question him tomorrow," he added. He left the compound but the two guards followed me to the doctor's hut and stood outside while I went in to get my hand wrapped. It took the doctor nearly an hour to stop the flow of blood. I felt terrible about the rice and wondered what the other prisoners were saying about me. I looked at the dysentery commode while the doctor worked on my hand. I decided that the only thing for me to do would be to escape through the drainpipe into the water of the chong. I could not stand the thought of being questioned again by the Japs the following day. I knew that I would lose my head and get into more trouble. I had visions of the Japs torturing me. I felt that as long as I stayed in the compound I would be doing something that would deprive the other prisoners of their rice. At that moment getting away from the compound, even if it meant being killed in the attempt, seemed to me to be the most important thing in the world.

I whispered to the doctor, "I'm going down that hole."

"You can't do that, man," he said in a low voice. "You'll get stuck in the slime down there. There are guards on the riverbank. If they don't shoot you the crocs will eat you."

The doctor's assistant, a Gurkha soldier whom we called Johnny, was listening to us. He tapped his chest, saying, "Johnny got *kukri*, *burosahib*."

He was telling me that he had a knife hidden somewhere.

"Let me have it, Johnny," I said.

He went to the side of the hut and slipped the knife out from under the palm leaves where he had hidden it and handed it to me. I put it inside my tunic. The doctor begged me not to attempt the escape. I looked around. It was already quite dark and the two guards were still standing in front of the hut.

"Look," I said to the doctor. "Allow me about four minutes. Then yell to the guards and tell them that you could not stop me from going down into the hole. That will protect you. And now stand in front of the doorway so the guards won't see me."

The doctor and Johnny blocked the view from the doorway and I opened the lid of the commode. The smell that arose from it almost knocked me over. I held my breath and lowered myself into the hole and dropped into the repulsive slop below. The flies and maggots buzzed angrily because I had disturbed them. To this day I do not know how I ever brought myself to go down into that hole. The Japs must have driven me somewhat insane to enable me to do it.

I found myself up to my waist in the steaming slime. I saw the opening of the drain before me and crawled through it. The fresh air at the opening of the riverbank was delicious. The sight of the churning black water of the river frightened me and my courage went away for a few moments. I crouched beside the bank and tried to pull myself together. Then I heard a whistle and shouts and I saw a figure of a man running along the bank between the barbed-wire fence and the water. I grasped the knife and leaped on him and pushed the knife into his neck. My strength amazed me. While the doctor was bandaging my hand I had felt weak and exhausted but now I felt as though I could cut down a tree with one stroke of the Gurkha knife. I ran down the bank away from the compound and I bumped squarely into another guard. He fell down, shouting in Japanese, and I plunged the knife into him and left it there and ran to the water's edge. A searchlight went on somewhere behind me at the compound. Just as it lit up the bank around me I dived into the water.

I went under and swam with a breast stroke for several yards before I raised my head for a gulp of air. I heard rifle shots and the chatter of a machine gun. The searchlight was on me. I went under again and swam under the surface until my lungs began to burst. I raised my head and heard the machine gun and felt something hit my arm. I rolled over on my side and swallowed a great deal of water. When I came to the surface I felt a bullet hitting my other arm. I tried to swim but I couldn't seem to move my arms. I let the current carry me downstream. My ears were roaring. I felt myself striking something and I thought of the crocodiles. My foot seemed to be stuck in something and I thought that the crocodiles had got me. I kicked with the other foot and it was stuck too. Then I raised my head and realized that I was not moving. I was lying in the mud by the side of the river.

I stood up and I sank in the mud up to my knees. I saw the searchlight playing on the water about two hundred yards up the river. The bank in front of me was steep and slippery and when I tried to climb it I slid backward. On the third or fourth attempt I clambered to the top of the bank and staggered into the bushes. When I tried to wipe the mud from my face I found that I could not raise my arms and there was something wrong with my shoulders. The muddy water in my mouth and my nose made me feel sick. I walked into a clearing and looked up and saw the stars in the sky. I walked on for a few minutes and then I fell on the ground and began to vomit. My arms were throbbing but I could not tell if they were bleeding because they were caked with wet mud. A feeling of great weakness came over me and I stretched out on the ground and closed my eyes. I remember thinking, "I got away but what good did it do me?" I was sure that I was going to die. That was the last thing I thought of as I lost consciousness.

CHAPTER 17

*W*HEN I AWOKE I WAS LYING ON MY BACK AND MY head was aching badly. My arms were throbbing with pain and they felt swollen. I closed my eyes again and my whole body seemed to rock and sway from side to side. I thought it was my head. Then I heard the creaking and crunching noise of wheels and opened my eyes and saw that I was lying on some sort of a cart that was moving along a road. I tried to sit up but I couldn't do it. I opened my mouth to shout but no sound came out.

The cart stopped moving after a while and around it I saw the faces of several dark-skinned natives with long, matted hair. When they saw that I was awake they began to babble among themselves with excitement. I opened and shut my mouth and ran my tongue over my dry lips to show that I was thirsty and they squeezed tomatoes into my mouth. The juice tasted good. They went away and came back with banana leaves and covered my body with them to protect me against the sun. The cart began to move again. I decided that it was being drawn by a bullock and then I went back to sleep again.

I have a dim recollection of someone lifting me from the cart and pouring water over me and bandaging my arms while a voice kept repeating, "You'll be all right, sahib." The next time I awoke I was in a clean bed in a cool bungalow. I went back to sleep. The next morning I found that the bungalow was owned by a planter, an Indian Christian named Ramarou. He told me that Burmese guerrillas had found me in the early morning while they were watching the Japanese prison camp from the opposite side of the river. He also said that he had heard reports that the war was over but he was not sure of it. He said that the Japs had moved far south and the guerrillas were attacking and plundering their columns as they retreated and burying the spoils.

"These guerrillas who brought you here work on my plantation in peacetime," he said. "When all the Japanese are killed, perhaps they may return and work for me again. But I don't know. They are doing so well with this plundering that they may not work again for the rest of their lives."

My arms were in bad shape. I stayed with Ramarou for six weeks. His ten-year-old daughter acted as my nurse. At the end of six weeks the swelling in my arms went down and I could move my right arm. The left arm was useless and my left hand would not open. But I was anxious to make an attempt to get to Rangoon. Ramarou gave me his elephant and two native guides and a hunting rifle and a month's supply of American K Rations which the guerrillas had taken from the Japs.

Ramarou's plantation was thirty-five miles north of the town of Pogwai and the Sittang River was between there and Rangoon. I had to make a detour one hundred miles to the north before I could find a place in the river shallow enough to cross. The guides took me as far as the river and I went the rest of the way alone on the elephant.

The elephant's name was Raffa and he and I became great friends. He understood conversation better than many human beings I have known. Every day at noon he would look for a palm tree and stand under it and nibble on the young leaves at its top. Every night at the same hour he would kneel down and refuse to move another inch. When I ate my breakfast of K Rations, I would save the lump of sugar and give it to him just before I climbed aboard his back to start the day's march. When the K Rations ran out I had a devil of a time trying to get him started in the morning. He thought I was holding back on the sugar.

I lived on bananas after the rations were gone. Sometimes I ate thirty of them in a day. I always thought that bananas were fattening but I was as thin as a skeleton when I finally met up with a detachment of British Dragoons on the twenty-fourth of November, about forty miles from Rangoon.

The Dragoons told me that the war had ended in August. You can imagine how I felt when I figured out the dates and estimated that the fighting in Burma had stopped two days after I made my escape from the prison camp. Two days more and all of us would have been set free.

Still, I did not know whether to be glad or sorry that I had made my escape. I feel that I would have got some bad treatment from the Japs the day before the war ended. The treatment might have been much worse than the machine-gun wounds in my arms.

Just before I was scheduled to return from Burma to India an epidemic of dysentery broke out in the camp where I was staying and I caught the disease and almost died from it. An Indian doctor gave me M and B tablets and ordered me to drink gallons of water. The next day when I was losing consciousness I heard the colonel in command of the camp telling the doctor that I had been given too many tablets. "He won't last long," the colonel said.

There was a Hindu bearer in the hospital and he and I had become quite attached to each other. He said prayers for me in Hindu every day. I was dying for liquid to drink but the chemical taste in the camp water made me nauseous. The Hindu bearer smuggled into the hospital a bottle of Pares gin, the white Indian gin that resembles arak. It is very strong stuff. I drank the whole bottle of it. The other patients told me later that I was found sitting nude under a palm tree outside the camp, singing songs at the top of my lungs. I was taken back to my bed in the hospital and I fell asleep and slept for twenty-four hours. I woke up almost completely cured of dysentery. The doctor could not understand it.

I went to India and spent three months in the mountains there, building up enough strength to travel, and on March 23, 1946, I boarded a ship for England. Lucille met me and we spent four weeks together and then I entered the naval hospital at Sherborne for treatments on my arms. During the next six months I went through nine operations and then electrical therapy treatments but my condition did not improve. My left arm was useless. I could move my right arm but it had no strength in it and I could not use the fingers. Finally the doctors told me that they could do no more for me and that I would never be able to use my arms for the rest of my life.

That put me in a bitter mood. I remember walking back to my bed after the doctors talked to me and when the fellow in the next bed asked me how I was feeling I told him to shut up and mind his own business. I sat on my bed, smoking cigarettes and brooding, and I refused to let the nurse do anything for me or even speak to me. That afternoon Lucille came to visit me, as she did every day. I could see from her face that they had told her the news.

"Don't worry about it, darling," she said. "I'll take care of you. To tell you the truth, I am a little glad because now you won't be able to be running off and leaving me any more."

She was trying to be kind but it was the worst thing she could have said to me. I hated the thought of being a burden on anyone. And above all I hated the thought of never going to sea again. I spoke cruelly to Lucille for the first time in all the years I had known her.

"You won't take care of me," I said. "You won't want a man who can't put his arms around you. Get out of here and leave me alone."

She started to cry. But I turned away from her. The nurse had to come and take her out. I was infuriated.

That night I sat awake and thought for a long time. I made up my mind to travel again, arms or no arms. There were too many places I wanted to see and too many things that I wanted to do. I remembered the promise I had made to Donald Gillies when he was dying to go to the United States after the war and see his mother and his sister. I remembered the dream I had had for years about exploring the Sargasso Sea, that untraveled and unknown doldrums in the Atlantic that was said to be full of strange creatures and lost ships. Now was the time to do it, I thought, despite the doctors and despite Lucille and despite everyone else. And then I decided that I wanted to do it alone. I would get a small boat that would be capable of crossing the ocean but still could be handled by me alone without the hindrance of a crew. The way I felt that night, I did not want the help of any member of the human race. I wanted to show the world that I could continue to live as I wanted to live without depending on another soul.

Even though the hour was very late when I arrived at this decision I climbed out of bed and put on my robe and slippers and went to the recreation room and wrote a letter to a friend of mine in the Admiralty who was in charge of the sale of surplus naval vessels. Because I couldn't use the fingers of my right hand I held the pen between my thumb and the side of my index finger. I held cigarettes that way and even buttoned my clothes that way too. I told my friend what I wanted: a small craft but a sturdy one, capable of ocean travel and still capable of being handled by one man. Perhaps it could be a tender. I also wanted a boat that could be outfitted with sails. I posted the letter and went to bed happy and slept soundly.

When Lucille came back to see me the next day I was a different person. I said nothing to her about the idea I had for making a voyage across the Atlantic. In a few days I heard from my friend in the Admiralty. He sent me a list of boats that were close to what I had specified and I selected one of them. It was a thirty-four-foot Scotch-built fifie, or small yawl, weighing seven tons with a draft of four feet and freeboard (height from the water line to the deck) of two and a half feet. The Navy had used her as a tender to ferry personnel from the big ships in the Firth of Forth. It seemed to me to be the kind of craft that would suit my purposes so I bought her. She had no name and she was lying at Dysart on the Firth of Forth.

That was in September. I was released from the hospital at the end of November. I appeared before a board of high-ranking officers, one of them an elderly admiral, and I was officially informed by them of my retirement from active duty in the Royal Navy. I was told that I would receive a pension for physical disability. Then they talked about my services in the war and all that sort of thing. I shook hands with them and the admiral asked me what I was planning to do next.

"I'm going to sea," I said casually. "I've bought a small boat and I'm taking her on an ocean voyage."

The officers looked at me in surprise.

"With whom?" the admiral said.

"With no one but myself."

The admiral looked at me for a moment and shook his head.

"Orsborne," he said, "you were born at the wrong time. You should have lived three hundred years ago."

I said to him, "Sir, perhaps I did."

CHAPTER *18*

*E*NGLAND SEEMED DIFFERENT TO ME WHEN I LEFT THE
hospital. The people who were so generous and friendly during the war
were gloomy and impatient and uncivil. I went to Kings Cross Station
and paid a porter to carry my luggage because I was unable to lift it
myself. We had walked about ten yards when he asked me what train
I was taking. I said I didn't know yet. He threw the luggage on the
platform.

"You ought to know," he said, "you bloody gold braids can't order
people about now. We're the government, you know."

He walked away, leaving the luggage where he had dropped it. I
could not carry it to the information office when I inquired about the
train and when I returned to the place where it had been left the
luggage was stolen.

"I'll be glad to get out of all this," I said to myself.

When I told Lucille about the voyage I was planning to make to the
Sargasso Sea and America she said, "I'm going too." I told her that she
could not go. We argued for a while and then she stopped talking. I
asked her what she was thinking about.

"Ration points," she said. "You don't realize how hard it is to buy
food in England now. I'm planning how I can scrape up enough
rations to stock that boat of yours. Now don't bother me until I figure
it out."

A little later she said, "I wish I was going with you, Dod, but I
know how you feel. I know how important it is for you to do it alone.
Now tell me the truth—do you have enough money?"

That was Lucille.

The next day I went to Dysart and looked up the place where the boat was lying. It was a soot-blackened quay with fifteen dilapidated craft bunched together in the mud-silted basin. I wondered if I had wasted my money. I walked around until I found the watchman, an old Scotsman named Peter Allen. I told him I wanted to have a look at the boat that was numbered N 30.

"You can have a look at her but it won't do you no good. She's been sold."

"I was the one who bought her. I haven't seen her yet."

"Well, sir," the watchman said, "I'll tell you. She was the only one of the whole lot that arrived here under her own power. And the only one that I haven't had to pump daily to keep afloat. She's the only one of them that I would put to sea."

I asked him how long he had been at sea himself and he said that he had done thirty-two years before he retired. That made me feel better. I figured that with so much experience he should be able to judge a boat.

When I looked at the boat I felt even better. She was covered with ugly black paint but she was strong and sturdy and the timber was the best hard oak. Although she had no masts she was built for sail. The watchman told me that a Scotch boat builder had made her just before the war as a sailing yawl for his own son and that naturally he had put the best quality of wood into her. She had been confiscated by the government at the start of the war for duty as a tender and the ship-builder's son had lost interest in her and had not bothered to reclaim her. She had a rather poor gasoline motor in her but I was not concerned about that. I was more interested in her sailing capacity.

The next day I hired two fishermen to clean her up and moved her away from the quay and beached her on firm sand in the outer harbor. When the tide went out I inspected her bottom. There was no sign of worms. We started to scrape her and I checked out of the hotel where I was staying and moved onto the boat. That night, with a cozy fire burning in the cabin stove and two candles serving as lights, I was very happy.

My two helpers and I worked steadily on the boat for the next two weeks. That was when I started to use my arms again. When I left the hospital I could lift my right hand up to my face and use it to smoke and eat with but it had no strength. If I wanted to put my left hand into my pocket somebody had to pick it up from my side and slip it into the pocket for me. I could not lift it. The first day we started scraping and chipping the old paint off the boat I used my right hand and arm a little. Then I bought the trunk of a pine tree with the bark still on it to make a mast. When we were planing the tree I pushed a plane with my right hand and let the limp left hand rest on the moving plane. After a few days of this the exercise strengthened my left arm and by the time the mast was finished I could lift it as high as my waist. While I was doing this work on the wood in the daytime I spent the nights in the cabin sewing sails. The labor exhausted my arms but it improved them greatly.

On the fourteenth of December the boat was ready for sailing. I bought at the Firth of Forth a cutter and two dinghies from the Admiralty's surplus property. I planned to give the cutter to Lucille's uncle, who needed one for transporting workers on his farm beside the Thames, and I was going to give one dinghy to Lucille and keep the other for myself. Although the weather was bad, I set out from Dysart on the sixteenth of December to sail to London, towing the cutter with the two dinghies in it. The next day the motor cut out and I put in at Dunbar to have it repaired. A mechanic from the local garage spent two days taking it apart and putting it together and assured me it was all right. The following day I ran into a bad storm off St. Abb's Head. The sea was breaking over the bow of the *Lonely Lady,* as I had decided to call her, and everything was upset in the cabin. The cutter foundered and broke loose from the towrope and went to the bottom, carrying the dinghies with it. That represented a loss of one hundred and forty pounds and I was in no position to be throwing money away.

But the *Lonely Lady* rode out the storm proudly. The engine went dead again and we ran into a calm and a fishing boat towed me into Arbroath. I left her there a few days and went back to London by train and then returned and sailed her through a really terrific storm to Yarmouth. The harbor officials did not believe that I had come to Yarmouth from Scotland. The storm had been so bad that it had driven a battleship, H.M.S. *Warspite,* up on the rocks. I was so fond of the boat then I decided to change her name from *Lonely Lady* to *Lovely Lady.* I was naming her after Lucille. Of course the earlier name would have suited Lucille too. Being mixed up with me, she was lonely as well as lovely.

When I brought the boat into St. Catharine's Dock in London the newspapers were on my trail. There were stories that said that the skipper of the *Girl Pat* was about to go out on another mystery voyage. Some of my friends visited the boat and with one of them was a young blond actress. There was a story in a newspaper a few days later with this actress's photograph and the following week there was a whole page of photographs of her in a magazine. The newspaper and the magazines said she was to accompany me on the mystery ship. One of the pictures showed her sewing on a sail and another pulling a rope. The pictures must have been taken in her own apartment. Lucille did not like it.

My money was rather limited. I put aside two thousand pounds to spend when I reached America and that did not leave me much to spend before I left England. I had decided to revisit the Phantom Islands off the West African coast on my way to the Sargasso Sea and to photograph the islands to back up my theory about the disappearance of the crew of the *Mary Celeste*. But I could not afford seventy-five pounds to spend on a camera. I discussed the islands with a friend of mine who was the editor of a newspaper and he suggested that I let a newspaper publisher buy me the camera with the understanding that I would turn over the pictures and the story to him for publication. I presented the idea to two newspapers and a magazine publisher but all of them refused to take the gamble. They said that I would not last at sea for more than one week.

She would not admit it, but I think that Lucille and her uncle and her friends went hungry for a long time to supply me with enough rationed food to stock the boat. She sailed down to Dover with me and kissed me good-by when I sailed from the Prince of Wales Pier there at three o'clock on the afternoon of June 25, 1947.

I had slow winds and I did not see the lights of Dieppe until the following night. I went along the French coast to Le Havre, which I reached at seven in the evening of the twenty-seventh of June. I did not stop, but kept going toward Normandy. That night I had a rather weird experience. When I was asleep I dreamed that a very beautiful woman in a pretty dress was pulling on my beard and saying, "Get up. You must get up." I awoke and felt disappointed when I realized that it was only a dream and went back to sleep again. I saw the same woman once more and this time she said more urgently, "You must get up at once. You're in danger." I opened my eyes and heard the ugly sound of a foghorn. I ran to the bridge and blew my small horn and beat on a bucket with a spanner. A big steamer was bearing down on me in the thick fog. For a moment I thought he was going to run over me. He just missed me and I heard somebody shouting, "It's a fishing boat on the port bow." I was still frightened when I heard his propeller chugging off in the darkness.

The next day I passed Cherbourg and headed for St. Peter Port in Guernsey in the Channel Islands. I tied up there and slept and the next day I went three miles to St. Sampson's to beach the boat and paint her bottom. I went ashore for a drink at the English and Guernsey Arms and met three friends, one from Burma and one who had landed with me in France and a chief engineer who had been a pal of mine in Grimsby. I sailed from Guernsey on the thirtieth of June and ran into a storm on my way to Brest. For two days I was too busy to make tea. One drum of water was washed overboard and the foresail was ripped and the mizzen sheet broke adrift. I had to run into a sheltered inlet on the Brittany coast and spend four days there repairing damages and sewing the sails. When I went out to sea again I ran into thick fog. I tried to get stores at Brest but I found food very scarce there and difficult to buy. On July 18, I left there and headed for Spain across the Bay of Biscay, which is a treacherous body of water. At night, as I steered through the darkness, I would see a long line of phosphorous-crested waves rushing toward me like a line of white horses. I would get frightened and think I was on a reef. Actually the strange behavior of the water there is caused by the rebound of the current of the Gulf Stream after it hits against the wall of the European coast. I began to use my crippled left arm as an alarm clock. I would lash the wheel to keep the boat on its course and wrap myself in a blanket and lie down on my left side with my arm under me. In a half hour or an hour my arm would get cramped and the pain would awaken me. I would get up and look to see if everything was all right and then lie down and sleep for another half hour. Sometimes I would go for two days in rough weather without a real meal and then when the water became calmer I would cook myself a tin of beans and a tin of meat and boil a few potatoes or make some fried potatoes and scrambled powdered eggs. I drank cocoa, tea, and coffee. The hard life was building up my arms rapidly. By the time I reached Spain the right arm was quite strong and I could lift the left arm as high as my chin and flex its fingers.

On the morning of July 24, I entered the harbor of La Coruña. The Spanish port official who came aboard advised me against lying beside the fishing boats in the north-side basin where I had tied up. He said that if I stayed there everything aboard would be stolen. He pointed at a British sloop at another quay and suggested that I stay next to her for protection. I shifted to a position beside the sloop but the captain of the sloop came out on her deck and requested me to move away.

"I'm having a hard enough time trying to watch this ship without watching yours too," he called. "Everything movable aboard here has been stolen."

I finally tied up ahead of the sloop near the Coruña Yachting Club. I slept the rest of the day and that evening I went aboard the sloop and took a shower bath. It was a British naval sloop that had been sold to a Chinese firm. Owing to crew trouble and engine trouble, she had been tied up at La Coruña for two months and it was beginning to look as though she would never make the voyage from England to China that had started ten weeks before. When something was fixed, something else would go wrong. Her name was the *Jaslock*.

The crew of the *Jaslock* was the lowest collection of dock rats I ever encountered in all my years at sea. While I was sitting on their mess deck, having a cup of tea, I heard one of them telling how he had stolen the ship's compass and sold it for five hundred pesetas and drunk the money. Another one described how he had been caught at two o'clock in the morning in the act of stealing the wardroom clock. Everybody thought it was very funny. "By the way," one of them said, "did they ever catch the chap who stole the clock from the bridge?"

The harassed captain told me later that they had even stolen one of his uniforms and the steward's cycle. They refused to work unless he paid them an advance on their wages and when he did give them money they went ashore and stayed there drinking for three days. The crew was out of hand and the captain could not cope with the situation. He had appealed several times to the British consul at La Coruña but the consul had long since refused to have anything to do with the *Jaslock* or her crew.

There were two Canadians aboard the *Jaslock* who were decent fellows. They had signed up with the ship to get back to their homes in Canada. The next day I went ashore with them. There were two things I wanted to do in La Coruña. I had almost no money left and I needed stores and some gasoline, so I sent a wire asking Lucille to send some of my money from England to the British Consulate. The other thing I wanted to do was to look up the fine girl in the brothel who had been so good to me after I had escaped from the jail at Corcubion in 1936. I sent the wire but I could not find the girl or anybody who knew what had become of her.

Spain had gone to pieces. It was not the same country I had known before the Civil War. Wherever a small crowd gathered in the streets of La Coruña, even if it was around an old woman selling fountain pens, five or six soldiers, armed with tommy guns, would march up and watch the people and disperse them. These armed soldiers and armed police were constantly patrolling the streets. The people looked poor and shabby and hungry.

The Canadians and I were sitting in a café, drinking white wine, when a well-dressed man approached our table and sat down.

"You are in danger here, my friends," he said.

I glanced at him. "We can take care of ourselves," I said.

"Perhaps. But I wish you would come with me to the café in the adjoining building."

My curiosity was aroused so I nodded to the Canadians to drink up and we went out with him. When we were seated in another café a little farther down the street he said to me, "I hope you will pardon my intrusion but I was only trying to help you. That café you were sitting in is a Communist gathering place. It is about to be raided by the police at any moment and I was afraid that you people might be injured. It is no place for strangers."

"How did you know we were strangers?"

He smiled at me. "Everybody in La Coruña knows you. You are the Capitán Solitario. You were in Spain before. Just before our Civil War."

I decided to admit nothing. "I was in Spain before but many years ago."

"But you are the Capitán Solitario? You did not wear a beard then."

"No, you are mistaken," I said. "I never heard of the Capitán Solitario."

I could see that he did not believe me. He invited us to go with him to another place to meet some of his friends. I got into an argument about Franco with one of them, a man who spoke English very well. I asked him what his nationality was and he said with indignation that he was a Spaniard.

"Born in what part of Germany?" I asked.

With that we arose and said good afternoon. The well-dressed Spaniard who had brought us there stayed with his friends but when we left the café I had the feeling that we were being followed. When the Canadians went aboard the *Jaslock*, I returned to my boat. As I passed the yachting club a man who was sitting alone at a table on the veranda called to me and invited me to have coffee with him. I thought he was English but when I sat down with him I found that he was a Spaniard who had spent twelve years in America and who had returned to La Coruña in 1934 to start a fruit business. The fruit business did well until the Civil War came. He was not a Franco sympathizer and he was put in jail for trying to leave the country. He started his business again when he got out of jail but it amounted to nothing. Now the Franco police visited him twice a week to check up on him. We sat and talked about Spain for three hours.

"Every man who walks freely in La Coruña has two men watching him," he said. "The ones with the green uniforms and the black hats and the German pistols, they are the real Fascists with the most power. They are like the Gestapo. When they knock on your door at night your family never sees you again. Then there are the ones with green uniforms and plain caps and tommy guns. They are the military police. The ones in blue uniforms are the ordinary police. The Fascists do not trust them. And then there are the listeners that you cannot recognize. They are everywhere. We Spaniards had great hope when your Mr. Churchill said on the radio that you would hunt the Fascists in every country in Europe. But then he said that Spain must find its own salvation. Now we have no hope. There are two thousand German Nazi fugitives today in La Coruña alone."

I told him about the man who had approached me in the café.

"Without doubt he was a Fascist who was trying to impress you with how efficiently the country is being run," he said. "He wanted to get you out of the first café you were in because he was afraid that you might hear there discontented grumbling."

The lights on the *Lovely Lady* had not been working well so the next day I took an electrician aboard to overhaul my switchboard. I left him at work on the boat and went to the *Jaslock* for a shower bath. He said that he could do the complete job in two hours. When I returned to the boat he was gone and so was the switchboard. I assumed that he had taken the switchboard to his workshop. But he failed to reappear in the next three days. Then I discovered that the generator and a twelve-volt battery were gone too.

I went to the electrical shop where I had hired the electrician but everybody there pretended not to know what I was talking about. There was a great deal of puzzled head shaking and shoulder shrugging. That night I had coffee again with the fruit dealer on the yachting club porch and I told him about the switchboard and the generator and the battery.

"*Amigo,* you made a great error when you stopped here in La Coruña," he said. "This place is a jinx for travelers. They come here and they go no farther."

"What do you mean?"

"Look at that ship near yours, the one that has been trying to get to Canada. It has been here for weeks. Two months ago four Dutchmen stopped here on their way to South Africa. They ran into so many difficulties that they sold their boat. Two of them have gone away. The other two are still here. Before them, there were three British adventurers in a small boat. In La Coruña they quarreled among themselves and also sold the boat here. They returned to England. This is the place, believe me, where everybody stops and turns back."

"But not me."

"We shall see. You wait here for your money to come from England. While you wait, one part of your boat goes ashore. Then another part. Soon you'll have nothing to sail with."

The next morning I was on my way to the British Consulate to see if a reply had come from London when I spotted the electrician with two other men walking down a side street. I followed them. After about a twenty-minute walk to the outskirts of town the electrician parted company with the other two men and went alone into a small house. I waited outside the house for an hour and then another hour. I saw no one but two small children who came out of the house and played in the street. Finally I went to the door and knocked on it. For a long time there was no answer. Then I began to bang on the door so hard that I rattled it on its hinges. I wanted that generator.

Finally a large fat woman came to the door, very excited. Before I spoke to her, she sputtered, *"No, Capitán. No hombre. No hombre."*

The fact that she addressed me as captain and her insistence about there being no man in the house told me that I was at the right place. She slammed the door in my face and locked it. I took down the address, 33 Oriente Bajo. I went to the consulate and got an interpreter and went to the police and told them the story. The police were indifferent until I told them I was planning to write a book about my travels and I planned to do a whole chapter on the thieves in La Coruña. Then they became rather nervous and promised me that everything would be returned to me the next day.

When I went back to the consulate with the interpreter I found a cable there from Lucille. She said she was having difficulty getting official permission to send my money out of England. That night I thought about what the fruit dealer had said about La Coruña being a jinx port for travelers. I made up my mind to get out of there as quickly as possible. But I needed stores for a month at sea, at least, and enough gasoline to get me out of the Bay of Coruña by motor. And I had no money. I decided to sell my radio and my extra clothing.

Three days later two policemen appeared at the boat, escorting the missing electrician. He claimed that he had been called away to the country but now he was ready to do the repairs. I told him to replace the switchboard and the generator and the battery within an hour. He went away and returned with the things he had taken. With him was one of the men from the electrical shop who had known nothing about the generator. I stood over them while they put everything back in its original place and then I ordered them ashore.

I spent the rest of the day selling my radio for five hundred pesetas and my best cream-colored drill uniform for two hundred and fifty pesatas. Stretching those seven hundred and fifty pesetas to buy food and petrol was harder than trying to cross the Bay of Biscay. I recalled with chagrin the month's supply of food that the officers of the American Liberty ship, *Fred E. Joyce,* had offered to give me for nothing while I was in Brest. But the night before I was supposed to go aboard and pick up the food the ship had been ordered to sail immediately for a German port and she had left at one o'clock in the morning without my knowledge. I was certainly having a great deal of luck on this trip.

Meat in La Coruña was thirty pesetas a pound, cheese was twenty-two pesetas a pound, and bread was thirty pesetas a loaf. I bought seven hundred pesetas' worth of food and hoped it would last me. It did not seem like much. Then I bought four gallons of petrol to carry me clear of La Coruña.

That afternoon I had a visit from one of the men on the *Jaslock*, a Liverpooler named Donovan. While I was making coffee for him I mentioned that I wanted to go to the market to buy some green tomatoes. He offered to stay aboard the boat and keep an eye on it while I was gone. I bought the tomatoes and then I went ashore with two cans to buy the petrol. It took me an hour to get it. I thanked Donovan for waiting for me. He was out of tobacco. I told him that I would buy him some that evening with the few pesetas that I had left. I was planning to sail with the tide that midnight.

Donovan came back to the boat about eight o'clock and we both went ashore. I took him to a café where I had made some good Spanish friends. I wanted to say good-by to them. Donovan got up to leave us about ten-thirty, saying that he was going back to the *Jaslock*. With my last ten pesetas I bought him a packet of tobacco. I had decided to give up smoking myself because I could not afford to buy enough tobacco to last me for the voyage. But when I said good-by to my Spanish friends at eleven o'clock they presented me with ten packets of tobacco, which was a pleasant and welcome surprise.

When I went back to the boat I saw that somebody had been standing on my box of green tomatoes. I looked around and saw that whoever had stood on the tomatoes had also entered the cabin through the skylight hatch. Then I searched the boat and discovered that my binoculars were missing. I decided that they were not stolen by a Spaniard because other valuables were untouched. I thought about Donovan and his friends from the *Jaslock*. They had evidently figured that they could take the binoculars safely because I would be sailing at midnight and I would be too busy to notice their absence until I was well out at sea.

I was furious. I made up my mind not to sail that night. I would stay in La Coruña and get those binoculars if it meant calling off the whole trip. I would not let those rats from the *Jaslock* put anything over on me.

I went to the *Jaslock*. Donovan had not yet come aboard. I waited until two-thirty and there was still no sign of him. I went back to the *Jaslock* in the morning and saw the captain. I told him about the binoculars and told him I wanted Donovan.

The first officer searched the ship for him and reported that Donovan and three others had not been aboard all night. I told the captain I was going ashore to have him arrested.

"Very well," the captain said. "He has a bad character and he's been stealing things here all along but we've never been able to catch him. I hope you do get him arrested."

I went to the British consul, who was not much help, and then to the Spanish police, who said that they could arrest Donovan if I gave them the authority in writing to do so. I gave them the authority in writing. Then I put a pistol in my pocket and went out looking for Donovan.

I went to several cafés. The proprietors had not seen him. I then went to the brothels. When I entered one of them the madam would come out bowing and smiling and line up the available girls for inspection. I would wave them aside, trying to explain that I was seeking a *mucho malo* English sailor.

After about an hour of this the word spread among the Spaniards and I began to be followed from house to house by an interested throng of spectators, mostly children. I went into seventeen houses on one street. As I was starting on the next street a small boy ran up and tugged my sleeve and pointed at a house. *"El Inglés,"* he said. I went straight to the house. I realized as I reached the door that I was running.

When I went inside Donovan was the first person I saw. He was sitting at a table, drinking with two other men and three women. I knew he was guilty from the way he looked at me.

"Come with me," I said. "You're under arrest."

He started to abuse me with filthy language. I forgot about my disabled arm. "Never mind the tongue," I said. "Come on." I put one hand on his shoulder.

When he started to swing I was ready for him. I pushed him with the hand I had on his shoulder. That turned him off balance and sent his punch swinging wildly. As he turned I drove my right hand into his face. I thought my fist was going down his throat. One of the other men jumped up and grabbed the cognac bottle from the table. I don't think he was planning to use the bottle on me. He was merely trying to protect the contents. But I was taking no chances. I put my left foot into his stomach and drove him and the bottle into a corner of the room. Donovan came at me again. He grasped my neck in both hands, trying to strangle me.

I lifted my knee hard into his groin and he went down, carrying the table and a few chairs with him. One of the women was trying to hold my arms and the other one was actually hanging with all her weight on the end of my beard. Donovan got to his feet and picked up a stool and raised it over his head.

I drew my pistol and fended off the stool and hit him on the head with the butt of the pistol. He went down, bleeding profusely, but he was not out. As he got up again I grabbed him around the waist and bent him backward until he groaned and dropped him to the floor and sat on his chest. I looked around. The doorways of the room were filled with fascinated Spanish faces. I yelled to them to get the police.

When the police appeared on the scene they shot the bolts on their rifles and leveled them at us.

"Arrest him and me too," I said. "Here's my pistol. As you'll see, it's empty."

The procession to the police station was quite a sight. First there were two policemen. Then Donovan, carried by his two friends and still bleeding, followed by two more policemen. Then me, between two policemen, with my shirt and my trousers stained with blood. Behind me marched a great crowd of Spaniards of all ages, every one of them explaining, with gestures, the fight to the other Spaniards who leaned out of windows and came to the doorways of shops and houses as the parade marched through the streets.

At the police station a doctor dressed Donovan's wounds and the British consul explained the case. Donovan was locked up and told that he would not be released until he revealed the whereabouts of the binoculars. I was set free. An hour after I returned to the boat a member of the crew of the *Jaslock* came to me and offered to return the binoculars in two hours if I agreed to call off the police and release Donovan.

"All right," I said to him. "But if the binoculars are not here in two hours I am coming aboard your ship with the police to arrest the three men who were with Donovan last night. Donovan told us who they are." I was bluffing of course. Donovan had said nothing.

After he left a plain-clothes policeman came aboard the *Lovely Lady* and told me that Donovan had admitted selling the binoculars but he could not remember where he had sold them. I told the policeman about the man from the *Jaslock* whom I had just talked to and asked him to wait with me for the return of the binoculars. The man turned up on time and handed me the binoculars. He said that the crew of the *Jaslock* had sold a suit and a wrist watch for four hundred pesetas to redeem the binoculars from a café owner.

I told the policeman to let Donovan go because I did not care to stay in La Coruña long enough to bring charges against him. But the policeman smiled and shook his head.

"You have broken the spell and the townspeople are no longer afraid of the Englishmen from the *Jaslock*," the policeman said. "One café owner has accused Donovan of stealing cognac and another has charged that Donovan and another man from the ship stole three hundred pesetas from his till last week. We have received a cycle that Donovan sold for five hundred pesetas a month ago. I think he will be in jail a long time and some of his friends will be with him."

An hour later a messenger came to the boat and said that the British consul wanted to see me. There was a cable at the consulate which said that my money had been transferred to the consul's bank and I could draw whatever I needed.

I was so mad about the general state of affairs and so fed up with La Coruña that I reached for a pencil and wrote, "Money not required. Sailed today, 6th August. So long." I handed the message to the consul and asked him to send it collect to Lucille the next morning. He looked at me in astonishment as I turned away abruptly and walked out without another word.

CHAPTER 19

I WAS STILL IN A BITTER MOOD WHEN I LEFT LA CORUÑA the next morning at four-thirty. Thanks to the delays in France and Spain, I was almost a month behind my schedule. That was bad. September is the hurricane season in the western Atlantic Ocean. And my supply of stores was very thin. I had already given up the idea of going south to Africa and revisiting the Phantom Islands. Without a camera there was not much point in that. And I realized now that I did not have enough stores to take the chance of wandering around in the doldrums of the Sargasso Sea. There was barely enough food in the boat to last for a straight trip across the ocean to America. I decided to go there by the most direct but the most difficult route, bucking the Gulf Stream currents instead of going north over the circle route. Perhaps I would be able to explore the Sargasso Sea on my return trip from America to England. I thought again about the hurricane season that was less than a month ahead of me. My prospects were not too good.

But when I found myself at sea with a good northeast wind pushing the *Lovely Lady* along steadily and the dim strip of the Spanish mainland disappearing under the overcast sky ten miles behind me, I began to feel better. It was good to be out of all the messy dishonesty and red tape that had been smothering me in Spain. I was tired of asking for cables at the consulate and conferring with the police and complaining to the weak-kneed captain of the *Jaslock*. I remembered the degrading conversation in the *Jaslock's* mess and the grease, almost a half inch thick, on its tables and I shuddered. It was a relief to put all that be-

246

hind me. I began to sing as I watched the *Lovely Lady* rushing forward, listing to the leeward with the sea just clearing the gunwale.

I thought I heard somebody shout. I stopped singing and listened. Visibility was poor and there was nothing in sight. I decided that it was an echo of my own voice. I shouted several times but there was no response. Then I decided that it was the wind in the sails and went back to work on the Scottish lullaby, "Turn Ye to Me."

But that afternoon I thought I heard another shout. I still could see nothing around me. Then I heard a faint moaning. I lashed the wheel and went into the cabin and searched it. The only place in the cabin big enough for a man to hide in was the water closet and there was no one in there. I went back to the wheel. It was set well and there was the right amount of tiller for the direction of the wind and it required no steering. It was getting cold and there was a light drizzle of rain. I put on a sweater and sat on the lee side of the hatchway and watched the boat furrowing her way through the water. I had had only a cheese sandwich since I left La Coruña so I decided to cook myself a hot meal.

While I was in the cabin, rummaging under the port bunker, I heard a whining noise. It sounded like a dog in pain. I looked around the cabin but it was still apparently empty. Then I noticed that the door of the starboard locker was moving slightly. I had kept potatoes in there but now it was empty. I went to it and opened it, expecting a dog or a cat to jump out at me. But inside the locker I found a man.

I don't know yet how he ever managed to get into the locker. It was only eighteen inches by four feet by nine inches so you can imagine how small and thin he was. He would have looked like a boy of twelve if it hadn't been for his mustache. He was pale and he had already been very seasick.

I had a hard time trying to pull him out of the locker. I propped him against the edge of the bunk but he kept falling to the floor and rolling from one side of the cabin to the other with the roll of the boat. I picked him up and threw him into the bunk and yelled at him, "What the hell are you doing here? How did you get in there?" He was frightened and he kept muttering, "No, señor!" Then I realized that he spoke no English. I sat down and stared at him. I could not believe it.

I was in a charming predicament now. I was forty or fifty miles off

247

the Spanish coast, heading for America across the Atlantic with barely enough food to last one man for thirty days if he did not eat much. And now I had a stowaway to feed too.

I wondered if it would be best to turn back. It would take me several days to regain the distance I had made that day in the favorable northeast wind. To hell with turning back, I thought. I've never turned back yet and it will take more than a stowaway to make me do it.

That decided, I went on with the preparation of my dinner of potatoes, peas, and bully beef. I offered none of it to the stowaway because it was obvious from the look of him that food was the furthest thing from his mind at the moment.

I let him stay in the bunk that night while I sat beside the wheel and listened to his groans. At two o'clock in the morning I made coffee and tried to force some of it into his mouth. He was sick all over me. I went back to the binnacle and sat there, disgusted. I tried to be charitable and told myself that the fellow was going through a terrible physical experience. But my first impression of him was that he was one of the lowest scum from La Coruña, which is saying quite a lot. And I saw no reason yet to change that impression.

Later in the morning I succeeded in getting him to swallow a little hot coffee and I talked to him slowly and patiently in my limited Spanish. Gradually I pieced together the story of how he had got on the boat. The English *amigos* on the *Jaslock* had put him in the locker for two hundred and fifty pesetas. They told him that after we got to sea I would put him aboard an English ship that was bound for Argentina.

The rats from the *Jaslock* had succeeded in getting in the last lick.

That afternoon the barometer fell to the deck and smashed. I did not mourn the loss, however, because a barometer was not particularly essential to me. It warned of approaching bad weather but I always had to be prepared for bad weather anyway. I wrapped myself in a blanket and lay down on the deck and slept for four and a half hours and awoke much refreshed. The boat was still speeding along on her course with the helm lashed. I made hot cocoa and tried to persuade the stowaway to come up on deck for a breath of fresh air. He was sicker than ever. I did not know his name so I decided to give him the name of McNasty.

I looked about the cabin for a can opener and could not find it so

I reached for my Commando knife to punch two holes in a tin of milk. As I took the knife from its scabbard McNasty leaped from the bunk and threw himself at my feet. He embraced my legs and screamed, "No, señor! No, señor!" He thought I was about to kill him.

I decided to write down a daily schedule of things that I should do and I did so and pinned it to the cockpit as a reminder. I still have a copy of it. It says:

SCHEDULE

Daybreak: Make sure pump is in good working order.
Look over running gear, stays, and canvas.
Make hot drink.
If possible, sleep. Let amount of sleep depend on weather.

Midday: Cook hot meal.
Transfer all penciled notes to logbook.
Trim all lights.

Night: Check pump.
Make hot drink.

The second dawn after I left Spain broke in the same murky sky. The wind had increased during the night and, looking aloft in the morning, I found that the starboard main topmast stay had parted four feet from the masthead. It would be difficult to fix it, I knew. But it had to be done if I was to continue to carry a full weight of sail. I stripped to the waist and took off my shoes. I hung a new stay over my shoulder and put a shackle in my month and stuck a marlinspike in my belt and climbed the mast, hand over hand. When I reached the top and looked down the tossing and rolling boat looked tiny. And I found it impossible to work. The mast was pitching so much that I had to hold onto it with both hands and both feet in order to keep from falling. Every time I tried to free one hand the mast would lurch madly.

I stayed up there for several minutes and then I slid back down to the deck. I found that I was trembling all over. I wondered if my nerves were giving out. I looked up at the mast. If only it would stay still long enough for me to get another shackle through the stay on the masthead, everything would be all right.

I sat and looked at the mast for twenty minutes. Then I lashed the wheel and lowered the mizzen, hoping that the foresail would keep the stern of the boat more to the wind and lessen the continual broadside tossing that was swaying the mast. Then I climbed the mast again. As I clung to it, waiting for the opportunity to free one hand, I realized that I was still trembling. I felt sure that if I fell I would land in the water and the boat would go on and leave me. McNasty would be of no help. He refused to move from that bunk in the cabin and he would never even know that I had fallen.

Finally I managed to get the shackles in place and then, between rolls, I was able to get a full turn on it. I waited until after another roll and made another turn. It was screwed securely home. I paused to congratulate myself. The next thing I knew I was falling from the mast.

It seemed as though I fell for a half hour. I landed on my chest on the windward gunwale. A wash of sea came over the side and struck me on the face. I rolled over on my back and passed out.

I don't know how long I was unconscious but it must have been for a long time. When I awoke the blood on my naked feet was caked and dried.

My mouth was also full of dried blood and when I coughed fresh blood came out from between my lips. It was painful to breathe and I could not raise my head. I tried to shout with no success. Then I realized that it was no good shouting. McNasty was probably unconscious from seasickness in the cabin. If he was well he would not have been any help to me. I must have passed out again then because the next time I looked at the sky it was clear and the wind had died down. I lay there looking at the blue sky and began to weep. I did not feel badly because of my pain but only because everything had gone so wrong and I seemed to have failed so miserably.

I tried to reconstruct what had happened to me on the mast and I decided that my crippled left arm must have collapsed. It was my fault. I had been overtaxing my arms, forgetting that a few months ago they were useless. As night came I looked at the stars and thought of a leopard hunt that I had been on in India on such a night as this. I remembered sitting in a native mud hut and eating wild boar and rice and then I realized that I was hungry. I thought of what my mother had often said: "If the bairn is hungry and can eat, there is really nothing the matter with him." That lifted my spirits. I thought about getting something to eat but I did not have the strength to face such a difficult project. I decided that some of my ribs were broken and I must have lost a lot of blood.

When dawn came I tried to stand up but the pain forced me back into a sitting position. I put my head on the hatchway and saw blood from my mouth dripping on the white paint. There was still no sign of McNasty. He might just as well have not been aboard. I sat and thought about various things that had happened to me over the years. I wondered what had become of little Nellie. She was a girl from the country who was staying near my home in Scotland and I was very sweet on her when I was released from the Navy after World War I. Many a night I kept her out until eight o'clock, which was then the curfew for seventeen-year-olds. One day when she was in my house I was teasing her and she threw a glass of water on me. I still remember how my mother's face went pale. Nellie, being from the country, did not know the superstitions of the Scottish seafaring folk. To throw fresh water on a seaman was to put him into misfortune. The next week I shipped on the *Dandani* and the entire crew was announced as missing at sea when the ship foundered in a bad storm. I can imagine how the townspeople blamed poor Nellie for the whole thing. She went away and I never saw her again. I often wondered what had become of her. She was a cute trick.

At dusk that day I gathered up enough strength to crawl into the cabin. McNasty was sound asleep on the bunk. I pulled a sheet away from him and took some bandages and iodine from the medicine chest and crawled out to the afterdeck. I did not have the energy to wet the sheet at the little water tank behind the bridge. I let it trail overboard. Then I wrung the sheet out over my leg until my trousers separated from the dried wound where they were stuck. When I pulled up the trouser leg I found that the calf was torn from the knee to the ankle. I must have caught my leg on the rigging when I was falling from the mast. I poured iodine over the wound and fashioned a bandage for it.

Then I tore the bed sheet into strips and wound them crisscross around my chest and shoulders. As I did so I could feel with my fingers parts of the bones moving loosely on the right side near the breastbone. A number of ribs were broken.

I crawled to the cabin again and took out a half-dozen oranges and ate them all in a half hour. That night when the stars came out I noticed that the ship was sailing southwest but I did not bother doing anything to shift her back toward the west. The next morning there were dark clouds in the sky and breezes from the north. I reached the tackle and managed to raise the mainsail by rolling along the deck, first pulling on the peak and leaning on it while I pulled a bit on the throat. Then a little more of the peak and again on the throat until the sail was up. I found an empty orange crate and put it behind the wheel with two cabin cushions and a folded blanket on top of it. Lying on the orange crate, I could see the compass and all about the boat. It was like having my bed at the wheel. I would sleep on it for a half hour or an hour at a time, waking with pain in my ribs. All day long I kept the boat headed west at about three and a half knots an hour. That night I drank two bottles of lime juice and ate some bread and cheese and biscuits. I saw that McNasty had been into the food and had done away with a half tin of biscuits. But he moaned about what he called his "stomach-achi." He moaned continually and I yelled at him often to shut up. His moans did not make it easier for me to endure my own pain.

On August 11, my sixth day at sea, the sun came out between the clouds and there was a fair wind from the northwest. The sea was not rough. A school of whales passed quite close to the boat in the morning and I thought how the sight of them would have overjoyed the rough heart of Screaming Jimmy, the skipper of the *Walpole*, the whaler that I had once shipped on. There were enough whales in the school to make Jimmy issue an extra tot of rum to each man. Toward evening the wind died down and the boat drifted silently. I fell asleep when it became dark and did not awake until two-thirty the following morning. It was the longest and the best sleep I had had since leaving La Coruña.

The wind was freshening from the south and I changed to the port tack for the first time. I did some calculating and estimated my position as about five hundred and fifty miles west and southerly from Cape Finisterre, the northwestern extremity of Spain. I figured that I had traveled two hundred and forty miles the first forty-eight hours and I had drifted about twenty miles to the southwest while I was lying on the deck after my fall from the mast. Then on successive days

I had done ninety and a hundred and four and a hundred miles. It was not bad.

At midday I cooked a meal of spinach, potatoes, and tinned ox tongue and McNasty made his first appearance on deck and joined me in eating it. He did not care for the potatoes and before I could stop him he threw three of them overboard. I tried to tell him that he would be longing for those three potatoes before the voyage was ended.

After we finished eating there was a thunderstorm and the rain came down in torrents. McNasty ran for the bunk in the cabin like a rabbit fleeing to its hole. I took a towel and a cake of soap and had a refreshing bath in the rain.

I never believed in the old saying, "Red sky at night, sailor's delight; red sky in the morning, sailor take warning." There was a red sky and rainbows in the morning of August 13 and it was the finest day I had on the voyage since leaving Spain. With the mainsail boom all the way out to port and the mizzen all out to starboard and a light wind from the east, the *Lovely Lady* glided toward the west like a bird. The sun was strong and warm. I would have gone to sleep but I felt that I would lose distance if I did not tend to the steering. In the evening it became calm and I tried to fish without success. I fell asleep watching the phosphorous flashes of the jellyfish.

A northeast breeze sprang up in the morning and continued to push me steadily west for the next three days. I tried some experiments in cooking. I made twenty-two little cakes and stored them in the bread box. Then I mixed flapjack batter and the flapjacks swelled wondrously in the pan. I discovered that I had used three spoonfuls of Andrews' Liver Salts instead of baking powder but it did not matter because the syrup disguised the taste.

McNasty continued to do nothing except sleep and eat. He did not even wash his own dishes. I tried to get him once to boil some water on the primus stove but he complained that the smell of the gasoline bothered his stomach-achi. And when he finished eating he invariably put his plate or his cup on the deck where it would roll overboard or break against something. Despite my complaints, he had lost three cups and two plates in this way.

At five o'clock on the morning of August 16, I estimated my position as fifty to seventy miles west northwest of the Azores. Thinking of the approaching hurricane season, I decided against taking the time to stop at the Azores.

At noon that day I cooked soup and bully beef and potatoes but McNasty refused to eat more than one small piece of meat and one potato. He complained of his stomach. But at evening when I was preparing tea I found out why he had not been hungry. Sixteen of the cakes I had put in the breadbox were missing. A small jam jar was lying empty on the cabin floor. And a teaspoon, sticky with jam, was on the cushion of his bunk.

I had a hard time keeping my hands off him. I felt like bashing his head in and throwing him overboard.

McNasty did not leave the cabin for the next two days. I moved the breadbox to the orange crate that I slept on at the bridge so that I could ration out its contents. I made more flapjacks and gave us each one of them with our morning and evening hot drinks.

Just before darkness on August 18, I looked over the running gear and found to my dismay that the mainsail topping lift was stranded a couple of feet from the block that is shackled five and a half feet from the top of the main topmast. In my physical condition it seemed impossible to climb the mast again. I wondered whether to leave it alone or whether to lower the mainsail and wait until finer weather before repairing it. While I was wondering about it darkness came and there was not much that I could do then anyway. All that night I expected the gaff to come crashing to the deck any minute. To make matters worse, the wind increased and there were angry squalls.

But at dawn the stranded rope was still holding. The top broken strand had unwound as far as the block and the bottom strand was unraveled about three feet toward the gaff. I spent that day with my heart in my mouth, watching for the line to snap. The foresail began to tear away at the throat and the mainsail started to come away from the rope at the foot. Still it held. At midnight the wind changed to the south and I had to change tack. I did it with my fingers crossed, expecting the gaff to come down as she swung over. But again it held.

The next morning I realized that I could not go on trusting to luck and decided reluctantly to repair the damage. It was hard work but I did it. Reefing a double tackle block is never easy. I had to go up the mast and splice and down again to reeve and up again to reeve the standing end. I went up the mainmast with the new halyard and a short piece of rope that I used to tie my body to the mast, after I had got a leg over each side of the spreader. I unshackled the block and then hung with my body upside down and my legs locked on the spreader and spliced the new halyard and lifted myself upright and reshackled the block. Then I made the two trips up and down to reeve without difficulty.

I replaced the foresail with a new one and patched the jib. I re-sewed the mainsail back onto the blot rope. The job was unfinished when darkness came and I carried it on by the light of a hurricane lamp.

The next three days passed with only one unhappy incident. The primus stove blew up in my face while I was pumping it and singed my beard and my eyebrows and scalded my left foot. But on the morning of the twenty-fourth of August, just after I had finished my calculations, a howling wind came up out of the northwest. The boat heeled over until the lee gunwale was awash. The jib flew away into the air like a handkerchief. The foresail was torn to ribbons. The cock-pit, where I was sitting, trembled and felt as if it would blow away. It was too late to reef the mainsail. If I had gone out on the deck the wind would have blown me into the water.

The wind made a sudden shift to the south and then came back again from the northwest. The mainsail was flattened against the mainmast. I heard a ripping and crashing noise. The mainsail tore down its middle and the boom swung from port to starboard and snapped into four splintered pieces and ended up trailing overboard with lines, blocks, and half the canvas clinging to it. The mizzenmast bent like a hoop and crashed to the deck.

In less than fifteen minutes the *Lovely Lady* had been completely dismantled and swept clean. Now she drifted broadside like a crab in the middle of the roaring hurricane.

I never saw such waves before and I know I'll never see such waves again. They rushed toward me, hissing, like great mountains. I ex-pected that each one would be the last one. I expected it to crush me. I ran into the cabin away from one particularly tremendous solid blue precipice of water. The orange box and pans and dishes and a great rush of water followed me. There was a roaring in my ears and some-thing hit me on the side of the head and there was blackness and I felt the boat shuddering. Then I opened my eyes and found myself in the cabin, standing in water up to my waist. I looked out and saw that the *Lovely Lady* was still on top of the water and riding directly into another great wave. As the wave came toward her she lifted her stern. Foaming water hit me in the face and knocked me back into the cabin. I remember seeing McNasty for a split second. He was crouched in the water-filled bunk and he was screaming.

I don't know how the boat ever came out from under that second wave. I thought she was breaking up but instead she was fighting for her life. She was setting a good example for me.

After that the main force of the hurricane lessened but the sea and the wind and the rain were still heavy and angry. I lashed a rope around my waist and while the boat rose and fell in the storm I worked until I had the remaining section of the aftermast stepped again in the tabernacle with eight square yards of canvas attached to it. I finished it at dark. It was not a pretty sail but at least it helped the *Lovely Lady* ride the seas with a port bow angle. I watched the little boat as she lifted her head proudly to meet each foaming wave and I could not help patting her tenderly as though she was a human being.

I pumped all that night although my arms were tired. There was a foot of oily water in the cabin and all my unpreserved stores floated in it. The flour, peas, beans, oats, biscuits, and most of the tea were a hopeless mess. I was able to salvage two small tins of stewed steak, one tin of lamb tongue, one tin of cocoa, two tins of dried milk, and ten tins of soup.

And more than a thousand miles lay ahead of me.

CHAPTER *20*

$\mathcal{S}$AILORS ARE ALWAYS TALKING ABOUT THE SARGASSO
Sea but very few of them have ever been there. The sailing ships stay
away from it because it is too calm and the steamships cannot go into
it because the seaweed is too thick for their propellers. The Sargasso
Sea is egg-shaped and about as large as the continent of Europe. It lies
in the Atlantic Ocean between the Azores and the Antilles in the cen-
tral whirl of the Gulf Stream. It differs from the ocean around it because of the seaweed, from which it gets its name, and because of
its strange circular currents and its lack of normal winds. The seaweed gives it the appearance of a tremendous swamp and the calm
atmosphere makes it one of the most silent places on this earth. I had
always wanted to visit the Sargasso Sea because of the strange stories
I had heard about the ancient hulks of ships, dating back for cen-
turies, that were said to be floating on its waters and about the rare fish
and sea animals that lived on its seaweed.

As I said before, I originally planned on exploring the Sargasso Sea
when I left England on the *Lovely Lady* but I gave up the idea when
I set out to cross the Atlantic from Spain because my stores were low.
But as it turned out I was forced against my will to follow the original
plan. The hurricane drove me several hundred miles south off my
course and into the northern extremities of the Sargasso Sea. It is one
of the very few places I have seen on this globe that I have absolutely
no desire to revisit. There was an unearthly air about it and it made
me feel as though it was unnatural and not a part of the world. It
seemed more like some place that a soul would pass through on its way

from life to hell or purgatory. You could not get me to go back to the Sargasso Sea if you put a gun at my back.

The hurricane struck the *Lovely Lady* on the twenty-fourth of August. After I pumped all that night I covered myself with two wet blankets and fell asleep, exhausted. The next day I sewed on a new mainsail until my right hand was bleeding from trying to push the needle through the wet canvas. I noticed then that McNasty was missing and I finally found him jammed in behind the water tank forward, under some cushions that he had taken from the cabin. He seemed to have a talent for squeezing himself into small hiding places. I imagine that he had devoted a lifetime of study to it. I dragged him out and pulled him to the pump in the cabin and showed him how to work it. He pumped for ten minutes. Then he sneaked, like a mouse, back into his hiding place behind the water tank. He did not even have the sense to pick a new spot. I dragged him out again. He claimed that the pump was out of order. I stripped it down and cleared out the beans that were clogging it and ordered him back to work. I told him with gestures that if he did not keep pumping I would throw him overboard.

That day after the hurricane we ate a tin of stew and the last seven potatoes and we shared a bottle of fresh water. I showed McNasty the remaining few tins of food in the locker and explained to him carefully that we could eat only one tin a day from now on and that if we ate more than one tin a day we would starve to death.

I felt sure then that I could reach the American mainland or Cuba or the Bahamas if I could get a passing ship to give me some food. The boat was moving southwest. With the wind as it was, blowing dead at me from the west, that was the best I could make her do with the one little sail that I had. The new mainsail which I completed and raised at seven o'clock on the night of the twenty-fifth of August merely helped me to keep her headed southwest. I could not expect to make her go straight west against the wind until I had a full set of rigging on her.

The day after that the sun came out and I hung the bedding and my clothes out to dry. The decks were so loosened by the hurricane that the spray from the sea trickled down into the cabin and we had to pump her for a half hour every four hours to keep her dry. My tobacco was ruined by the hurricane and, dying for a smoke, I tried tea leaves wrapped in toilet paper. The dishes were nearly all smashed. I gave McNasty a pudding basin to eat from and used a pan for myself.

I put up a new jib, which increased the boat's speed to four knots, and rebuilt the mizzenmast. It was four feet shorter than it should be but it still was capable of carrying a fairly hefty sail. I sewed all night to make the mizzen. On August 27, I had up as much rigging as I could produce but I still could make no progress westerly. I kept going southwesterly and prayed that the wind would shift from the west to the north because I realized that the southwest course was taking me toward the Sargasso Sea.

In the early morning of the twenty-ninth, the wind shifted from the west to the west northwest and began to blow at gale force. The sea became rough and heavy. I had all I could do to hold the boat on the southwesterly course. The waves became tremendous. As the boat coasted downward into the valley between two of the waves the sails would lose the wind for a moment and hang slack and empty. Then, as the boat rushed upward to the top of the next incline, the sails would fill out with a snap. I could do nothing but hang onto the wheel. Each roaring wave that advanced upon me threatened to smash across the deck. I would pull the wheel to the leeward and take the wave on the stern and then run before it and try to swerve back onto my original course. I could not reef the sails because when I remade them after the hurricane I had put no reefing points in them. I was soaked to the skin but I dared not leave the wheel for a moment all that day. I shouted to McNasty at noon to take a can of milk from the locker for himself and to bring one to me.

The gale did not blow itself out for twenty-four hours, finally dying down at daybreak on the thirtieth. The jib was gone again and every sail was ripped and torn. I made a third jib from the canvas mattress covers from the two bunks, undoing the seams with a safety razor blade as we had done on the *Girl Pat*.

The next day was the warmest yet and there was not a breath of breeze. I sat on the deck, sewing on the sails and listening to McNasty complaining about the lack of food. You would have thought by the sound of him that he had paid for a first-class passage.

The seaweed became plentiful and I could tell from the brown appearance of it and from the unnatural calmness of the weather that I was nearing, if not already in, the Sargasso Sea.

I dragged a bucket over the side and pulled it in and examined the seaweed. It was full of small brown creatures that were shaped like tadpoles. There were lots of porpoise and many sharks that came alongside and rubbed against the side of the boat, as cows will against a tree.

As it grew dark I watched the jellyfish with fascination. They were clearly outlined in the dark water by the phosphorous and they were as big as the top of a large, round dining-room table. The water was so thick with them that it appeared as though I could get out of the boat and walk.

The ocean seemed motionless but a check with the compass showed that I was traveling in circles. In ten minutes the boat would move from north toward the port side and around to north again. It was so calm that I put a bed on the afterdeck and slept there. I realized that it was the first time I had slept on a bed or a bunk since I had left Spain. The little sleep I had got had been in snatches half standing at the wheel or in a half-sitting position on the orange crate on the bridge. When morning came I felt like staying the rest of the day in that bed.

The weather on the next day and every day that I was in the Sargasso Sea was always the same. It was hot and humid and there was always a light mist with the sun shining dimly above it. When the boat was not passing through seaweed or jellyfish I could see clearly to a great depth in the water.

There were sharks around me always, several of them representing types that I had never seen before. One fellow stayed next to the boat with his head against the side just under the surface of the water. He stared up at me with his dead gray eyes. Then he would dive under the boat and come up on the other side and lie there and stare at me again. He seemed to be measuring me.

The shark made me uneasy. I went to the cabin and got a pistol and loaded it. While he stared at me I leaned over the side until my hand with the pistol in it was only two feet above his head. I pulled the trigger and fired twice. The shark's tail lifted with a swish out of the water. I thought he was coming up onto the deck after me. Then a dozen or more other sharks came from nowhere and began to tear him to pieces. I watched them diving at him, weaving and swaying and rolling in one big involved mass, and they all went down and down and down into the depths of the ocean. I could see them fighting and maneuvering and dipping and whirling around the crippled shark until they blurred slowly out of sight at about ten fathoms under the surface.

In the evening the sun would set as though it was in a fog and after dark the mist would be somewhat heavier. The only good thing about being in the Sargasso Sea was the uninterrupted sleep I had there at night. There was absolutely no sound or no wind or no storm to disturb my slumber.

Luckily I had plenty of sewing to do to keep my mind occupied. I also dried out a pack of cards on the afterdeck and played a few games of solitaire. The cards had been given to me by a friend in London who said that they might serve to pass the time when I was lonely. I noticed some writing on the edges of them. It was blurred by the water that had stuck the cards together during a storm and I could not make it out until I looked at it through a magnifying glass. My friend had written messages of encouragement on the cards. Things like, "Be brave and keep going" and "Keep your chin up" and "You have weathered many storms in life." I must say that I felt a lift in my spirit when I read these messages and I am grateful to the friend who wrote them. They did me a lot of good.

The seaweed was incredible. It grew as high as a foot above the water in some places and in other places it was higher than the gunwales of the boat. It had a heavy, sickening smell and it was horrible to look at and more horrible to touch. It felt slimy and almost like wet human flesh. There were small suckers on it that clung to my hand. Where the suckers ate the dirt on the palm of my hand they left white spots. Where they ate the flesh they left blood. The seaweed was also alive with brown beetles, about two inches long, that crawled up the sides of the boat and onto the deck. There were also snails, six or eight inches long, and lice that were a nightmare.

I will never forget the night of September 3. I looked out from the bridge in the darkness and saw what seemed to be a great white serpent rolling sideways across the deck toward me. It was a thick strand of seaweed, crawling with phosphorous-lighted insects. The whole deck began to glow with them. I walked about chopping at them desperately with a flat piece of wood. Then I poured paraffin on the deck. It did no good. The seaweed clung to the side of the boat and brushed up on the deck and the insects swarmed aboard, using it as a gangplank. Before the night was over and I reached a patch of clear water I thought I would lose my mind.

The hunger became unbearable. On September 4, I was preparing to mix hot water with dried milk and cocoa for our slim daily meal. The cocoa drink and one can of soup, to be divided between the two of us, would make up our complete bill of fare. I felt an impulse toward extravagance that day, however, and I decided to open two cans of soup instead of one.

I went to the locker and opened it. The first can I reached for was empty. I presumed that it had been put back there by mistake and reached for another. It was empty too. Every one of the cans had been opened and drained dry and replaced in the locker upside down. Thirteen cans of milk and soup were gone. All that remained were two one-pound cans of spinach.

At first I felt sick from dismay and sorrow. Then I began to feel an overpowing desire to kill McNasty.

I went to him and reached for him, grabbing him by the collar of my blue sweater, which he was wearing. I was so deranged by fury that I do not remember what he said or whether he struggled. I lifted him and carried him across the deck.

But just as I was lifting him higher to throw him overboard the whole boat was suddenly filled with a terrible smell. It was a stench so bad and so strong that it turned my stomach.

I dropped McNasty and forgot about him. I looked about to see what was the cause of the smell. In a clear patch of water, not much more than ten yards off the stern, I saw a deserted lifeboat. It was sunk almost to the gunwales. It had been once painted light gray but now it was bleached to its natural color by the heat of the sun. At the water's edge on the boat's bow there were some faded numbers that were originally painted in white. One of them was either a 2 or a 9 and I could not make out the rest. I tried to get a look inside the boat to see what was making the unbearable smell. I ran and got my binoculars and focused them on the lifeboat. There was sluggish water inside it and although I could not be certain I thought I saw something floating in the water that looked like a dead human body.

I watched the lifeboat come abreast of me and then float past me. Then it dawned on me that it was moving in the opposite direction from the one that I was moving toward, despite the fact that there were only about ten or fifteen yards between us. Before it went out of sight I took a bearing on it with the compass and saw that it was headed southeast. The surface of the water was placid and told me nothing. I tried to figure why the lifeboat and the *Lovely Lady* were drifting in opposite directions. Perhaps I was standing still and the lifeboat was moving to the southeast. I doubted that. I was passing through patches of clear water and masses of seaweed and I was sure that I was in motion. Perhaps the lifeboat was in a current of water that was moving to the southeast and I was in a second current that was moving in the opposite direction, namely, to the northwest. That seemed strange because our respective paths had almost touched with no change in our respective directions. Or the third possibility was that the lifeboat was standing still and I was moving to the northwest. I favored either of the last two theories. One thing was certain: I was in a current of water that was moving me to the northwest.

That gave me hope. I figured that I was on the northern edge of the Sargasso Sea and, if I was moving to the northwest, I stood a chance of getting out of this calmness and back into the normal winds of the ocean. After being in the still Sargasso Sea, I almost would have welcomed another hurricane.

The stench of the lifeboat seemed to stay with us a long time after we lost sight of it. I did not bother discussing the missing food with McNasty because the mere thought of food was unbearable with that odor in my nostrils. That afternoon we moved into a clear patch of water and I saw a strange type of fish that I had never seen before. The largest ones were about twelve feet long and they had heads like ox cobras and bodies like eels. They moved along on the surface of the water at a terrific rate of speed, with their heads held up like a swan's, twelve or sixteen inches out of the water. They were black with bright blue stripes across their bodies and I noticed no movement of their fins while they swam. At dusk the mist grew thicker as usual and the seaweed closed in on the boat again. I went around the boat, chopping it away from the gunwales. I don't know why but the stuff frightened me. I could still smell the lifeboat.

At five o'clock the next morning I drifted into another clearing.

The sun came up in the ever-present mist. I saw a number of flat objects lying on the surface of the water. As I watched them they moved now and then. I heard a loud clapping noise. I watched again and saw one of the flat things lift and drop its sides, like the pages of a book. As the sides dropped, there was a sharp clap. The objects were gigantic rays. As they clapped their sides they would descend into the water. The first one I saw was at least twenty feet across.

As I passed the rays I noticed a large expanse of open water to my right beyond an extensive mass of seaweed. I had a strong feeling that it was the edge of the normal ocean. Far ahead of me there was a narrow opening that led into it from the patch of water that I was on. I ran quickly and found the rubber dinghy paddle and attached it to a boat hook. I put a round file into one of the holes in the side of the gunwale that is intended for the rods of safety lines. Using the file as an oarlock, I rowed with the boat hook. I was able to move the boat slightly. I changed to the other side and rowed there awhile. It was tiring and I had to stop and rest several times. The channel leading into the open water started to close and I began to give up hope of steering and rowing the boat through it. After several hours of rowing I reached the channel. For about one hundred and fifty yards I rowed frantically on one side and tried to push back the seaweed on the other side. At last I pushed the boat out of the channel and drifted into the open sea. It had taken six hours of rowing but I felt a great joy and satisfaction. I was sure that I was now clear of the Sargasso Sea.

To celebrate, I lit the stove and heated both cans of spinach and mixed four pints of cocoa and dried milk with boiling water. I gave a pint of the drink to each of us and we ate all the spinach. It was the last meal that was served on the *Lovely Lady*.

The next day it was still calm. My body was aching from the exertion of rowing. The bed that I had been sleeping on had become infested with Sargasso Sea insects and I was forced to throw it overboard. I gathered up the small pieces of canvas that were left over from my sailmaking and made a pillow of them and slept on them for four hours. When I awoke I remembered that I had stowed away in a small recess on the starboard four small tins of a special vitamin-rich ration that had been issued to the Commandos during the war. I had put those tins away before I had left London and I had not thought of them since. As I was thinking about the rations the sails filled out with a light breeze from the southeast. "Boy," I thought, "your luck is changing."

I fixed the sails and lashed the wheel and went to look for the tins of rations. They were not in the place where I had put them. I thought that perhaps they had been tossed about when the boat was in the hurricane.

I went below and explained the tins to McNasty and described them to him. He grinned and nodded.

"*Sí*," he said. "Chocolate. Very good. Very good." He had eaten them all himself.

I was too discouraged and tired to knock him through the bulkhead as I should have done. I went up on the deck and sat down. I wondered why I was getting kicked below the belt so often. It seemed as though I met opposition every time I turned around. I thought about my situation and my prospects for a long time. I was far from the shipping lanes. The transatlantic traffic was due north of me. If I went westward toward America I might travel for another month without seeing a ship. Without food I could not last that long. Food was the thing. The only thing for me to do was to sail north for two weeks and try to beg some food from a passing ship. Then I could turn westward toward America.

On the next day, September 7, the wind changed to the west southwest and I set a course to the northwest. I sailed like that for five days, dozing occasionally at the wheel with my head resting on my folded arms. The hunger pangs were bad but I knew from my experience on the *Girl Pat* that the worst ones were still to come. The water supply held up but I had to boil the water before drinking it because the water tank was rusted. On September 9 the wind shifted to south southwest, which cheered me a little. On that day I saw some birds, which reminded me that I had seen no bird life at all on the Sargasso Sea.

On September 10, the fifth day without food, I began to have dreams about standing in front of a baker's shop and seeing fancy cakes in the window. The winds backed a little to the south and became stronger. On the afternoon of September 11 the wind increased to gale force. I decided to stick it out with the sails up. I was being pushed north faster and faster. There was danger of damage to the sails but the idea of getting north into the shipping lanes appealed to my hungry stomach. I decided that the speed was worth the risk.

But that night about ten o'clock I was hit by another hurricane.

It was worse than the first one. When I coasted down the side of the waves it seemed as though I was rushing into a bottomless precipice. I lashed the wheel hard aport. It was difficult for me to see in the utter darkness but I heard the canvas ripping. I was too weak from hunger to do much about it. I lay down in a daze and tried not to think about what was happening to the boat. I thought that daylight would never come.

When dawn broke at last I found the jib and the foresail in ribbons. But to my astonishment the mainsail and the mizzen had held. The boat was full of water. I began to pump. At first I did one hundred strokes with the right arm and one hundred strokes with the left arm. But I had to cut this down to eighty strokes and then to sixty and forty. After a while I could do no more than ten strokes without changing hands.

But the wind blew hard all that day and that next night and at dawn I was adrift on a roaring sea without a sheet of sail. The sidelights had been washed overboard and part of the cockpit was gone. The wind was blowing from the west with a heavy rain and driving me eastward. I was unable to keep up with the pumping and there were two feet of water in the cabin. I searched every locker over and over again, hoping that McNasty might have overlooked at least one small tin of food but I could find nothing.

At dusk that day while the *Lovely Lady* was riding on the crest of a high wave I saw a faint light in the northwest. It went out of sight when I went down between the rollers but when we rode to the top of the next one I saw it again. I continued to catch glimpses of it and then I made it out as the light of a ship that was coming straight at me.

I quickly chopped up a piece of rope and put the pieces in a bucket and covered them with oil and lit the bucket. It blazed brightly. I then lashed two shirts with rope to the end of a boat hook and dipped them in creosote and made a flaming torch and waved it. The ship signaled to me with its blinker, "What ship?" I had no signal lamp to answer with and I tried to make an S.O.S. by swinging three dots and three dashes with the boat hook torch. The ship slowed and stopped, well to the windward.

266

Someone shouted at me, "What do you want?"

I yelled weakly above the whine of the wind, "Food! I've had no food for eight days!"

The ship laid to and I drifted to the leeward. I thought that he had heard me and was launching a lifeboat to come to my assistance. I could not see the ship well in the darkness but it seemed to be a cargo type, about sixteen thousand tons. There was a long wait and then he maneuvered closer to me. Then I heard a voice that sounded different from the first one.

"What's the matter?" it shouted.

I shouted, "I've had no food for eight days!"

There was a pause. Then another shout from the ship.

"Do you wish to abandon?"

I took a deep breath and tried to make it as loud as possible.

"No! I want food so that I can carry on!"

He shouted something back at me but I had drifted out of earshot. There was another long delay and then he edged a little closer to me and called again.

"What ship is it?"

"*Lovely Lady* from London!"

"What ship is it?"

"*Lovely Lady*. I'm from London."

"From where?"

"London."

Then he turned his searchlight on me and examined my boat from stem to stern. It must have been a pathetic sight. He shouted at me again.

"Can you sail that ship?"

I took another deep breath and made another attempt to make myself heard above the wind and the water.

"Not now. But if you give me food, I can make sails and carry on."

"Are you alone?"

"Yes."

I considered being with McNasty the same thing as being alone, only much worse. Besides, if I had ever tried to explain McNasty, the captain of the ship and I would have been standing there shouting at each other for another week. The ship drifted leeward. Then after another wait it came up to my bow and turned the searchlight on me again. I felt as though I was standing in the noonday sun.

He shouted, "Do you want me to send a message?"

"Yes," I called. "Send out my position and say that I am slightly injured and slightly waterlogged. And now, if you'll pass me some food, I'll refit and head for the States."

He thought that over for a few more minutes. "What is this?" I said to myself.

"All right," he shouted. "I will drop a float with food on it. But it will be up to you to get hold of it. You'll have to do your best."

"Fine," I shouted. "I'm ready."

I expected him to fire a line to me with a rocket so that I would be able to pull in the float. But no. Apparently that would have been too much trouble. He lowered the float from his stern and steamed by my bow and dropped it on the water about one hundred yards from my port bow, a little to the leeward.

"There you are," he called. "I'm going on now. You'll have to do your best to get that float."

I wondered what he expected me to do. Jump into the water and swim to the float? He turned around to the southeast and steamed away into the night. There was a calcium water light on the float and I watched it helplessly as it bobbed away from me. I thought of swimming for it but to swim in my weakened condition in that heavy sea would have been suicide.

I thought about the captain of the steamship and wondered what in the name of God he had been thinking of when he dropped that float. In his place I would have lowered a lifeboat. Perhaps he did not have seamen who could handle such a boat. More likely he did not want to risk his men on the rough water. Surely he must have had equipment for firing a line to me that he could have attached to the float so that I could pull it to my boat. Why hadn't he done that? And if he had to drop the float on the sea with no line on it, why did he drop it to the windward of my boat? Any fool knows that a heavier object drifts faster in the wind than a lighter one. And the captain of the steamship should have realized that my boat would drift faster than the float. Instead of the float drifting to me in the wind, I drifted away from it.

I brooded about the food on the raft and the stupidity of the captain all that night and all the next day. My hunger did not make the disappointment any easier to bear. I had reached the stage where it was difficult for me to stand upright without feeling pain and dizziness in my head. I made myself work on the sails because I knew that in a few more days I would not have the strength to do anything. I dragged some seaweed into the boat and tried cooking it in oil from the medicine chest. But it was impossible to swallow. Even McNasty could not stomach it.

At two o'clock that next morning I saw another ship far to the windward. I burned flares again but he did not notice me. To make a set of sails, I sewed together two ground sheets, four bed sheets, two tablecloths, two tea towels, the covering of a waterproof cushion, and two pairs of drill trousers. Sewing was an ordeal because everything was so wet. I undid the strands of fishing line for thread. My hands were so sore that I had to stop frequently and soak them in a bucket of sea water. Finally I had to use a pair of pliers to pull the needle through each individual stitch.

That afternoon, the afternoon of September 15, I saw another ship on the horizon but he did not see me either. Toward dusk I raised the last mainsail that I would be able to make. The wind changed to the east, which was encouraging. I pulled up the last foresail at ten o'clock the following morning. Just as I had it set a ship appeared in the northeast. I lowered the sails so that he could see the daytime distress signals that I was flying. But he paid no attention to me. I raised the sails again and lowered them several times in an attempt to catch his eye. He was so close that I could make out the shapes of men on the deck. But he kept on going.

At three o'clock that afternoon I had all the sails up. Only one needle was left and I had to sharpen the point of that one with a file in order to finish the job.

That was the eleventh day since I had eaten the last can of spinach. I was bothered incessantly by thoughts of food and I had cramps and pains in the stomach when I remained in one position for any length of time. The winds were fair and still blowing from the east. The sails seemed to be holding up well. Just before dark another steamer came at me from the southwest. I burned the flares in the bucket and waved the boat-hook torch again but he ignored my signals. I wondered bitterly what kind of officers were running the ships these days.

269

My mind began to wander after that. I forgot to do the routine things, such as winding the clock, and I stared at myself for long periods of time in the cabin mirror. My hair and my beard were turning white. My cheekbones were sticking out and my body was wasting to nothing. My stomach filled with gas and I smelled badly when I belched. I found a half package of mildewed tea in one of the bunks. I brewed it and gave half of the liquid to McNasty. We drank it and tried to eat the tea leaves but it was difficult to get them down. Three more ships passed me on September 16, two heading west southwest and one going east northeast. They ignored my distress signals. I was too tired at that point to lower the sails so that they could see the signals more distinctly.

On September 17, I saw some small fish following the boat and tried to catch them, using silver paper as bait, but I had no success. I found one pipeful of moldy tobacco in a silver pot from India that was hanging up forward. I dried it on the stove and filled my pipe with it and sat down to enjoy a smoke. When I took the first puff the pipe fell from my hand and my heart felt as though it had stopped beating. I passed out on the deck. After I recovered I thought what a lovely way to die. I picked up the pipe and I was about to light it again but instead I called myself a coward and threw the pipe overboard and staggered back to the wheel.

Then I saw a ship coming from the east and I became determined to stop it. I tried to sail across the captain's bow so that he would run me down if he did not stop. As he came toward me I stood on the cockpit, holding onto the after stay, and waved a white shirt at him.

He altered his course and carefully went around me.

Later in the day another vessel passed about a mile to the north of me. I saw several ducks in the air and I decided that I was probably a hundred miles or so from Bermuda. The wind died down. I had lost track of the hours because all of the three clocks on the boat had stopped running.

The wind freshened just before daybreak on September 18. It started to blow briskly from the northwest. Then there was a heavy rainstorm. I was able to collect about three gallons of water before it stopped. The sky cleared and the wind backed to the southwest. And within an hour I was trying to save my canvas from another gale of hurricane force.

I did not have the strength to struggle against the fierce wind. I did my best to secure the jib and foresail but they were beaten to pieces against the bowsprit and the deck windlass. The mizzen split in half and the top half of it blew into the sea. I tried to lower the mainsail but something jammed in the running gear. The gaff refused to come more than halfway down. I had to edge along the deck on my stomach to keep from being washed overboard. I lashed the wheel hard aport and I sat down in the cockpit and put my face in my hands and wept. I knew that this storm had destroyed my last hope of reaching the American mainland. McNasty crawled out of the cabin, which was filling with water rapidly, and sat down beside me. He looked at me for sympathy.

The gale lasted only a few hours. When it was dying down I found myself drifting broadside with the mainsail half hoisted and jammed but, miraculously, still intact. The rain was falling heavily and the decks leaked like a basket. There were three feet of water in the cabin. I worked the pump until I became exhausted and still I seemed to make little impression on the water.

The next day, September 19, I saw no ships. I took my logbook out of my suitcase and wrote in it that if I was found dead on the boat I did not wish to be buried at sea. "The sea has won enough from me already," I wrote.

The following day I succeeded in raising the mainsail. I also made a sort of mizzen from two blankets, sewing them with fishing line and a sacking needle. I don't know why I bothered with all that work because I had no hope of getting anywhere.

I thought seriously about eating McNasty. I decided that he would not have enough flesh on his bones to make the effort worth while and then I realized that I was losing my senses. I looked at myself in the mirror and saw a white-haired old man who looked about seventy. I pulled out my pistol and smashed the mirror.

A ship passed me. I watched in a daze and did not even wave.

I reached over the side and caught a piece of seaweed that was floating by. Then I noticed that the barnacles on the side of the boat had grown much larger. I pulled one off and ate the sucker inside the shell. It tasted good. I scraped off more barnacles with a silver fork tied to a piece of brass piping. I cut off the suckers with a safety-razor blade and gave a cupful of them to McNasty instead of murdering him as I had planned. He said they were good.

I found it increasingly difficult to sleep as the days went by. I would find myself sinking into periods of semiconsciousness in which I had a lapse of memory. After one of these lapses I would search for McNasty to make sure that I had not killed him without knowing it. A vessel passed me on the night of September 22 and another came close to me on the night of September 23. While I was burning a bucket of gasoline to signal to the second ship I knocked the bucket over and set the afterdeck on fire. I had to throw several buckets of sea water on it before I was able to put it out.

Early in the morning of September 25, I saw a faint light in the west. I stood up and looked at it and said aloud, "This is the last ship that will pass me by." I went to the cabin and took out my pistol and put two bullets in it and went back to the deck and watched the oncoming ship. I made up my mind to shoot myself if it did not stop.

Then I saw that the ship was altering its course and coming toward me. I suspected at first that I was dreaming. But I realized it was a real ship. I ran below to the cabin and dragged McNasty to the deck and pushed my jacket into his hands and yelled, "Wave! Wave!" I pulled off my own sweater and stood on the foredeck and waved it too.

The vessel was an American Liberty ship, the *Jose Bonifacio*. The first officer of the *Jose Bonifacio*, Ted Davies, of Malden, Massachusetts, wrote in his personal logbook an eyewitness report on what happened during the next hour. Ted was in better command of his senses than I was that morning. Let him continue the story in his own words:

> *At 0610 I came out of the chartroom where I had been working out our position. Upon reaching the flying deck I noticed a small boat on the starboard bow. I knew that something was unusual and without making out the details I called the captain to the bridge. He ordered a change in course to investigate. The engine room was called and told that we might have to stand by. I saw that the boat was a schooner or ketch and the only sail up was the mainsail and it was in a scandalized position. Several small flags were flying from the shrouds and the captain recognized one of them as a British Navy Reserve pennant. Two men were hanging to the starboard shrouds and not attempting to*

272

sail her. With the engines going full astern, we passed them slowly and the captain asked if they were in trouble. One man, who wore a British officer's cap, shouted that they had had no food for twenty-one days.

The captain shouted back that he would stop. We turned around, putting the engines ahead to bring our ship alongside the boat. While we were doing this, the steward was called to the bridge and told to prepare some food for the two men. A heavy swell was running from ESE and we tried to bring them alongside on the port, lee side. After they slipped by our bow, several lines were thrown and fell short. The one with the officer's hat was doing everything he could to get the lines on board with a boat hook. The other man, who was bareheaded, merely made begging gestures to us. The captain put our ship's engines astern again and I managed to throw out a heaving line that the officer on the small boat reached with his boat hook. We bent a larger line to the heaving line and as the skipper of the small boat struggled to make it fast, the other man, who was making the begging gestures, got in his way. I heard the skipper say, "Get out of my way, you bastard. You're the cause of all my troubles." I thought to myself, "This certainly has been no pleasant week-end cruise."

I noticed that the hull of the boat was solid but her rigging and decks were in shambles. The leech of the mainsail was ragged from the peak to the clew and the gaff was hopelessly tangled. We lowered to them a burlap bag full of food and I asked the skipper his destination. He said, "The States." We were about to cast off the line when the skipper asked me how far he was from land. I told him the position in longitude and latitude and he asked me again the mileage to land. I said he was at least twelve hundred miles from the United States.

He said, "We can never make it."

The bosun was preparing to cast off the line. I shouted to him to hold on and asked the skipper if he wished to abandon his ship.

He said, "Yes, I can do no other. I have no more canvas and I am half full of water."

We hauled the boat in again and the bosun put a short pilot's ladder over the side. The bareheaded man made a frantic grab for the ladder. I yelled for someone to grab the damn fool before *he killed himself. Several hands reached downward and an upward roll of the sea picked him up bodily and threw him on our deck.*

The captain threw a few things into a suitcase and came up the ladder. I reached for his hand and the captain also took hold of him. I noticed that he did not look back at his boat after he left it and I can understand his reluctance to do so. After we let go the line, it broke my heart to see the little vessel drifting astern all by itself. Having always wanted to make a journey across the Atlantic in a small boat myself, I hated to see someone else's dream go smash. That boat was a forlorn sight as it disappeared in the distance.

CHAPTER *21*

PRACTICALLY EVERYTHING OF VALUE THAT I OWNED DRIFTED away on the *Lovely Lady.* My money was on the boat but I did not mind losing that. It was the loss of the other things that made me sad: the cigarette lighter that had been given to me by the first class of two hundred Commandos that I had trained on the Isle of Wight, the luggage made from the skin of a bison that I had shot in India, pictures and letters and mementos that I had collected through the years. I saved my logbook and a few odds and ends of clothing and my binoculars, that I treasured, and a marvelous German instrument for taking sights and elevations that had been used by the Nazis for aiming buzz bombs. It had been given to me by a man on the Isle of Jersey who had been a prisoner of the Germans. It had remarkable lenses that could pick out all the details in color of a ship twenty miles away at sea. I gave it to the captain of the *Jose Bonifacio.*

As soon as I boarded the *Jose Bonifacio,* I ate a tremendous meal of ham and eggs. I knew it was the wrong thing to do but I did it anyway. The pleasure of eating that meal more than compensated for the illness that came afterward. McNasty stuffed himself, not only on that first day but every day afterward. Although there was plenty of good food to be had whenever he wanted it McNasty would always eat everything in sight and what he could not eat he hid under his shirt and carried back to his bunk.

The day after our rescue I received countless messages from all over the world. Some were from Lucille and my friends and others were from news agencies who wanted my story. The destination of the *Jose Bonifacio* was Bremen in Germany. When we arrived there on October 6, I was besieged by reporters. They had been writing all sorts of strange tales about my voyage. When they learned that there had been a passenger aboard the *Lovely Lady* some papers said that it was a girl and others claimed that my stowaway was Martin Bormann, Hitler's aide. Some people even said that McNasty was Hitler himself. The same papers that had refused to give me seventy-five pounds so that I could buy a camera at the start of the voyage and photograph the Phantom Islands now offered me fantastic sums for the right to publish my logbook. I took great pleasure in turning them down cold.

It had been reported earlier in England that the *Jose Bonifacio* would land me at Dover. Lucille went to Dover with a doctor and an ambulance and waited with them at the dock for several days.

After I started to eat again my hair changed from its white color back to its original brownish red. But I was in pitiful physical condition. My weight had dropped during the voyage from a hundred and sixty pounds to ninety-five pounds. I was afraid to go back to England because I knew that the naval authorities would insist upon putting me back into a hospital for convalescence. I dreaded the thought of returning to a hospital. I felt that I could regain my health much better aboard the *Jose Bonifacio*. I wanted to go back across the Atlantic on her and to carry out my original plan of visiting Donald's sister and his mother in the United States. I talked to the captain about this and it was agreeable to him, if I could clear myself with the port officials at Bremen. I needed a visa for my passport but I could not get it there because it was the American zone of Germany.

The editor of the British newspaper, *News of the World,* was a friend of mine and he offered to fly me to England to see about a visa and to fly me back again to Bremen to catch the boat before it left. The first officer of the *Jose Bonifacio,* Ted Davies, went along with me. I had a big reunion with Lucille and with Bill Gillies, Donald's brother. Getting the visa took a lot of doing. We went back to Germany and finally straightened it out.

Before we sailed from Bremen, McNasty was taken ashore under guard. It turned out that while he was held on the ship somebody ashore in Germany had sent him messages in German which were found on his person. While he was questioned about the messages by American counterintelligence agents he told several conflicting stories and gave several wrong names before they found out the right one.

The Americans finally established that he had served as a German stool during the war. He was one of the Spaniards who went into prison camps in France, disguised as a prisoner, and talked groups of prisoners into escaping to Spain. At the border he would tip off the Vichy French or German authorities and the prisoners would be rounded up and shot. I was not particularly surprised at this revelation because I never felt that McNasty was a particularly admirable character.

The *Jose Bonifacio* was headed for the west coast of South America, via the Panama Canal. I decided to leave the ship at the canal and to work my way to the United States from there. I asked the captain to loan me a hundred dollars, offering my binoculars, which were worth three hundred, as security. The captain loaned me the hundred dollars but would not hear of accepting the security. I left the binoculars anyway with Ted and he delivered them to me later.

I said good-by to the *Jose Bonifacio* at Cristobal on the Atlantic side of the Panama Canal. One of the officials at the British Consulate there turned out to be one of the agents I had worked with in the Mediterranean, back in the days when I was dodging the Spanish and the Italians on the *Mon Amour*. He made the arrangements with the American officials for me to get permission to fly from Panama to Miami. I had a few quid of English money, enough to pay for my hotel expenses at Cristobal. That left me with a hundred dollars. I made friends with a pilot at Cristobal who took me with him while he was guiding a ship through the canal and that saved me the expense of paying train fare to the airport at Panama City. The plane fare from there to Miami was ninety-nine dollars. I bought my ticket and boarded the plane.

We had gone about three hundred miles over the Caribbean when one of the engines went out and the pilot decided to turn back to Panama. We did not arrive in Panama until late that night. "Good God," I thought, "this does have to happen to me." After several hours it was announced that a two-engined plane would make the trip to Miami. Most of the other passengers who were with me on the original flight in the morning had left the airport. I could not leave because all the money I had in the world was tied up in that plane ticket.

I arrived finally in Miami late at night. I was hungry so I bought a cup of coffee and a piece of cheesecake at the airport cafeteria with my last dollar. The waitress gave me fifty cents' change. Then I put

277

in a telephone call to my sister Betty, in New York. I had not seen her in several years. I told her where I was and the financial spot I was in and she said that she would wire money to me immediately. I had to wait at the airport until the money came. I walked about all night and toward dawn I went back to the same cafeteria for another cup of coffee and another piece of cheesecake. I was waited on by the same girl. I handed her the fifty-cent piece that she had given to me as change earlier in the night. She picked it up and looked at it and flung it back at me.

"What are you trying to do, brother?" she said. "You can't con me."

I picked up the fifty-cent piece and looked at it. It was undoubtedly a counterfeit. I blushed and stammered an apology. I saw that the other people in the cafeteria were looking at me. I stood up and walked away.

Betty's money arrived at ten o'clock that morning and I went into Miami and booked a room in a hotel and fell asleep. The next day I took a train to New York.

About a week later I was having a drink with a friend of mine in the men's bar at the Waldorf-Astoria and he asked me what I was planning to do next.

"I want to buy a schooner with a Diesel engine," I said. "I'll gather about twenty friends of mine and we'll take a tour around the world. The tour will last for about two years. We'll go to all the places where I've been and where the tourists never go. We'll go to the Barawi Islands and the Godavari River. I'll show them the place in the West Indies where Nelson participated in a bigamous marriage ceremony with Lady Hamilton. We may even visit that inlet in Argentina where Scoush and I found the pearls. When we find a place we like we'll stay there until we feel the urge to move on to someplace else."

"Sounds good," my friend said. "But it also sounds expensive. What will you use for money?"

"I don't know," I said.

"Have you ever thought of writing a book?"

"That's an idea," I said.

So I sat down to write the book and this is it and when I get through with this paragraph it will be finished. I hope it makes some money because I do want to get that schooner and make that trip around the world.

278

Girl Pat.

	DATE DUE	

THE MENNINGER STORY

The
Menninger
Story

By WALKER WINSLOW

Doubleday & Company, Inc., Garden City, N.Y., 1956

Library of Congress Catalog Card Number 56–6531

Copyright ©, 1956, by Walker Winslow
All Rights Reserved
Printed in the United States of America

First Edition